The Romance of Adventure

Douglas Fairbanks in *The Three Musketeers* (1921)

Studies in Popular Culture
M. Thomas Inge, General Editor

The Romance of Adventure
The Genre of Historical Adventure Movies

BRIAN TAVES

UNIVERSITY PRESS OF MISSISSIPPI
Jackson

Copyright © 1993 by the University Press of Mississippi
All rights reserved
Manufactured in the United States of America

96 95 94 93   4 3 2 1

The paper in this book meets the guidelines for permanence and
durability of the Committee on Production Guidelines for Book
Longevity of the Council on Library Resources.

Library of Congress Cataloging-in-Publication Data

Taves, Brian, 1959—
    The romance of adventure : the genre of historical adventure
movies / Brian Taves.
        p.   cm. — (Studies in popular culture)
    Includes bibliographical references and index.
    ISBN 0-87805-597-5 (acid-free).—ISBN 0-87805-598-3 (acid-free :
pbk.)
        1. Adventure films—United States—History and criticism.
    I. Title. II. Series: Studies in popular culture (Jackson, Miss.)
PN1995.9.A3T38   1993
791.43'658—dc20   93-19458
                                                                  CIP

British Library Cataloging-in-Publication data available

To my mother

with affection and appreciation

CONTENTS

ACKNOWLEDGMENTS

During the fall of 1978, while completing my freshman year at the University of Southern California, I took the course in classical Hollywood cinema that turned me toward film studies as the path I would follow. One of the professor's shorter lectures discussed adventure films, noting at the outset how they seemed to be poorly understood and little analyzed in the literature of the field. At that moment, the inspiration for this book was born. I had enjoyed many such pictures and felt I could make a contribution toward a better comprehension of them. Over the ensuing years, the same professor, Rick Jewell, fostered the project, through undergraduate research in 1979 and its eventual evolution into my dissertation, completed in 1988. I owe him many thanks, and am also grateful for the support of my committee member for American history, Frank Mitchell, who provided the key that unlocked the ideas that became Chapter 9 of this book.

In addition, I owe a debt to the many friends who patiently video-taped countless adventure films from obscure cable channels. I also enjoyed and benefitted from the input received from many of my fellow students in film history and criticism at USC. Martin Green, professor at Tufts University and author of several books on literary adventure, provided encouragement and a rigorous reading of early drafts of several chapters. I should also mention a different kind of contributor, the writer Talbot Mundy, whose philosophical brand of adventure literature provided many of the ideas that became the basis for my approach to the genre. All illustrations are from the Robert Florey collection and the personal collection of the author.

Finally, I should thank my patient editor at the University Press of Mississippi, Seetha Srinivasan, who saw the potential in an earlier version of this manuscript and allowed the time for it to be reworked into its present form.

INTRODUCTION

Historical adventure movies form one of the most enduring and mythically significant American film genres. Whether swashbucklers, tales of pirates, the sea, or the building of empires, adventure includes films as diverse as *The Mark of Zorro; The Three Musketeers; The Count of Monte Cristo; Mutiny on the Bounty; Moby Dick; Captain Horatio Hornblower; The Charge of the Light Brigade; Gunga Din; The Man Who Would Be King;* and *Around the World in 80 Days.* Ranging from exploration of the world's remote regions to Robin Hood–style rebellions against totalitarianism, the cinema's adventurer is impelled by an idealistic worldview and a belief in patriotism, chivalry, and honor. A political consciousness underlies all of these activities; the plots of these films follow a pattern of despotism, subversion, and the establishment of a governing system to protect the rights of its citizens. Human history is portrayed as a progression toward democratic egalitarianism, illustrating the development of responsible self-government as a historical phenomenon.

There has never been a comprehensive study of adventure films, even though the genre has a strong tradition of unique conventions and the films have been popular from the early days of filmmaking through the present. This lack of attention may be the result of a certain confusion over what comprises the genre: it has been described so narrowly as to include swashbucklers exclusively and so broadly as to encompass virtually any film. I offer an original definition of adventure movies, emphasizing the importance of the period setting and its attendant characterizations and codes of behavior.

The genre includes not only swashbucklers but also similar related adventure forms, such as films of empire and sea stories. One of my central goals is to demonstrate what these movies have in common. At the same time, I clarify the differences between historical adventure and other action-oriented types of films.

Hence, the primary goal of this book is to answer the basic question, "What is an adventure film?" by describing and analyzing the elements that comprise the genre. The organization reflects this basic purpose, with the initial two chapters delineating some of the proposed boundaries of historical adventure, distinguishing it from other genres sharing similar elements. The first chapter, "What Is Adventure?," discusses the possible definitions of adventure and how it must be understood in order to be examined as a genre. Chapter 2, "Five Forms of Adventure," divides the genre among its principal manifestations, the swashbuckler, pirate, sea, empire, and fortune hunter forms. This taxonomy highlights the hero's character and purpose together with the geographical locale, and each type has its own mythology, narrative expectations, and conventionalized settings. Chapter 3, "The Evolution of the Adventure Genre," notes the genre's own historical context and how it has developed over time, from its literary beginnings through its commercial development at the box office and on television.

Building upon this structure, subsequent chapters elaborate the themes and motifs appearing throughout the genre, discussing its elements in terms of the unifying conventions of setting and characterization. Chapter 4, "The Era of Adventure," investigates the spatial-temporal realm in which historical adventure takes place. The label "historical" is a reminder of the specific temporal period found to be favored in films of the genre, from the Middle Ages through the end of the nineteenth century. (The word *adventure* is used throughout these pages as a shorthand for historical adventure.) Adventure belongs to an era long past, and history is often presented more as myth than an accurate re-creation in order to show morality drawn in sharp relief.

Chapter 5, "Characters and Their Traits," discusses the types of individuals who appear in the genre and how the hero interacts with friends, women, and indigenous peoples as secondary characters. Adventurers are altruistic characters, exemplars of gentlemanliness, chivalry and honor, characteristics that distinguish them from villains. Chapter 6, "The Adventurer's Code," elaborates on these themes to examine the pattern of ethics and behavior that governs the adventurer's conduct. Leadership, the military, and the conflict between camaraderie and solitude are all important aspects of his life. Revenge is often a key motive, and the hero's resources are tested in a type of initiation as he undergoes trials and survives the pressures of circumstance and locale.

The chapter on the adventurer's code and the remainder of the book are a discussion of the "philosophy of adventure," a term that best sums up the complexities of the various facets of the genre. Four principal avenues of expression are explored: the adventurous life-style, service to country, and the political and spiritual beliefs underlying the character's activities. The genre's predominant themes and motifs are manifested in behavioral and political topics, centering around a viewpoint asserting the importance of fighting dictatorship and achieving freedom. Chapters 7 and 8, "The Politics of Adventure Films" and "Colonialism and Adventure," dissect these multifaceted aspects of the adventurer's beliefs. The same values that celebrate individualistic, armed rebellions that restore justice to endangered societies are used to form a colonial ethic, condoning an imperialism portrayed as benevolent yet paternalistic, which benefits natives and is administered by officers who love the foreign land. Chapter 9 suggests an explanation of the seeming incongruities in this philosophy by examining adventure movies as a unique expression of the various political crosscurrents and contradictions in the American experience, especially the political perception of our own revolution.

Until now, only individual films or facets of the adventure film have been approached; adventure literature has been discussed only slightly more. While these various studies have contributed to this book, my primary source has been adventure movies themselves. I have viewed more than four hundred different films, many on multiple occasions, along with hundreds of hours of television series. This endeavor hardly qualifies as a labor of love; to sample adventure thoroughly, I have not only enjoyed the best of the genre but also suffered through some of its worst examples. I have seen all the available movies, but there are many more that are inaccessible. Related sources, such as reviews, plot summaries, and even scripts, are not reliable representations of what appeared on screen. I have tried to avoid the twin perils either of producing a veritable catalog or relying excessively on a few works; the appendix provides a chronological list of hundreds of titles of English-language adventure films. A representative sample of around fifty movies produced from the 1920s through the present has provided the core of references for this study. These readily available films are significant either for their content or for their major commercial success. At the same time, I have sought to move beyond the canonical "great films" methodology that seems to have hindered the larger understanding of the genre. (My forthcoming book on Talbot Mundy will take a different approach by tracing the career of an unusual adventure author as well as exploring in-depth the production and structure of the media adaptations of his work.)

I discuss television series, miniseries, and made-for-television films as well as theatrical movies. While emphasizing movies, the need to discuss the genre in both mediums is indicated by the interchange of adventure storytelling on the large and small screens, whether as made-for-television pictures or re-edited television shows theatrically released as features. However, radio programs, shorts, documentaries, and animation are separate forms and mediums and are not included here. As a genre study, I have limited myself largely to Hollywood and its formulas. Far less susceptible to such influences are adventure films made in non-English-speaking countries. They are grounded in their own cultural and filmic traditions, both in terms of production and consumption; they also more readily merge with the fantasy genre, such as the foreign adventure movies *The Red Tent* or *Lancelot du Lac*. *The Castilian*, which emerged from the less confined generic tradition of European coproductions, changes course midstream from a historically based swashbuckler to a fantasy, with the sudden appearance of two saints who help Spain defeat the Moors in battle. On the other hand, pictures from the various English-speaking countries share much in common, including heritage and culture, and so are discussed interchangeably. For instance, the Walt Disney version of *Treasure Island* (1950), and its Australian-made sequel, *Long John Silver's Return to Treasure Island* (1954), both directed by Byron Haskin and starring Robert Newton as Robert Louis Stevenson's notorious pirate, are virtually identical despite the different countries of origin.

Examples are offered throughout the text; titles mentioned in parentheses are films that exemplify the preceding sentence. Unless indicated by a date, such as *The Four Feathers* (1977), reference to a title implies equal applicability to all film versions of that story.

Only in Chapter 3, because of the emphasis on chronology, has it been necessary to provide dates for every production. In the first mention of a picture in each chapter, any alternate titles are listed following a slash mark, with the best-known, the American, or the initial release title having precedence—from the extreme example of *The Soldier and the Lady / Michael Strogoff / The Bandit and the Lady / The Adventures of Michael Strogoff* (final release title / initial and British release title / theatrical reissue title / television title) to the more typical case of *Flame over India / Northwest Frontier* (American title / British title).

Adventure has certainly tended to be sexist and imperialist, casting individuals into social, psychological, and sexual stereotypes. The films emerge from a patriarchal context and offer extremely limited and unsophisticated options for both masculine and feminine behavior. For me, this is adventure's greatest flaw, its most pernicious result, and I certainly do not applaud these aspects of the films. Imperialism and nationalism have been partially acknowledged and questioned in adventure movies, although both are still invoked in a disturbing manner. Nonetheless, the films are profoundly polysemous, offering a mix of often conflicting themes and ideas. For instance, I believe adventure movies avoid the charge of militarism through their emphasis on individualism, stylized violence, and a fluid interpretation of patriotism. Adventure films stress human liberty and freedom, with a powerful and potentially radical penchant for showing the overthrow of the political status quo. In a typical case, *Captain from Castile* presents a very moving portrait of a man's flight from the tyranny of the Spanish Inquisition, yet he joins Cortés's conquest of the Aztecs, and the movie largely overlooks its effects on the native people.

Overall, adventure's many backward sentiments are sufficiently recognized and obvious that it is not necessary to annotate a critical commentary. My aim is to elucidate the genre rather than to produce a polemic, and this does not imply agreement with the content of the films I discuss. Instead, a form of popular culture is analyzed, one that has all the limitations and drawbacks of most such entertainment. Even though the narrative content of a genre now lacks credibility, it should not be overlooked or simply disparaged; changing mores make it all the more valuable as a cultural relic. Just as it has been important to study the western, with all of its inherent faults, so it is necessary to understand adventure, no matter how skeptically we may regard its ethics. In describing the genre, I have sometimes also had to use its own terms, such as *Oriental* and *native,* to describe the people and principal locales of colonial Africa, Arabia, India, China, and the Pacific islands. While such words have become an anachronism, the connotations of foreign, non-white otherness and cultural difference are precisely the attitudes of adventure I am highlighting.

In laying out the parameters of the adventure genre in film, I am aware that many other avenues could have been followed. Adventure may prove amenable to anthropological, psychoanalytic, semiotic, Marxist, or other perspectives in later studies. Nonetheless, considering the paucity of attention adventure films have received to date and the status of this book as a first step toward conceptualizing the genre in its entirety, my objective must be to identify a group of films that forms the basis for further discussion. Without a resolution of the question of what an adventure film is, there will be little chance for a cogent and coherent series of studies to develop. (This same fact has precluded making any comment upon the more abstract questions intrinsic to genre studies.) Having provided a definition, I hope my work can serve as a springboard to many more theoretical, and no doubt differing, interpretations of this genre. I look forward to the work of others approaching this genre with new ideas, methodologies, and conclusions. If this book provokes a greater recognition and discussion of adventure films, I will have achieved my goal.

The Romance of Adventure

CHAPTER 1 What Is Adventure?

Ask six different individuals—lay person, scholar, critic, or filmmaker—to name the first adventure film that comes to mind, and there will probably be a half-dozen widely divergent answers. One person mentions *Raiders of the Lost Ark*, the second champions *Star Wars*, another replies *The Guns of Navaronne*, a fourth cites *Quo Vadis*, a fifth champions the James Bond movies, and the sixth suggests *Robin Hood*. I believe that of these examples only *Robin Hood* is truly an adventure film. The others represent genres that are distinct in their own right. *Raiders of the Lost Ark* is a fantasy, wherein the dark powers of fascism are defeated by the Old Testament magic of the Arc of the Covenant. *Star Wars* is science fiction, telling a story set on distant planets in a time of advanced technology. *The Guns of Navaronne* is a war movie, part of a whole genre centering on twentieth-century combat, especially World Wars I and II. *Quo Vadis* is a biblical epic, portraying the decadence of ancient Rome in order to reveal the redemptive power of Christianity. James Bond is a spy whose exploits are set in a world of espionage and secret agents whose conflict substitutes for the more overt and explosive confrontation of warfare. *Robin Hood*, by contrast, deals with the valiant fight for freedom and a just form of government, set in exotic locales and the historical past. This is the central theme of adventure, a motif that is unique to the genre.

It is essential to determine what comprises an adventure film, to analyze the genre's central tenets, and to distinguish its borders from other forms with similar elements. In the case of historical adventure, few film genres are so thoroughly misunderstood. The label has been applied to a seemingly endless number of better-defined genres, everything from westerns, war, crime, science fiction, fantasy, epics of ancient and biblical worlds, to thrillers, disaster, samurai, and kung-fu movies. Indeed, the term has been so broadly used and misused that it has become encrusted with a multiplicity of meanings and preconceptions. If it were possible, I would use another word to label the genre, but unfortunately there is no alternative that better expresses my meaning (Noyce, 19).

There has always been a general uncertainty about the dynamics of historical adventure on the part of journalistic critics, scholars, industry, and perhaps even audiences. Adventure, whether as a literary or cinematic form or as a mode of experience, is usually painted in broad strokes, defined in a loose, general manner. A typical description is offered by Trentwell White, equating fiction, diversion, escapism and adventure. He writes that practically all fiction is adventure—a voyage into the unknown or beyond the horizon (White, 930). Ian Cameron epitomizes this attitude in his book, *Adventure in the Movies*, writing that adventure is distributed in varying amounts throughout the cinema, so that nearly all movies can be described as adventure. Taking this thesis to its logical extension, Cameron mentions the historical love story, *Gone with the Wind*, and the musical biography, *The Glenn Miller Story*, as containing elements of adventure (Cameron, 71, 16).

Adventure, in this sense, is so generalized and vague as to be meaningless. Fortunately, other interpretations are more helpful. The usual definitions of *adventure* stress elements of the unusual, overcoming obstacles with narrow escapes, and vanquishing villains. In this sense, *adventure* becomes linked with *action*, a word attached to any film with a greater emphasis on action than emotion. Indeed, *action* is a more appropriate word than *adventure* to describe the style of storytelling that runs through many genres, a male-oriented approach dependent on physical movement, violence, and suspense, with often perfunctory motivation and romance. Action tends to shift sentiment, character, dialogue, and family to the background. In action films a hero succeeds by facing death, courageously overcoming dangers and adversaries. Better than adventure, the term *action* indicates the relationship between a variety of genres sharing these characteristics, including westerns, war, aviation, science fiction, ancient world–biblical, martial arts, spy, and all types of crime films.

While adventure may be amorphous in its descriptive sense, usually implying action, as a name for a genre it necessarily becomes narrower and more precise. The basic traits of action are not specific enough for a generic approach that will sort out the films that appropriately belong to adventure. Genre criticism divides the massive number of entertainment films into types sharing various traits, a prerequisite to discussing adventure movies as a distinct entity. Genres are a form of categorization into which art forms may be grouped by content and technique; motion pictures in a particular genre share subject matter, characters, and themes. Other common elements include point of view, setting, shots, locales, icons, social milieu, and the costumes, dialogue, and physiognomy of the players that combine to create the characters (Ed Buscombe in Grant 1977, 27; Altman 1984, 16). Similar situations and concerns reappear continuously, and the generic perspective stresses what is common among them. These largely thematically oriented devices form the primary, linguistic elements of the film, and the first task is to discover character types, atmosphere, archetypal situations, and themes. Afterward, their implications are probed; from the structure of the various combinations of these elements emerges the manner in which a genre conveys its meaning (Altman 1984, 10–12). Genres are named by the various aspects of the movies: character (gangster movies), pivotal event (disasters), mood and purpose (horror films, comedies), target audience (women's films), setting (westerns), or style (musicals). Certain genres are expected to address different audiences and concerns: family problems in melodrama, marriage in the women's picture, international tensions in the spy movie, psychological fears in the horror movie, lawlessness in the suspense thriller.

Genre criticism provides the most satisfactory approach to adventure; many other approaches have proven inappropriate. Adventure is not recognizable by a distinct and unique style, like the musical with its diegetic music, science fiction with its need for special effects, or ancient world–biblical tales with their typical epic treatment. No particular filmmaker made his or her reputation in the historical adventure; it has been overlooked by *auteur* critics who preferred other action genres. Biographies of famous players identified as swashbucklers, such as Douglas Fairbanks, Errol Flynn, or Tyrone Power, tend to be misleading, often combining discussion of their adventure films with the movies of other genres in which they appeared. A resulting side effect is to ignore key adventure films featuring players not readily identified with the form (Parish and Stanke; Cameron, 120). By contrast, genre study allows us to depart from the canon of cinema history to discuss the escapist products of popular culture in a systematic manner. The generic approach allows the most comprehensive look at the range of adventure films and their meaning as an enduring form, revealing the background from which they emerged and the cultural, social, and political significance of the themes they have developed.

Genre's methodology is suitable for discussing the commercial tendencies of the American cinema, as opposed to the individual, artistic proclivities of European filmmaking. The mass production of films requires invoking formulas, patterns of characterization, plot progression, and themes that have become predictable. In a sense, genre films tell the same story over and over, repeating essentially the same narratives, allowing audiences to become adept at instantly recognizing the specifics of a type. It is easy for the viewer to determine with virtual certainty how the narrative will develop, the behavior that will be involved, and the temporal and spiritual underpinnings that will be in place. For instance, a gangster film and a western will offer fundamentally different types of behavior and spatial-temporal settings. Neither would be expected to cross over into the supernatural or the gruesome that becomes possible with the horror film. The notion of genre and the expectations it offers allow the film goer a reassuring shorthand for choosing at least the basic type of entertainment he or she prefers. As well, using archetypal plots offers the film industry some economic security beyond that provided by stars and other personnel, since audience appreciation of a certain type of plot can be roughly gauged by past examples.

The predictability of a genre indicates a shared understanding of the various ingredients that define types and categories between an entertainment's consumers and producers. The "pure" story may not exist in any single film but assembles collectively in the viewer's mind through the experience of a variety of similar films (Basinger, 73). A picture's meaning arises in part out of the relationship between audience expectations and a movie's treatment of them (Sobchack in Grant 1977, 39–40; Grant 1977, 1). The tradition of past story construction largely governs the ways its elements can be rearranged. Through the popularity of individual examples of the form, genres evolve over time, as patterns of motifs and ingredients are established, explored, repeated, codified, and varied. These conventions create expectations that are usually flexible to only a limited degree (Sobchack in Grant 1977, 43). In this sense genres are formulaic, and the making of such movies is bound in advance by an interlocking set of unwritten but implicit rules (Paul Willemen in Neale, 1). Some genres share a narrative structure, with a standard introduction, development, actions, and climax repeated even as the details of the plots change. Yet genre films do not all aim to tell the same story, only to use similar forms: not all westerns deal with Indian wars and the cavalry, or sheriffs and gunslingers, or cattlemen and rustlers, but at least one of these oppositions is likely to be found. While much repetition is involved to retain generic recognition, changes on the standard theme are provided to keep each example sufficiently individual in order to avoid boredom or satiation on the part of the audience. Films within a genre must be fresh enough to generate sufficient interest to draw new audiences by alternating patterns of repetition and difference in its story and/or style (Neale, 49–50). Genres are also not static, and may evolve into forms very different from their predecessors, as demonstrated by the development of the hard-boiled private detective mystery out of the classic mystery sleuth.

Genre study has implications for understanding how audiences have absorbed movies, since, in determining which types of film to attend, audiences tend to validate certain beliefs in what may become almost a ritual manner (Altman 1984, 8–9). The concerns addressed by genres may serve as a psychic mirror, reflecting the national character and culture, its aspirations, and insecurities. By observing the repeated myths, themes, and images that were absorbed by film goers, one may tentatively deduce how and why they embodied the beliefs, hopes, and fears of their audiences. Some genres have been clearly impacted by their times; horror and science fiction pictures, for instance, altered dramatically during the first decades of the atomic age to reflect its concerns. The western presents the continental expansion in America's past, and the movies of the genre offer changing views on American destiny and supposed national virtues. Hence, a genre approach can provide a measure of the specific traditions from which various types of pictures have developed.

A single genre is not an isolated, separate entity, but often linked with other types by similar concerns, icons, or styles. Characteristics from one genre may be adapted to create new meanings within another, to merge motifs, character types, or settings—a strategy typical, for instance, of science fiction (Basinger, 155, 277). Although each genre contains variable combinations of anticipated ingredients, few belong exclusively to any specific type (Andrew, 110). In historical adventure, the audience finds period settings, exotic locales, exploration, imperialism, voyages, duels, battles, wars, revolutions, colorful characters, mysterious benefactors, love stories, abductions, pursuits and escapes, treasure, suspense, intrigue, royalty, and even a measure of politics. None of these elements is found solely in adventure, but each is handled with varying thoroughness and importance in a manner unlike other genres (cf. Green 1979, 315; Kiely, 20). An individual ingredient may be part of many genres, yet in each it will appear in unique conjunction with other concerns. Unrelated genres may intersect at various points, yet some of the borderlines help to determine where these genres end and adventure commences (Todorov, 270). While violence is a motif shared by gangster, war, western, and historical adventure movies, each of them approaches it differently—from brutally in gangster films to stylishly in the swashbuckling adventure.

To reserve the label "adventure" for a specific genre requires the recognition of precisely where the borders lie with other action types. James Bond, Shane, the Thief of Bagdad, Luke Skywalker, and hosts of heroes of other action genres all belong to their own type, different from adventure. All of these types involve their own visual techniques, themes, plot conventions, and temporal and spatial settings. The western, although set in the latter part of the period of adventure pictures, is distinct by virtue of its locale and conventions. Military conflicts including and subsequent to World War I fall within the purview of the war film, the technological violence and disillusionment of bombs and trenches replacing adventure's jousts and sword play. By contrast, science fiction typically takes place in the future, with narratives speculating on future technological possibilities and their effect on humanity.

Crime movies and thrillers, whether stories of spies, detectives, or gangsters, provide some of the sharpest dichotomies. Crime settings are most often contemporary, and the key features are suspense and mystery, not a conscientious battle for liberty and proper government. There is a descent into the criminal underworld to discover whodunit or who stole the object of value, a search that is involved with syndicates and criminals—not nature and natives, as in adventures such as *Kim*; *King Solomon's Mines* (1950); or *Treasure of the Golden Condor*. Similarly, although Sir Arthur Conan Doyle prefaced numerous Sherlock Holmes stories with the title "The Adventure of," they hardly qualify as adventure. Movies in another category, adventure thrillers, adopt some of the trappings of adventure, including exotic locales and the search for wealth, but they portray very different characters in a contemporary period, attuned to their modern age, less redeemed by their search for treasure, and involved with syndicates and gangsters; examples include *Four Men and a Prayer*; *Valley of the Kings*; *Bengazi*; *Mara Maru*; *Boy on a Dolphin*; *Beyond Mombasa*; *The Deep*; *Sphinx*; and *Romancing the Stone*. *The General Died at Dawn*; *Barricade*; and *The Left Hand of God*, depicting heroes who stand for freedom against corrupt Chinese warlords, resemble the hard-boiled thriller and are primarily concerned with espionage and suspense, not adventure's triumph over political oppression.

One form that is often confused with the adventure genre but lies distinctly outside its tradition is fantasy (Fisher, 9; Gove 62, 74; Tony Thomas, 1; Richards 1977, 271). Unlike adventure, fantasy presents a netherworld where events violate physical reality and the bounds of human possibility, trespassing the laws of nature and mixing the otherwise separate worlds of the natural and the supernatural (Todorov, 25–27). The violation of these bounds is fantasy's motif and highlight, indicating that the genre is fundamentally opposed to the inherent limitations and verisimilitude of adventure, with its historical concerns. Unlike adventure, fantasy is often set in bizarre, imaginary lands, with monstrous creatures representing the divine or the diabolical (*The Golden Voyage of Sinbad*; *Conan the*

Barbarian; Ulysses; Clash of the Titans). Fantasy suspends known physical laws: slowing the process of aging in *She* and the *Lost Horizon* of Shangri-La, revealing weapons with supernatural properties in *Excalibur* and *The Magic Sword,* changing man into an animal in *Ladyhawke,* or exploring the relationship between Mowgli and his anthropomorphized animal friends in *The Jungle Book.* Arthurian settings are used in both fantasy and adventure, yet the distinction remains clear between the two genres. *Knights of the Round Table; Prince Valiant; The Black Knight; Sword of Lancelot / Lancelot and Guinevere;* and *King Arthur—The Young Warlord* are all adventure films, while a highlight of the fantasy *A Connecticut Yankee in King Arthur's Court* is the display of Hank's nineteenth-century "magic" in pretechnological times. Similarly, the equally fantastic *Excalibur* is less politicized than steeped in supernatural lore, as one priestly order gives way to another. The difference between adventure and fantasy is that which separates Rafael Sabatini's *The Historical Nights' Entertainments* and the *Arabian Nights.* Sabatini tells fictionalized tales of authentic individuals in specific periods of the past, stories of courage and daring that are physically possible—never entering the world of the genies and magic as found in the *Arabian Nights.*

The indulgence in fantasy, as opposed to adventure, also has ideological implications, implying a wider focus than adventure's world. Unlike the adventurer, limited to earthly powers, the larger-than-life fantasy hero undergoes mystical experiences, depending on devices and allies outside of himself—such as the gods in the tradition of Homer, Greco-Roman mythology, the Bible or the Arabian Nights (Cassiday, 13; Zweig, 8). In adventure, ideals are achievable within the real world; in fantasy, humankind must ultimately call upon more powerful forces. For instance, *The Thief of Bagdad* emphasizes the initiation into the supernatural, until he flies away on a magic carpet. Unlike its television counterpart, *The Young Indiana Jones Chronicles*, the movie trilogy (*Raiders of the Lost Ark; Indiana Jones and the Temple of Doom; Indiana Jones and the Last Crusade*) does not draw on any of the five established adventure types. Instead it uses the ingredients of fantasy—religious relics, lost races, and secret cults, with Nazis summoning an ultimate destructive power associated with divine retribution. Little of adventure remains intact in fantasy; each genre is based on contradictory assumptions, and the genres have been separate throughout literary and film history, from Aladdin and Sindbad the Sailor to Superman.

There are other difficulties in reserving the label "adventure" for a specific type of picture, rather than for the wide range of movies to which it has been applied. What is regarded as an adventurous experience in life may not be readily transferrable to a recognizable genre of adventure films; for instance, *The Dove* (1975), dealing with a teenager who sails around the world, subordinates this theme to the melodramatic tale of his difficulties falling in love. Likewise, a person may have a deeply adventurous experience on a hike or a camping trip, but this internal emotion is hardly material for the narrative of a generic Hollywood film. Only when such an episode highlights the adventure itself, as with a *Robinson Crusoe*–type story, may it truly be described as material for the genre.

One initial aspect of adventure is the expectation of the hero's exhibition of courage with a willingness to meet whatever perils may occur. There is the implication of "a physical challenge, a confrontation with bodily risk"—the view that all an adventurer needs is "an enquiring turn of mind and a profound contempt for scurvy and Spaniards" (Zweig, 223; Moth, 531). The adventurer is never passive, having an "appetite for life" and relishing hazardous and exciting occurrences, overcoming seemingly invincible obstacles and the apparent rules of probability (Bolitho, 238–239, 214–215; Nerlich 1987, 4). The adventurous experience occurs outside the usual mundane continuity of existence, encompassing travel and the dangerous, unexpected, and sometimes extraordinary undertaking (Simmel, 243; Nerlich 1987, 3, 373). The hero's life also depends on cunning, endurance, and the skill to survive (Green 1991, 1). Much suspense derives from seeing how adventurers measure their own strength against the world, with the result that the ultimate dimension of adventure is the possibility of death (Cameron, 128; Hawthorne, 179; Lill, 848). Consequently, the history and literature of adventure encompass both the noblest, the most thrilling, and the most inspiring human endeavors, as well as the shoddy, brazen, and disreputable (Hanson, vii). Indeed, both facets are often evident, whether in a swashbuckler, an imperialist, or an explorer, from Christopher Columbus to Robert Falcon Scott.

There is more to adventure films than the style and spectacle of a battle at sea or the clash of armies. What ultimately makes this aspect into something beyond action, into an adventure, is the experience beyond the physical challenge—its moral and intellectual flavor (Fisher, 319). The adventurous experience often leaves its characters matured and changed. Although frequently a superficial genre, adventure is potentially as enlightening and emotionally stirring as any other form, usually to the very degree to which the genre's traditional limits are stretched or overridden (Fisher, 136, 36). Indeed, many of the truest and most interesting adventurers are those for whom the physical element is the least significant part of their adventure (Green 1990, 61). Quasi-spiritual experiences are found in movies such as *Stanley and Livingstone; Kim; El Cid; Khartoum;* and *The Man Who Would Be King*. In attempting to overcome the merely physical, the adventurer's quest may include a metaphysical, philosophical dimension, although remaining in the realm of the possible and avoiding the supernatural occurrences of fantasy films. The hero in historical adventure has limited, earthly powers, without the option of calling upon the otherworldly or magic to aid his cause; the adventurer's trials and goals are part of a romantic yet realistic approach to the world. The adventurer must rely on those human qualities possessed within; even when promoting Christianity, as in *Stanley and Livingstone,* the spirituality is of a secular, nationalistic, and humanitarian variety.

To speak of adventure in terms of a film genre, we must move beyond simply a definition of adventure toward what gives the genre its cohesiveness and depth. Adding "historical" in front of "adventure" clarifies the distinction between the genre and other action types. Adventure's settings, not only temporally but geographically, are remote from what is mundane to the intended audience. The plot moves toward a mythical realm, where dates and locales are almost legendary, handled more as myth than factual re-creation (George Orwell in Green 1990, 2). Adventure movies take place from the Middle Ages up to the commencement of World War I, after the fall of the ancient world and prior to war movies. The genre allows the viewers to escape from their contemporary world into a historical past where right and wrong are presented unambiguously, when morality was drawn in sharp relief dividing heroes and villains (Cohen, 44).

Adventure films are united by the thematic consistency with which they treat history, characters, and a code of conduct and values. The everyday is replaced by an enlargement of life through imagination, the majesty of larger issues and greater conflicts in a historical setting in which nobility of character is evident (Fisher, 19, 408). The genre calls for deeds that accomplish some laudable goal and are performed for altruistic reasons, inferring models of admirable behavior for emulation. Adventure dramatizes the exploits of actual historical figures or famous incidents that fall into its generic domain, the challenges faced in the past of kings and battles, rebellion, piracy, exploration, the creation of empires, and the interplay of power politics between the individual and national authority. Only in this genre does Hollywood combine these subjects. Adventure movies not only adopt these standard meanings of adventure but also are linked by a thematic commitment to certain ideals, giving them a political dimension. Ultimately, the genre is less concerned with military exploits per se than with the worthiness of struggling for freedom and proper governance. Adventure in the cinema deals primarily with liberty and overcoming oppression as a historical phenomenon. The same ethic directs the hero's action, whether he is Robin Hood or an adventurer in a colonial setting, where he is portrayed as the selfless protector of native peoples from the threat of tyrants or religious fanatics. The occupying race, not the rebelling natives, is portrayed as representing the move toward a freer society and believe that they are bringing enlightenment to primitive lands.

The genre's fundamental tone is one of optimism (Bloch, 143; Green 1991, 17). Appealing to the imagination and the heart, human faith is vindicated, good triumphs, and justice prevails (Fisher, 408). Within the world of adventure, humankind's past is conceived as a progression toward equality, depicting as a historical phenomenon the triumph of the political values supporting democratic institutions (Bloch 139–43). The narrative movement keynotes freedom and throwing off shackles to create a new, more just society, following a sequence of tyranny, subversion, and the establishment of a government protecting the rights of its citizens. Adventure transforms the setting from one of oppression and dishonor to one of liberty, dignity, and independence; the goal provides a reason for the sacrifice and the taking of life, the willingness to resort to warfare. Adventure movies arrange history to reveal, by the end, a more romantic view than the film opened with—whether *Mayflower: The Pilgrims' Adventure* or *Ali Baba and the Forty Thieves*. Adventure is important not only as a major Hollywood genre but also because it deals with the western world's past attempts to broaden civilization and to develop responsible self-government in a political philosophy that reflects the American experience. Through the vehicle of adventure movies, Americans see aspects of their own development and national virtues reflected in the portrayals of other countries and their social systems (cf. Durgnat in Grant 1977, 108). Adventure becomes a metaphorical depiction of the American Revolution, casting the conflict's essential issues in various times and places to indicate the timeless need for liberty and freedom. So central are these analogous traits, imputing American ideals to past foreign struggles for freedom, that I will conclude this book by examining how Hollywood adventure pictures may be read as allegory, a metaphor of the American experience, particularly the Revolution. Instead of portraying directly this pivotal event in the American experience, it is offered in a mythic, parallel manner through representations of similar events in terms of the adventure genre.

CHAPTER 2 **Five Forms of Adventure**

Adventure is usually packaged in one of several different forms, and the similarity and diversity of the genre is best understood by a division into five principal types: the swashbuckler, pirate, sea, empire, and fortune hunter.[1] For instance, *The Three Musketeers; Captain Blood; Mutiny on the Bounty; Gunga Din;* and *Around the World in 80 Days* are all adventure films, yet each belongs to one of the five separate types. This typology highlights the principal activities of the main characters, along with their basic locales—whether in the castles of medieval Europe, the piratical Spanish Main, a ship on the high seas, or colonial India and Africa. The types of adventure are distinguished not only by narrative patterns, iconography, and various conventionalized locales but also by the nature of the hero's efforts and the attitudes of the characters toward political issues. The fluidity in temporal and geographical settings ultimately amplifies the underlying unity of the genre, since the overriding themes remain the same regardless of time and place. Each type of adventure illustrates a different aspect of the historical conflict between injustice, oppression, and revolt—the empire adventure depicts destructive rebellions, while the swashbuckler portrays benevolent ones. The swashbuckler and empire builder, and now and then the pirate and sea adventurer, are involved with revolution or its suppression, while the sea story, pirate, and fortune hunter often undertake exploration or the search for wealth. (Within each section, films are mentioned whose qualification for that form has been confirmed through the author's viewing; the appendix includes other titles that research indicates likely belong to that form.) The five types of adventure are discussed in a specific order, from the swashbuckler, the most easily understood form, through the least formulaic variety, the fortune hunter. The progression also illustrates a gradual shift from a liberating viewpoint to the more conservative perspective of adventures whose colonial settings require justifying an imperialist presence. Only by tracking these various strands, the disparate manifestations of a variable genre, does the term *adventure* acquire a comprehensive and generic meaning. Later chapters will explore in more detail the principal issues—characterization, history, politics, imperialism—raised by the various forms of adventure.

The Swashbuckler Adventure

The swashbuckler is the best-known and most recognizable type of adventure film. This form usually opens with oppression imposed on a peaceful land, resulting in a rebellion that, as in *Son of Monte Cristo*, calls forth a leader dedicated to the rights of the people. The distinctly political overtones of the conflict are clear in the words of the preface to the 1920 version of *The Mark of Zorro*. "Oppression—by its very nature—creates the power that crushes it. A champion arises—a champion of the oppressed—whether it be a Cromwell or someone unrecorded, he will be there. He is born." The swashbuckling hero typically spearheads a popular revolt against a tyrannical pretender, such as Prince John, or a royal minister attempting to usurp the proper authority, as in *Adventures of Casanova*. Through a series of confrontations, power alternates between the forces of change and the status quo until the conflict eventually gives birth to a new era of freedom (Nerlich 1987, 391). With the hero's aid, at the conclusion of the swashbuckling adventure either a just regime is restored or a new, improved establishment is created, replacing one liable to transgression by tyrants. While the prototype of the swashbuckler is the myth of Robin Hood, the figure has been elaborated historically through more recent manifestations in popular literature, from the Scarlet Pimpernel to Zorro, and the implications of such a figure will be discussed in the subsequent chapters.

Some swashbucklers have a more conservative tinge and focus on keeping the status quo in power rather than glorifying rebellion. Such reactions are provoked by the threat of an even worse regime attempting to seize power, a theme also found in empire adventures. An imperfect monarchy may be threatened by authoritarian and corrupt forces seeking power for their own ends, whether Cardinal Richelieu in *The Three Musketeers* or Black Michael in *The Prisoner of Zenda*. The French revolutionaries in *The Scarlet Pimpernel; The Black Book / Reign of Terror;* and *The Purple Mask* (1955) have become as cruel as their predecessors. Similarly, the *Moonraker* (1958) fights the Roundheads, hoping to restore a monarchy that was more beneficent than its Cromwellian successor.

Swashbucklers are often made aware of injustice as one displaced by the new hierarchy, as in *The Saracen Blade.* Their personal enemies may be the same as those who menace society at large, as when young Dick Shelton discovers the conspiracy of his traitorous uncle, Daniel Brackley, in *The Black Arrow.* While not desiring a political role, a swashbuckler seldom requires more than minimal persuasion to assume leadership, as in *Robin and Marian.* The readiness to defend good against evil is often both empowering and a crucial redeeming virtue; adopting a political cause redeems those who initially appear to be scoundrels in *Lorna Doone; Don Juan* (1926); *The Lady and the Highwayman;* and *The Bandits of Corsica / The Revenge of the Corsican Brothers.*

The swashbuckler offers the appeal of characters who briefly but justifiably succeed in transgressing the law, yet whose ultimate impact is to uphold justice and morality. Anarchy is never an option, and even as the adventurer subverts the existing authority, he is paving the way for a newly constituted social order. The outlaw deeds are ultimately given official sanction and pardon, since the actual lawbreakers are those who have attempted to seize power (Thomas Sobchack in Grant 1977, 49; Green 1979, 86). By contrast, the swashbuckler has remained a gentleman dedicated to a just cause, never seeking personal gain, whether *The Highwayman* or *The King's Thief*. The duality of this approach to law is based on the conscience of the hero, who upholds personal ideals that always parallel political justice and are more reliable than the power structure.

Swashbucklers stress the purity of the hero's motives, his physical and mental agility, impeccable manners, and often witty speech. The aristocracy in the swashbuckler is one of bearing rather than inheritance; whether a noble or commoner, the hero is a gentleman and patriot, with humor, charm, and gallantry underlying the devotion to justice (Richards 1973, 4–5). The villain, despite any surface display of similar characteristics, is inevitably a boor, such as Louis XI in *The Beloved Rogue*, *If I Were King*, and other renderings of the François Villon story. For the knight, who was one of the earliest swashbucklers and often a veteran of such "Christian" quests as the Crusades, armor is not only a shield but the concrete symbol of these unwavering ideals. Violating this code of conduct in any way can have dire consequences, both for the hero and for the society of which he is a part, as when *The War Lord* takes advantage of archaic noble prerogatives over a newly wed bride, provoking a peasant revolt.

The swashbuckler offers the comforting myth that any tyranny, no matter how formidable the military forces on its side, can be defeated by civilians with a sense of strategy and a belief in justice, even if their weapons are inferior. The magnetism and skill of the hero's leadership, rather than force of arms or number of followers, brings victory in *The Mark of Zorro*; *Robin Hood*; and all their various progeny—*Don Q Son of Zorro*; *The Bold Caballero / The Bold Cavalier*; *The Sign of Zorro*; *Bandit of Sherwood Forest*; *Rogues of Sherwood Forest*; *Son of Robin Hood*; *Sword of Sherwood Forest*; and the like. These somewhat simplistic qualities of the swashbuckler have also rendered it the form of adventure most open to humorous and satiric treatment, with films such as *The Court Jester*; *Start the Revolution without Me*; and *Zorro—The Gay Blade*.

The swashbuckler elevates the importance of the individual. Although heroes usually have a small band to assist them, the interaction among the group is slighted in favor of attention to the hero; camaraderie is more important in other types of adventure. Many swashbucklers function virtually alone, with minimal assistance from others, as in *Mark of the Renegade*. A measure of isolation may be essential to the task, even one of its most heart-rending requirements; *The Scarlet Pimpernel* must keep his exploits secret from his French wife, exacerbating a rift in their marriage. Plots frequently end with a duel in which the hero single-handedly kills the principal villain.

The swashbuckler is set throughout the era of adventure, from the Middle Ages through the nineteenth century, most often in Europe. For instance, thanks partially to the vitality of the historical fictions of Alexandre Dumas, many of the movies take place in France during the reigns of Louis XIII and XIV and Cardinals Richelieu and Mazarin (*Richelieu; The Three Musketeers; The Fifth Musketeer / Behind the Iron Mask; At Sword's Point / Sons of the Musketeers; Under the Red Robe*) or the Napoleonic era and its aftermath (*Captain Scarlett; The Sword of Monte Cristo; The Duellists*). A Spanish setting evokes more historically conscious pictures, whether in the Moorish period (*El Cid*) or the wars against the first Bonaparte (*The Pride and the Passion*). Other countries include the Netherlands (*Prince of Pirates*), Italy (*The Affairs of Cellini*), and even Russia (*The White Warrior*).

England is perhaps the favorite locale for swashbucklers; as the preface to *Robin Hood* (1922) notes, "Her chronicles tell of warriors and statesman, of royal crusaders, of jousting knights. Her ballads sing of jolly friars, troubadours, of gallant outlaws who roamed her mighty forests." The home front during the Crusades has achieved a legendary status, with Prince John usurping the absent Richard the Lion-Hearted, triggering the formation of Robin Hood's band in Sherwood (*Ivanhoe*). The British Isles as a locale for swashbuckling adventure first appear during the era of knighthood (*The Black Shield of Falworth; Quentin Durward / The Adventures of Quentin Durward; Siege of the Saxons*), beginning with King Arthur (*Knights of the Round Table; The Black Knight; Prince Valiant; Sword of Lancelot; King Arthur—The Young Warlord*). The frequent wars between England and France over the centuries are also a favorite subject (*The Warriors / The Dark Avenger; Sea Devils* [1953]), as are the struggles for independence of smaller nations. Scotland is portrayed as a wild, freedom-loving land whose fights against England for independence are viewed sympathetically (*Kidnapped; The Master of Ballantrae; Bonnie Prince Charlie; The Scarecrow of Romney Marsh / Dr. Syn Alias the Scarecrow*), as are those of Ireland (*Cap-

tain Boycott; Captain Lightfoot; The Fighting Prince of Donegal) and French-speaking *Quebec.*

As the most formulaic of adventure forms, the swashbuckler evokes the expectation of swordplay, often pitting the hero against several adversaries simultaneously, since the term *swashbuckler* properly indicates the sound of sword striking sword or shield in battle (Cohen, 4). However, many swashbuckling adventure pictures emphasize battles or hand-to-hand fights yet are swashbucklers by their shared plot concerns, such as the American Revolution drama *Johnny Tremain / Johnny Tremain and the Sons of Liberty.* The primary importance of a sword fight is as an embodiment of the plot conflict, and only secondarily a display of physical agility, as indicated by the significance of the accompanying sprightly dialogue. Swashbuckling action is merely one aspect of an overall expression of a larger way of life, an entire philosophy, and the swashbuckler is a narrative form rather than a style of filmmaking, with action growing out of themes that must be discussed within their context. There are many other icons and motifs in the swashbuckler, such as archery, jousting, castles, coronations, renunciations, royal intrigue, escapes from dungeons, battles alternating with humorous and romantic interludes, and chases on horseback where the pursued escape by hiding while the pursuer races by (Jones, 43).[2]

All of the classic, archetypal elements of the swashbuckler are contained in the 1937 movie of Anthony Hope's 1894 novel, *The Prisoner of Zenda*, a story also filmed in 1912, 1915, 1922, 1952 (an exact remake of the 1937 version), and in a 1979 comedic version. *The Prisoner of Zenda* is built on the theme of a kingdom whose safety is threatened by a plot to usurp the throne by an illegitimate ruler. The setting is a typically vague period, some time in the late nineteenth century, "when History wore a Rose and Politics had not yet outgrown the Waltz," as the movie's preface relates. Already verging on legend, the emphasis on myth over historicity is further emphasized by placing the tale in an imagined southeastern European country, Ruritania—a principality where old values and kinship still hold sway. As the preface continues, "Toward the close of the last century . . . a Great Royal Scandal was whispered in the Anterooms of Europe. However true it was, any resemblance in 'The Prisoner of Zenda' to Heroes, Villains or Heroines, living or dead, is a coincidence not intended." (The capitalization is used on screen.) Already the story has been transformed into simultaneous fiction,

Rassendyll (Lewis Stone) and Flavia (Alice Terry) must deny their love out of duty to the kingdom, as Sapt (Robert Edeson) reminds them in *The Prisoner of Zenda* (1922).

myth, and history-as-it-might-have-been; a similar foreword is found in the 1937 version of *The Prince and the Pauper*.

Loyalty is owed to the rightful king, Rudolf V (Ronald Colman), although he is inclined to drink irresponsibly. Rudolf's downfall is plotted by an illegitimate older brother, Black Michael (Raymond Massey), who seeks the kingdom for his own glorification. The Englishman Rudolf Rassendyll (Colman again, in a dual role), like all adventure heroes, agrees to foil the plot. He carries royal Ruritanian blood, through the centuries-past indiscretion of a monarch, so his appearance is identical to that of his distant cousin, Rudolf V. Rassendyll comes literally to act out his part with initial reluctance but recognizes the call of duty and honor. His tasks will bring him no reward beyond the satisfaction of fulfilling an obligation that fate has imposed on him.

The Prisoner of Zenda offers several sets of parallel characters, with casting that accentuates each of the oppositions: King Rudolf and Rassendyll, the legitimate king and the potential usurper, Rassendyll and Rupert, and Flavia and Antoinette. Rassendyll, although noble only in spirit rather than birth, becomes the opposite of Rupert of Hentzau, an aristocrat by lineage but truly a blackguard. Rupert (Douglas Fairbanks, Jr.) is a fortune hunter who aids Michael's cause not from duty but rather the promise of reward; ultimately he tries to seduce Antoinette and quarrels with Michael. A similar dichotomy separates the two women. The dark Antoinette (Mary Astor), mistress of Michael, lives only for him, and fearing Michael's plot will cost him his life, endangers herself by revealing the conspiracy. On the other hand, the blonde Flavia (Madeleine Carroll), destined to be queen and keenly aware of her duties, is willing to sacrifice even love for the kingdom.

The Prisoner of Zenda follows the swashbuckler's narrative pattern. A country's peaceful existence is shattered by the threatened imposition of a false political authority, and an outsider who becomes an outlaw must restore the old order. While Rassendyll has two assistants, Sapt (C. Aubrey Smith) and Fritz (David Niven), his exploits are largely undertaken alone, and in crises he must rely entirely on his own resources. As a hero, Rassendyll is a man of both intellectual and physical abilities; the climactic duel with Rupert is one of wit as well as saber. Rassendyll must relinquish the throne he temporarily occupied and fought to preserve, as well as Flavia who, while she could never be his wife, would always be queen in his heart. Although Queen Flavia and the commoner who acts like a king fall in love, they cannot be united; the call of honor, patriotism, and politics must be paramount over the emotions of the heart. As a result, unfulfilled romances occur in a number of swashbucklers, such as *The Exile* (1947) and *Adventures of Don Juan*, even though the genre more often favors a satisfying fulfillment of the romantic ideal that parallels the political settlement.

During the 1940s and 1950s, a distinct but short-lived branch of the swashbuckler developed that demonstrated the underlying unity and adaptability among the different adventure forms. The Oriental swashbuckler merged three different types of adventure into a new hybrid by transferring traditional swashbuckler motifs to the locale most typical of empire and fortune hunter adventures, the Near and Far East, especially Arabia (Richards 1977, 270). Yet the Oriental swashbuckler is different in one key respect: it relinquishes any pretence of the realism found in the similar locales of empire and fortune hunter adventures. Instead, it evokes a lure and mystique that creates a transparently imaginary and artificial Far East (*Son of Sinbad / Nights in a Harem*). The emphasis is on a surface exoticism, abandoning the facade of historicity in favor of temporal indeterminacy, located some time in adventure's general era.

In this respect, the Oriental swashbuckler emulates the iconography of *A Thousand and One Arabian Nights* and *The Thief of Bagdad*, yet remains within the limitations of physical reality, without fantasy's magic and supernatural. In place of flying carpets or genies, the Oriental swashbuckler substitutes traditional adventure motifs centering around the struggle for freedom against oppression. The characters in the Oriental swashbuckler have different titles— caliphs, sheiks, sultans, and viziers replace kings, knights, and vassals—but the heroes and the conflicts are the same. Individuals are borrowed from the Arabian Nights but taken out of their original context, conforming faithfully to the conventional stereotypes of the traditional swashbuckler. Many of the figures portrayed are simply King Arthur or Robin Hood by another name; *Ali Baba and the Forty Thieves* become a band of political outlaws.

The post–World War II decade saw brief popularity for the Oriental swashbuckler because its bazaars, mosques, and dancers were ideally matched to the bright, sumptuous technicolor that was no longer limited to the highest budget pictures (cf. Richards 1977, 270, 282). These movies gave the illusion of costing more than they actually did, becoming a specialty of the Universal and Columbia studios. One screenwriter, Gerald Drayson Adams, coauthored more than one-third of the Oriental swashbucklers: *The Desert Hawk; Flame of Araby; The Golden Horde; The Prince Who Was a Thief; Son of Ali Baba;* and *Princess of the Nile.* The form also offered a purer, more lighthearted escapism at the time when the more straightforward swashbuckler, together with other adventure forms, was entering a phase of greater realism. The Oriental swashbuckler appealed chiefly to juvenile audiences and allowed for the continuance of the basic swashbuckler form at its most naive and stylized, as in *Son of Ali Baba* and *Arabian Nights* (1942). The plots are highly variable, able to contain more improbable overtones and incidents; for instance, a princess marries a barber in *The Adventures of Hajji Baba.* In the increased tendency for princes and princesses to use disguise, often as slaves or commoners, the Oriental type took an established swashbuckler convention to new extremes, as in *Princess of the Nile* (Jowett, 802).

The Oriental swashbuckler combines the swashbuckler formula with an Eastern setting. In *Omar Khayyam*, the secret head of the "brotherhood of assassins" (Michael Rennie) pays homage to the shah (Raymond Massey); at his right is Omar (Cornel Wilde).

The Prince Who Was a Thief contains the standard swashbuckler situation of a young monarch (Tony Curtis), unlawfully denied his throne, who hides from his enemies amidst the lowest classes. From such people he finds the support to regain his rightful position and eventually chooses his princess from among them. *Omar Khayyam*, on the other hand, clearly displays the Oriental swashbuckler's debt to the use of the Far East in the empire adventure. In a variation on the terrorist theme used to justify the conservative politics of empire, *Omar Khayyam* tells of a "Brotherhood of Assassins," a conspiracy of fanatics committed to murder and suicide who threaten the legitimate regime in Persia. Their portrayal, and indeed the entire narrative, are reminiscent of the cult of Kali, portrayed in *Gunga Din* and elsewhere. Otherwise, however, *Omar Khayyam* sets out the milieu and conflict typical of the Oriental swashbuckler, epitomized by its narrated preface.

A thousand years ago the Persian empire stretched from the Mediterranean Sea all the way to India and down to Egypt. This great empire was ruled by a warrior shah. He had the absolute power of life and death. Even the most exalted bent at his feet. Yet this mighty ruler would now be forgotten but for the work of a man who was among the humblest of his subjects, Omar Khayyam. He was a happy man, with friends among both the lowly and the great in the ancient city of Neschapur. The motto of those dangerous and exciting days was "think as your master thinks." But Omar Khayyam thought for himself. He was a lover of life and of wisdom, a poet when the mood was upon him, and a mathematician when it was not. He was a student of the stars, and of those things written in the stars. Omar Khayyam had an understanding of human nature and a philosophy which has conquered the hearts of men—and of women.

The title character in *Omar Khayyam* is portrayed by Cornel Wilde as not only an eloquent poet and fabled philosopher but also a scholar, mathematician, and astronomer, devising a new and accurate calendar by observing the stars. Like most adventurers, Omar is both practical and a dreamer. However, he is also a wily adventurer, who risks death by penetrating the secret mountain lair of the assassins to learn their weaknesses and ultimately destroys them through his knowledge of science. Yet Omar is also a lover, who reaches above his station, only to be frustrated by social inequality. After much unhappiness at seeing his love (Debra Paget) married to the shah, Omar's loyalty is rewarded when, as a widow, she is allowed to break with royal tradition to return to him.

The Pirate Adventure

While the pirate film often has been lumped with the swashbuckler because of certain iconographic similarities, the contrasts in tone, characterization, and narrative are enormous. These point the pirate at least equally in the direction of the next distinct type, the sea adventure, and the pirate tale in fact occupies a berth midway between the swashbuckler and the sea story. For instance, unlike the swashbuckler, operating within a group is essential to seafaring life, and the pirate's relationship with his crew is vital.

The predominant atmosphere, as well as many of the typical recurring plot elements, is carefully described in the preface to *The*

Black Pirate (1926), reproduced as it appears on the screen. "Being an account of *Buccaneers* and the *Spanish Main*, the *Jolly Roger*, *Golden Galleons*, bleached skulls, *Buried Treasure*, the *Plank*, dirks and cutlasses, *Scuttled Ships, Marooning, Desperate Deeds, Desperate Men*, and—even on this dark soil—*Romance*. It was the custom of *these pirates, to subdue* their *prey, loot* the *ship, Bind* their *captives* and *Blow them up*." Pirate adventures tend to center on the geographic regions where such activity actually occurred: the South Pacific (*China Seas; Nate and Hayes / Savage Islands*), the Mediterranean (*The Sea Hawk* [1924]), and especially the Caribbean during the period of the Spanish Main. The last is the most frequent setting, with the conflict not only between pirates and government officials but often between pirates of English versus Spanish or French background. Tales occasionally take place at the beginning of the nineteenth century, centering on French Louisiana and the early years of American control (*Yankee Buccaneer*). Other pirate pictures, such as *Treasure Island*, are involved simply with the timeless search for wealth and are not so temporally or geographically specific. In some cases, otherwise honest individuals may become accidentally involved with pirates, as in *Shipwrecked* (1991).

Although not part of the political establishment, the pirate operates from a position of strength; European countries and their overseas representatives are powerless to rid the seas of them. Many of the local magistrates are already thoroughly corrupted and survive in office not only at royal pleasure but also at the whim of the pirates themselves (Nerlich 1987, 398–99). Some pirates, while overtly condemned in Europe, are privately encouraged by one country to prey on the ships of an enemy nation. In this way the pirate's life is acknowledged and occasionally sanctioned, his activities turned to a useful purpose. Such pirates could become heroes, instead of outlaws, shifting such films as *The Sea Hawk* (1940) and *Seven Seas to Calais* out of the pirate category and into the sea story. Piracy is defined less by specific acts than by an individualistic rebelliousness and refusal to submit to any outside domination (Nerlich 1987, 428 n. 123).

In *The Fortunes of Captain Blood*, Blood announces "We're freebooters and privateers, with no land of our own. But we fight for something more precious than land—freedom." Although sometimes unconcerned with government, even conspiring to manipulate rulers for profit, pirates usually discover that they share a love of

liberty in common with other rebels, as in *The Crimson Pirate;*
Caribbean / Caribbean Gold; and *Pirate Warrior / Black Pirate /*
Rage of the Buccaneers. Pirates move to such locales as Maracaibo
or Tortuga to build a new, exclusive society of their own, with a code
of honor and an aristocracy unrelated to the old world. The more
egalitarian rules are reflected in the racial mix of the crew, which
nearly always includes a black or an oriental. As in the historical
case of Sir Henry Morgan in *The Black Swan,* the pirate may even be
sworn into the king's service to root out former allies. Reformed
pirates may become civilian leaders and a force to be reckoned with,
tempering firmness with a knowledge derived from their own outlaw days. Yet there remains a reluctance to undertake royal commands, indicating the pirate will only remain in office so long as
official policies serve goals compatible with their own views.

Even when cast in the heroic mold, pirates are not as clean living,
patriotic, or moral as most other adventurers, and they are allowed
greater deviation from the norms of gentlemanly behavior (*Moon-
fleet; The Black Swan; The Spanish Main*). The pirate life is one of
few commitments and rapidly shifting loyalties: the title character
in *Captain Blood* (1935) kills his temporary partner, the evil
Lavesseur, ending a pact that "should never have been signed." Isolation often becomes a problem for the pirate captain: if a minimal
distance and respect from his crew is lost, he often faces rebellion, as
in *The Crimson Pirate* and *A High Wind in Jamaica.* Like *Hurricane
Smith,* pirates are usually commoners belonging to the lower
classes, without the education, gentlemanly manners, and the
noblesse oblige typical of the more aristocratic swashbuckler.

Two widely divergent behavior patterns emerge for different types
of pirate. Some are only temporarily disaffected, alienated because of
an injustice, or exiled by a dictatorial regime. The life of a privateer
is little more than a means to an end, a final refuge; as Jean Laffite's
second in command, Dominique You, remarks in *The Buccaneer*
(1958), "When a man loses everything else, he still has the sea."
Although a pirate may become weary of his outlaw status, he may
have little choice. Such a life is ultimately the only one available
unless political regimes change (*Morgan the Pirate*) or are willing to
pardon their previous behavior. Great anguish results from the inability to call a homeland one's own, and the pirate proves willing to
serve his country should it call on him (*Captain Blood*).

In contrast to these gentlemanly pirates is another type, pirates who never wish to become integrated into respectable society, like Long John Silver in his various exploits—the many versions of *Treasure Island* and the cinematic and television sequels. For them, patriotism and romance are incidental to self-interest; they are simultaneously a virtual anarchist and a materialist. They value both the hunt for and the spending of treasure—prized less as property than for whatever quick pleasures it can buy in the tavern. This pirate willingly becomes an outcast, a status that carries with it the freedom and unsettled existence he thrives upon. The ultimate outsider, he becomes a permanent outlaw, whose questionable past, lack of ethics and uninhibited life-style bar him from the ordinary society of the Old World. Relishing their unrespectable status, pirates range from disgruntled nonconformists to antisocial dropouts and undesirables who find themselves unable to live by ordinary laws or means. A few pirates are distinct villains, especially the vicious wreckers, who lure ships onto deserted coasts in storms, killing all on board and ransacking the hulk for profit (*Jamaica Inn; The Wreck of the Hesperus; Fury at Smuggler's Bay; The Light at the Edge of the World*).

The modern trend in pirate films has been toward deromanticizing the genre, introducing a greater element of realism. Pirates are portrayed as being as depraved as they probably were, rather than as legend and novelists such as Rafael Sabatini have painted them. The streak of cruelty apparent in such movies as *Captain Kidd; Anne of the Indies;* or *Blackbeard the Pirate* has been amplified to include a sense of degeneracy and mental deficiency. *The Pirates of Blood River* turns into a statement denouncing their senseless greed. Pirates today are pictured as foolish, quarrelsome, socially maladjusted misfits, lecherous rather than as the romantic figures of earlier films. These characteristics of the revisionist pirate adventure became pronounced in the 1960s with *A High Wind in Jamaica* and were amplified in *The Light at the Edge of the World* through *Pirates* (1986) to feature an emphasis on the protagonist's peculiarities and brutality, aspects foreign to the classical pirate mythology.

One of the penalties of the pirate life for a gentleman corsair is a greater difficulty in finding love than is experienced by other adventure heroes. In exchange for freedom, pirates must sacrifice the honorable reputation so prized by adventurers, and frequently, at least for a time, the possibility of acceptance by a member of the opposite sex. The aspiration felt by some pirates to re-enter proper society often becomes bound up with love for a person who is initially socially above them but also offers an opportunity for redemption (Jowett, 804–5). For instance, Captain Blood anguishes over the apparent impossibility of his union with the Lady Arabella, and only a change in the political conditions governing his actions allows the couple to come together.

Despite the problematic nature of love in pirate films, it also permits some of the most important roles for women in the adventure genre. The pirate adventure brings together diametrically opposite types of women, fellow adventurers and those who become objects and remain basically passive. The form is rife with women who occupy a background role, often abducted and won over by the pirate captain (*Raiders of the Seven Seas*). Yet the ranks of pirates also include an unusually large number of fiery women of the sea who take active roles as the equal or superior of men (*Frenchman's Creek; Buccaneer's Girl; Anne of the Indies; Against All Flags*) (Cohen, 61). Nonetheless, the independence of such characters is frequently undercut through their portrayals in situations where they become largely dependent on men.

Like the swashbuckler's Oriental form, the pirate film has a subtype, although in this case it never has achieved such popularity. The depiction of Vikings has become a variation on the pirate formula, as in *The Vikings* and *The Long Ships*. Despite the surface iconic differences and change in period and locale, their activities are strikingly similar to those of later pirates, emphasizing looting, brawling, wenching, and superstition. Like their successors, Vikings place a high value on loyalty to the ship, their band, and the search for gold.

The Buccaneer (1958) sums up the various inclinations of the pirate film but more strongly reflects the philosophical aspects of the genre than the 1938 version or the recounting of the same incidents in *The Last of the Buccaneers* and a 1953 television dramatization, *Cavalcade of America: The Pirate's Choice*. In *The Buccaneer* (1958), Jean Laffite (Yul Brynner) is unquestionably a heroic corsair, one who has always maintained certain standards, never attacking American ships. Tired of being a man without a country, he now seeks one to which he can belong. He controls his unruly men with a fair but iron hand, convincing them to follow his new inclinations, however reluctantly, by the force of his example and oratory. His motivation stems from two factors: an abstract admiration for the Declaration of Independence, frequently quoting "all men are created equal," and his blossoming love for the daughter of Louisiana's governor.

Throughout the movie Laffite is paralleled with Gen. Andrew Jackson (Charlton Heston), a bona fide American hero. Jackson is preparing, with minimal resources, to defend New Orleans against a well-armed British invasion during the War of 1812. Laffite tries to convince the suspicious governor to accept his assistance, but the offer is not conveyed to Jackson, and the original order to attack Laffite's island base is carried out. With his pirates imprisoned, Laffite does not abandon his original scheme or go to the British, who have attempted to bribe him, but instead negotiates directly with Jackson. Jackson rectifies the error and, thanks to the aid of Laffite, the British are defeated at New Orleans and the young America is saved.

As the victory is celebrated and Lafitte becomes engaged, the former pirate's past comes back to haunt him: a renegade captain had sunk an American ship that carried the sister of the woman he loves. Although Laffite hanged the miscreant, his new-found American friends turn on him, with the sole exception of Jackson, who can only grant him the chance to escape. Gathering his followers, Laffite sets sail, having lost both his newly adopted country and the love of the governor's daughter. The pirates have discovered, in the words of his lieutenant, that "our only home is the deck beneath our feet." The pirate's existence is found inevitably unsatisfying, sowing its own future disillusionment, and only the possibility of a renewed commitment to patriotism provides hope.

The Sea Adventure

The next step among adventure types is the sea story. Not only does this form share much of the locale of the pirate adventure, aboard a ship on the high seas, but the content often relates one of the ways people were driven to piracy. The pirate's life is often the result of a mutiny; for instance, Fletcher Christian adopts a pirate-like scarf when he selects Pitcairn's Island as a refuge in the sea adventure *Mutiny on the Bounty* (1935). Sea and pirate adventures are also linked by the use of naval iconography, such as the battle scenes, sailing vessels coming around to aim their guns at one an-

As part of the bargain to save his men, but also because of his admiration for the United States, the pirate Lafitte (Yul Brynner, with pistol) offers to help Gen. Andrew Jackson (Charlton Heston) in the Battle of New Orleans, in *The Buccaneer* (1958).

other, sweeping the deck with broadsides to the sound of cannon fire and the collapse of masts and rigging.

However, the sea adventure is differentiated by a manner that is considerably less romantic than swashbucklers and pirate films. Contrasting reality and mythology, the sea adventure becomes inherently more authentic, if not quite mimetic, especially in its grim portrayal of life aboard ships in the historical past. There are magnificent visuals, backed by musical scores, of the intricacies and majesty of ships gracefully leaving port to a musical score, yet the aesthetics of wind, sails, and rigging are counterpointed by the cruel law of the sea that governs the routine of ocean-going life. A number of conventionalized but harsh plot incidents stress the rugged life of the sailor. During a funeral at sea, a comrade is summarily dumped overboard from beneath a flag for a shroud, to the accompaniment of drums and a perfunctory prayer from the captain. Later in the voyage the ship is trapped in the doldrums with the hot sun beating down, the sails slack, and the currents still. To extricate themselves the crew must row the small boats to tow the huge ship to safety. Frequently reefs, collisions, and wrecks provide more distress. Individuals fall overboard and are drowned, or drop to their deaths from the rigging high atop the masts down to the deck below. There are hand-to-hand fights in the sailors' quarters, a few of them good natured, together with brief moments of camaraderie among the brethren of the sea, providing respites from the daily drudgery.

For most sailors and officers, this adventure type supports the myth that a person is improved by going to sea—as in the case of *Midshipman Easy,* Byam in *Mutiny on the Bounty,* Stewart in *Two Years before the Mast,* and the reformation of Harvey Cheyne in *Captains Courageous.* The experience proves to be the making of one's character; during the voyage the boy, whatever his age, becomes a man (*Down to the Sea in Ships*) (Green 1979, 150). In *Captain China,* a Pacific storm offers the opportunity for two disgraced, once-drunken officers to redeem themselves and resume their proper command, as well as impelling an ambitious first mate to reject the opportunism that once caused him to usurp his superior's role. The alteration can be either literal or metaphorical, changing the heroes into more responsible, concerned individuals, less isolated and self-centered. The ocean serves as a locale inducing more contemplation than awe, the voyage becoming a testing ground for the complexities of command and responsibility and the maturation it may produce in individuals of every station (Milne, 19, 23). Indeed, in sharp contrast to most other adventure types, especially pirate films, sea stories dwell on serious and complex themes, with an almost literary density. Among the frequent sources are history (the *Bounty* retellings, Richard Henry Dana's *Two Years Before the Mast*), respected classics (Jack London's *The Sea Wolf,* Herman Melville's *Moby Dick* and *Billy Budd*), or novels of a higher standard than most adventure fiction (Rudyard Kipling's *Captains Courageous* and C. S. Forester's Hornblower series). Sea adventures tend to become character studies of the captain, officers, and crew, their leadership abilities, motivations, relationships, and actions. Events inevitably lead to self-revelation, the baring of one's true nature. As Ishmael narrates in *Moby Dick* (1956), the sea is a place "where each man, as in a mirror, finds himself." The sea comes to represent a basic challenge, where humankind may learn to fulfill its potential and reach a greater understanding of itself and nature (Milne, 19).

The sea adventure concentrates on a microcosm, groups of people in isolated conditions, living amidst the elements and outside the normal social interaction of other adventure settings (Milne, 25; Fisher, 25). This group has similarities to the regiment in the empire adventure or the war film. Separated for lengthy periods from civilization, each member of the crew experiences a longing for home. Compressed in cramped quarters, tired of one another's constant presence, officers and sailors alike are faced with exhausting labors and find themselves hard-pressed to maintain self-control. The sea story is also the adventure type with the least opportunity for women to participate, a result of the practical matter of the locale; romantic interludes seem an improbable intrusion on the veneer of historicity in *John Paul Jones*; *The Sea Wolf* (1941); *Two Years Before the Mast*; and *Botany Bay*.

Among all adventure types, none etches more vividly the stratification between superior and subordinate, extending the ruler-peasant motif of land-based adventures (Milne, 25). The distinctions between the officers and crew are accented, rather than diminished, despite their similar backgrounds. Seldom is either nobly born, usually belonging to the lower and occasionally middle economic class. The members of the crew tend to be lifetime sailors or individuals compelled into service by impressment; many are homeless drifters without families, who are seen in only one other conventional habitat, the tavern. They are depicted as a superstitious lot, poorly educated, for whom the sea is a refuge. Beginning with cynical expectations, the sailors are habituated to a harsh life where only the hardiest survive. They are restless from the start, grumbling against authority and tempted toward mutiny, whether provoked or not.

The political hierarchy on board establishes the captain as more powerful than any king, ruling by tradition and a handful of officers. The most successful voyages are those where the crew feels at one with the captain and his aims (*The Sea Hawk* [1940]); the lack of such an understanding portends disaster (*Mutiny on the Bounty*; *The Sea Wolf*). Hence a central concern is communication, or its failure, between captain and crew. The captain must be able to transmit his goal and vision to convince the crew to follow him. In only a few cases is this ideal achieved; it often breaks down, not because of a lack of respect for discipline but because of a heartless officer with an uncaring attitude toward his crew.

Like the other types within the genre, the sea adventure has an important political element. The voyage often turns on the question of proper authority; the strength and wisdom of a command is measured by the captain's sense of justice and mercy. While avoiding the extreme of anarchy by supporting the need for discipline among a motley crew, the sea adventure's sympathies are clearly with the right of the members of a crew to free themselves from an oppressive command. Sea adventures often include a callous and misguided authority figure who has lost all grasp of human values—whether William Bligh, Wolf Larsen, Ahab, or Claggart in *Billy Budd*. Verging on madness, his obsession allows the goal of the voyage to justify any act, no matter how ruthless—whether in the service of the British empire (Bligh) or on some personal mission of revenge (Larsen and Ahab). He will be faced with either a mutiny or a similar reaction—or find his goal overcome by a combination of natural circumstances that seem to resemble the intervention of fate, as in *Moby Dick*. The sea adventure often depicts a small-scale allegory of revolt, reflecting basically the same political view as the land-based swashbuckler, the ocean-going vessel serving as a kingdom in which the captain reigns.

A number of recurring incidents provoke mutinies. The captain may commence the voyage by addressing his men from the ship's bridge, warning of his harsh ways. Sadistic officers enjoy ordering and inflicting punishment. All hands are repeatedly summoned to witness keelhauling and flogging, the strokes of the lash counted to drumbeats, concluded by pouring salt in the victim's wounds. The crew survives on meager rations; scurvy often breaks out. The common sailor has no reason to respect the tradition of the sea, only to fear and overcome it. At first there is hope that a captain's excesses will be remanded by the admiralty on the return to home port, but ultimately his maliciousness becomes too much to bear. Mutiny never involves random vengeance but is always directed at the most malevolent. As a result, the line between officer and crew will be transgressed, the captain lowered from his mighty position.

Like the pirate adventure, rebellions at sea are potentially far more destabilizing and radical than within a conventional land-based political order or class structure. This is partly endemic to the ship and to the ocean itself, which by their very nature underline the shared characteristics of all those involved in the voyage, whatever their capacity. The participation together, the isolated environment in which they interact, and the sympathy for the common sailor all promote an ideal of brotherhood (Bender, 10). In this sense, sea adventures, whatever the background or nationality of the characters, are the most profoundly democratic of adventure forms, the type that most clearly endorses American notions of equality and social values (Bender, 7, xi). Indeed, the genre's inclination toward rebellion reaches its highest ebb in sea adventures; this is why the narrative politics of *Mutiny on the Bounty* are more faithful to American morals than the actual British naval values of the time.

Although the sea adventure offers the most thorough and violent upheavals against the status quo of any adventure form, compensatory figures among the officers are usually apparent. For at least one, acquiescence is steadily more grudging, until the need for mutiny is finally recognized, respect for tradition overcome by the demand of conscience to end the abuse. Most often an alliance between the crew and certain officers is crucial to initiating a mutiny; not only sailors but officers as well receive a taste of the law of the sea. However, the urge toward mutiny must spring from the sailors and flow up through the ranks; attempts to overthrow the captain cannot be initiated from the top down. Such direction will fail, as in *Moby Dick*: despite Starbuck's agitation against Ahab, the others continue to follow the captain. In *The Sea Wolf* (1941), Humphrey Van Weyden begins as a believer in the land-based law, turning a girl who seeks his protection over to the police. Later, when fate has allowed Van Weyden to be rescued by the *Ghost*, then forced into its service, he learns to despise the law and the vicious authority on which it rests.

The sea adventure does offer a less frequent though notable range of admirable captains, epitomized by *Captain Horatio Hornblower*. An individual with all the charisma of Ahab and the seafaring skill of Bligh, unhappy in love, yet refreshingly humane, he turns his talents to the needs of his country. Discipline is strict, but he convinces the officers on board that the flogging of sailors is unnecessary, thereby winning the devotion and loyalty of both groups (Richards 1973, 183). Hornblower embodies the same strength of character associated with Ahab and others but uses it to outwit England's enemies, not just his own, overcoming enormous odds to assist the Royal Navy to victory against the French. There are even some positive, almost redeeming aspects to the more obsessive captains. Bligh accomplishes the miraculous goal of steering his small boat of loyal followers across the Pacific to safety after the mutiny

The ideal sea captain earns the unwavering respect and confidence of his crew, who become ready to follow him through any ordeal, such as this sea battle with Gregory Peck (center) as the title character in *Captain Horatio Hornblower* (1951).

on board the *Bounty*. Ahab, for all his evident insanity, directs his wrath at Moby Dick, never the crew; he skillfully convinces the sailors to share his mania for the white whale, and they are devoted to the crazed but charismatic captain. Yet there is also recognition of Captain Ahab's folly in taking the crew of the *Pequod* down with him.

The locales and purposes of sea adventures are often joined. As with some pirate movies, many sea stories are initiated in America during the nineteenth century, such as *Down to the Sea in Ships*; *Little Old New York* (1940); *Souls at Sea*; *Captains Courageous*; *Reap the Wild Wind*; *All the Brothers Were Valiant*; *Two Years before the Mast*; *The World in His Arms*; *Moby Dick*; and *The Sea Wolf*. The motives for these voyages are primarily profit and private benefit, not nationalistic interest. However, the War of 1812 and the conflict against the Barbary Pirates have been featured in such American naval adventures as *Mutiny* (1952), *Captain Caution*; and *Old Ironsides*. Another frequent setting is in the eighteenth century or during the Napoleonic wars as in *Captain Horatio Hornblower*;

Billy Budd; and *Damn the Defiant! / H.M.S. Defiant.* Many voyages originate from Britain, usually as an imperial accessory to extend her overseas domain and carried out under the aegis of the Royal Navy, including versions of the *Bounty* mutiny; *Botany Bay; Captain Cook* and *Drake the Pirate / Drake of England; Seven Seas to Calais* and *Drake's Voyage.* (Rowse, 54). The 1940 version of *The Sea Hawk* also belongs in this category, involving a patriot acting in the national interest, labeled "pirate" for political convenience and taking orders from Queen Elizabeth.

Damn the Defiant! (1962) embodies characteristics of two types of sea stories—those concerned with naval adventure as well as those dwelling on a conflict between officers and crew resolving into mutiny. There is a consciousness of the ship's activity as an arm of the empire, set on board the British warship *Defiant* during the Napoleonic wars. However, the vessel's role in the European conflict is secondary to the drama on board ship, pivoting around the confrontation between a duplicitous officer on the one side, and the captain and crew on the other. In a manner similar to *Billy Budd,* there is a twist in the conventional plot since it is not the captain who is the villain but a subordinate whom the captain must struggle to control and eventually repel with the aid of his crew. Again the question of legitimacy does much to define the nature of authority, as in other adventure types.

Rapport and respect exist between Captain Crawford (Alec Guinness) and his crew, represented by Vizard (Anthony Quayle), a leader among the sailors and a moderating influence. Crawford commands by example rather than by inflicting punishment, and between captain and crew is a knowledge of the law of the sea. The sailors' lives are hard, and expectations are low, but by allowing them dignity the captain can win their allegiance. Crawford sympathizes with their lot but is unaware of a planned strike by the entire fleet to improve conditions, an action that Vizard is promoting aboard the *Defiant.* Thrusting himself between them is vicious first officer Scott-Padgett (Dirk Bogarde), whose mother is the mistress of a British noble and has instigated the courts-martial of his previous captains. The first officer and captain represent divergent attitudes toward the crew, one savage, the other paternal.

Scott-Padgett seeks to advance by usurping the captain's prerogatives, his cruelty goading the sailors into outright mutiny. Even the presence of the captain's adolescent son on board for his first voyage as a junior midshipman is exploited by Scott-Padgett, who hazes the boy so ruthlessly that the captain places his son out of danger on another vessel. With a sudden change in the fortunes of war, Scott-Padgett tries to force Crawford to follow his own advice rather than admiralty orders. His only goal is a command of his own, and subversion and treason are no obstacles. The sailors realize Scott-Padgett's purpose, and proper authority has been undermined. While the captain can rely on the crew he trusts, even when he must lead them on an apparently suicidal mission, the mate's insubordination is exacerbated by his refusal to follow military orders. The struggle of the crew for just treatment comes to a climax in the final confrontation between captain and mate. Scott-Padgett's murder by a sailor, while technically mutinous, becomes a patriotic act, lauded by all. The strike by sailors throughout the fleet has taken place while the *Defiant* has been distracted with its own difficulties; the result in both instances has been a greater recognition of sailors' rights on English ships and a restoration of justice aboard the *Defiant*. As Vizard proudly tells the captain, there are no mutineers aboard the *Defiant*.

The Empire Adventure

Moving away from the initial, more lighthearted, and upbeat adventures of the swashbuckler and pirate, the sea story began a shift toward the genre's more serious forms. This trend is continued with the empire adventure, one of the most polysemous of the genre's types, revealing some very complex and contradictory themes. Empire adventures encompass many clashing beliefs—particularly the depiction of imperialism as a liberating experience, a contradiction that becomes increasingly apparent in those films produced while empires were collapsing in the decades after World War II. In this chapter the primary concern is outlining the narrative formula of empire adventures; the issues involved will be more fully addressed in Chapter 8, on the motif of colonialism throughout adventure. Meanwhile, this description of the filmic rationale of empire should not be construed as acceptance of the obviously obsolete attitudes expressed in them.

Most empire adventures are set in the period of European domination over the emerging nations of Africa and Asia, the lands sometimes today referred to as the Third World. Since England was the dominant global colonial power at the time films began to be made, various portions of the former British empire were most often seen on screen. However, the imperial ventures of many other nations also appeared: France (*Suez*; *Fort Algiers*; and the numerous Foreign Legion adventures—*Under Two Flags*; *Beau Geste*; *Beau Sabreur*; *Beau Ideal*; *The Foreign Legion*; *Renegades*; *The Legionnaire*; *Legion of Missing Men*; *Adventure in Sahara*; *Outpost in Morocco*; *Ten Tall Men*; *Desert Legion*; *Desert Hell*; *Legion of the Doomed*; *March or Die*), Spain (versions of the Christopher Columbus story, *Captain from Castile*; *7 Cities of Gold*; *The Royal Hunt of the Sun*; *The Young Rebel / Cervantes*; *The Mission*), Italy (the films of Marco Polo's travels), the Mongols (*The Conqueror*; *Genghis Khan*; *The Tartars*), the Boers (*Untamed* [1955]), and Russia (*Michael Strogoff*; *Charge of the Lancers*). In *Stanley and Livingstone*, Henry Morton Stanley is portrayed as a man of primarily American background, and the imperial drives of the United States, in various settings at home and abroad, have also been seen in *A Message to Garcia*; *Laughing at Life*; *The Real Glory*; *Tripoli* (1950); *Yankee Pasha*; *The Wind and the Lion*; *Plymouth Adventure*; and *Mayflower: The Pilgrims' Adventure*. *Robinson Crusoe* and other castaway stories reveal shipwrecked settlers who survive on barren locales; since they originally set out to expand their country's domain and continue this goal in isolation despite adversities, they are another form of empire (*Swiss Family Robinson*; *Man Friday*; *Strange Holiday* [1969]; *The White Dawn*). Pictures such as *55 Days at Peking*, *The Sand Pebbles*, and *Shogun* or that feature the Crusades have told of the efforts of an assortment of world powers. This range of films indicates the cinematic reflection of the multinational nature of the impulse to explore and colonize, with representatives of many countries roaming over different areas (Wilkinson, 5). The similar treatment given this wide assortment of empires makes it clear that all movies of this type—whatever imperial nation the hero may emanate from and wherever the action is set geographically—are fundamentally interrelated, indeed virtually interchangeable.

Empire adventures portray the colony as ruled not for self-interest but from an altruistic desire to bring peace and justice to a land where both are endangered. The imperial presence is invariably justified by depicting the ruling administration as holding in check the inherent propensity toward civil conflict in the colony. Fighting, whether among native tribes or against the colonists, is provoked by blood-thirsty, power-hungry khans, self-serving maharajahs (*Drums / The Drum*), or religious fanatics, whether on the side of Thuggee (*The Deceivers* [1988]), Kali (*Gunga Din; The Bandit of Zhobe*), or Islam (*Khartoum*). Their goal is not to promote liberation or the best interests of their people but personal ambition, to substitute themselves as the replacement for the colonial master. On occasion, native despots ally with outsiders fomenting discontent for their own territorial aims. Such an undesirable foreign intrusion is illustrated through Russia's regional designs on the Indian subcontinent in *Kim, Rogue's March*, and *The Charge of the Light Brigade*.

Adventure films endorse the colonial system by portraying it as a way to protect imperiled natives from domestic and foreign enemies. Quelling the threat of rebellion becomes justifiable as an unfortunate necessity, the empire builder maintaining order in the countries they govern. Although often a soldier, his or her role is ultimately that of promoting the long-term peace. While rebel figures become dangerous rather than heroic, by subduing revolts empire builders are still enacting the genre's basic political view, since (in the film) they free the people from local oppression (Richards 1978, 125). Empire adventures convey their ideology through the genre's framework, avoiding a celebration of the sort of blatant, conquering imperialism typical of the western. Taking up "the white man's burden" in the empire adventure is perceived as a form of service, protecting the native peoples, earning their affection and respect rather than fear. There is usually little personal reward beyond the satisfaction of serving a foreign land and a people that are now loved as their own (Richards 1974, 87). Empire building is a means of spreading the advantages of Western civilization, whether the suppression of disease, of torture, of slavery, or of suttee (*The Real Glory; Killers of Kilimanjaro; Drums of Africa*) (Richards 1973, 149). Indeed, the seriousness of the task is indicated by the frequency with which empire adventures conclude on a note of sadness. One or more of the heroes may be killed as a prerequisite to final military victory (*Khartoum; Zulu Dawn*) or partially defeated, as in the foreshadowing of the struggle for independence in *Flame over India*.

Accordingly, the attitude toward natives, whether Arab, African, or Asian, must be more paternalistic than exploitative. Only the leaders of the native revolts, the dissipated or power- hungry chieftains, are thoroughly villainous. Otherwise natives are not regarded as primitive or evil but as good people, worthy of respect and assistance. The Occidental heroes often encounter courageous and sophisticated natives and do not look on the Orient and its culture or races as inferior—and if they do, their attitudes are corrected, as in *Gunga Din*. Indeed, the genre is sufficiently flexible to allow for only a lukewarm endorsement of colonialism or questioning of its political effects, sometimes even going so far as to contradict imperialist beliefs. This tradition goes back at least to 1928 and the notable production of *White Shadows over the South Seas,* and the motif becomes frequent in the post–World War II decade (*Outpost in Morocco; King Richard and the Crusaders; King of the Khyber Rifles; 7 Cities of Gold*) until the revisionist strain became dominant during the 1960s and beyond (*The Brigand of Kandahar; The Long Duel; The Royal Hunt of the Sun; Burn!; The Wind and the Lion; Zulu Dawn; Christopher Columbus* [1985]; *Walker; Mountains of the Moon*).

Politics is further obscured and shunted into the background because the adventurer is seldom a conscious proponent of imperial policies, often apparently almost unaware of them. Empire adventures concentrate on the romance of exploration and the broadening of horizons, the imperial endeavor itself remaining in the abstract, almost an unintended side effect of the adventurer's life-style. Indeed, empire plots often shift adventure away from the political impact of the action, toward a more contemplative, reflective tone. Concerns outside the genre's usual focus are addressed, including loneliness (*The Lost Patrol*), loyalty (*Beau Geste*), guilt and the nature of heroism (*The Four Feathers*), alienation and disillusion in love, religion, politics (*Outpost in Morocco; The Mission*). The adventurer is usually attracted to empire not out of some enthusiasm for spreading his country's domain but because he is an outcast, hoping the new land will offer the refuge denied by his own country. *Captain from Castile* only associates with Cortés because he is a refugee from the Spanish inquisition, while *Beau Geste* and his brothers join the French Foreign Legion to save their family's reputation.

The empire builder may be one of two types. First, there is the explorer of new continents, regions, or seas who discovers unknown lands and establishes his homeland's claim to territory. The second type is more frequent, a soldier securing an empire already created, as in French Foreign Legion pictures or those set in British India.

These two tasks, first of creating an empire and then of preserving it, are not always compatible and demand different types of heroes; individuals combining both these necessary traits are a rare synthesis. Explorers are the individuals who discover and map new, uncharted lands, with a readiness to face the perils of nature and the unknown. Exploring and annexing territory requires an imaginative mind and the ability to inspire others. The heroes with these characteristics are dedicated to a vision of what the new empire can become, a trait displayed by Livingstone and that Stanley must learn in order to equal him in *Stanley and Livingstone*. Cinematic depictions portray Christopher Columbus as an explorer who proves too much the impractical dreamer to maintain control over his new domain, and Robert Falcon Scott as a man who falls tragically short of his goal. Having explored and brought order, the colonist remains to promote peace and to ensure that these benefits of civilization are not lost or corrupted (Richards and Aldgate, 16). This second stage, of keeping the empire once it has been won, requires a simpler, more anonymous individual, whose training and dedication reflect the regimental system, preserving the adopted country against change. Yet such a person, while a commonplace soldier or similar figure, could become as much a heroic image of daring and destiny as the more unusual explorer (Katz, 28).The fact that life in the empire is often one of dangerous exploration or military endeavor reduces the role of women, love taking a smaller thematic role than in the swashbuckler. By comparison with the passionately committed and romantic swashbuckler, the empire builder may be alienated, a "man's man," a relatively unexceptional figure whose glory is derived from being part of the larger colonial endeavor.

Empire reverses the pattern of the swashbuckler, which glorifies the power of the individual and group of private citizens who voluntarily band together to secure liberty and oppose the established hierarchy. Empire accents the mystique of the military: loyalty, tradition, honor, courageous deeds, and the willingness to sacrifice and undergo ordeals. For empire builders, the only satisfaction may be in the military life, and one of the highest aspirations is belonging to the regiment or its equivalent, groups forming an indissoluble unit but welcoming anyone with the requisite courage and dedication—a pattern evident in pictures as seemingly divergent as *Scott of the Antarctic* and *Zulu*. Even where the hero is a lonely district commissioner rather than a member of the military, he is clearly a member of the colonial system's governing bureaucracy.

Partially mitigating the accent on military life is the frequent requirement for the hero to prove resourcefulness by undertaking a lone mission, accompanied at most by one or two comrades. Briefly disobeying orders or acting as an irregular, the hero may sometimes risk disgrace by pretending to desert or go over to the enemy. Eventually, however, his course is accepted because the endeavor ultimately serves the greater needs of the empire. For instance, after the shame of losing the flag because of his love for the princess, Kenneth of Huntington temporarily joins Saladin in *King Richard and the Crusaders*. Going in disguise behind enemy lines also reveals the degree to which the adventurer has become steeped in the culture, learning local customs and language in order to lose himself amidst the native peoples. A few empire adventures, such as *Alfred the Great* or films enacting the crusades, are related to the swashbuckler by common iconography, but their thematic concerns are clearly those of building empires as opposed to the adventures of Robin Hood back in England. However, the empire builder usually avoids the sword, and occupies a later temporal niche that favors the rifle, machine gun, and cannon.

India has always been one of the most popular locales for empire adventures, and perhaps the most influential movie with this setting was *The Lives of a Bengal Lancer* (1935). There were previous empire adventures placed in India (*The White Panther*; *The Black Watch*; and *Clive of India*), but *The Lives of A Bengal Lancer* substituted the autobiographical, philosophical implications of its literary source for a plot lifted directly from the conventions of contemporary pulp fiction, with which several of its screenwriters were involved. The popularity of *The Lives of a Bengal Lancer* turned its elements and narrative into a formula, inspiring a whole series of adventures in India, a cycle that returned after World War II before largely dying out in the 1960s. Titles during these years and after include *The Charge of the Light Brigade*; *Storm over Bengal*; *Drums*; *Gunga Din*; *Kim*; *Soldiers Three*; *Rogues' March*; *Bengal Brigade / Bengal Rifles*; *Flame of Calcutta*; *Khyber Patrol*; *King of the Khyber Rifles*; *Zarak*; *The Bandit of Zhobe*; *Flame over India*; *Kali-Yug—Goddess of Vengeance*; *Temple of the White Elephant*; *The Brigand of Kandahar*; *The Long Duel*; *Fury of the Khybers /*

The empire builder learns to love the colony as an adopted home; Gary Cooper as McGregor in *The Lives of a Bengal Lancer* (with Lone Pine, California substituting for the landscape of India).

Slaughter on the Khyber Pass; The Deceivers; and the 1950s television series *Tales of the 77th Bengal Lancers.* All deal basically with the same situation, a threatened native revolt, often from the Khyber Pass on the Northwest frontier, which must be quelled by an irregular military operation.

The Lives of a Bengal Lancer is structured around two key elements, the inculcation of the regimental ethic and the mystique of India (Richards 1974, 82). Each of the three heroes finds a moment of glory in performing their duty for country and at the same time acting outside the confines of regimental orders. At the end of the film the heroes resemble each other as members of the regiment, but they begin as quite different individuals. McGregor (Gary Cooper) is a Canadian expatriate and an experienced soldier on the frontier who has made India his home. Forsythe (Franchot Tone) is a virtual fop, transferred to the Bengal Lancers from a fashionable regiment; he must relearn the soldier's life at a more dangerous outpost. Young Donald Stone (Richard Cromwell) is just emerging from boyhood. At this point, McGregor is newly initiated into the code of conduct required of an adventurer engaging in military life. He comes to realize the importance of command, as well as the proper care of his comrades, especially the inexperienced Donald. Donald must also gain understanding, and he and Forsythe acquire the obligation to duty and to India that McGregor and Donald's father, the regiment's commander (Sir Guy Standing), already embody. Both McGregor and the elder Stone love India and would gladly sacrifice their lives in her service. The affection for the land is shown in their involvement with local activities and the growing willingness to risk hardship in performing their duties, together with the picture's commencement with documentary style location footage.

McGregor begins as the rebel, labeling his commander "ramrod" after urging Colonel Stone to change strategy and fight, rather than retreat before tribal gunfire. However, Stone fears that this action will provoke a wider conflict; a true empire builder, he prefers peace to dominion. McGregor later acquires a familial interest in young Donald after observing the impersonal and cold treatment by the father: the successful commander is a failure in his parental role. The naive Donald fails the call of duty when he is trapped by a Russian spy. Forsythe mocks McGregor's conscious drive to help Donald but later proves himself equally willing to risk his life and disobey orders to save the lad; the heroes disguise themselves as natives in an effort to rescue the kidnapped Donald.

The audience comes to recognize the rationale of the colonial endeavor from the viewpoint of the characters as they learn their vital tasks. At the beginning the motives and actions of the colonial presence are vague. McGregor, Forsythe, and Donald are basically selfish outsiders, caring little for the regimental ethic and the justi-fication for colonialism. In the course of the ensuing adventures they come to realize the importance of acting as a team, even when distanced from the military unit. They realize their duty to India through their encounters with Mohammed Khan (Douglas Dumbrille), who unites tribal chieftains to threaten a massacre of the Bengal Lancers and their fellow countrymen. The Lancers have been willing to force information from Moslem natives by threaten-ing to bury them in pigskins, but this is placed in juxtaposition to the even more vicious methods of the villain Mohammed Khan, who tortures McGregor, Forsythe, and Donald until the lad breaks down. Donald's shame brings him to a realization of duty, as he joins Forsythe and McGregor in a spectacular escape and the killing of Khan. However, the sense of victory is muted, having cost the life of McGregor, who sacrificed himself; it is only by his example that Forsythe and Donald grow to full maturity, with father and son finally united.

The Fortune Hunter Adventure

The fifth adventure type, the fortune hunter, partakes of elements of all the preceding groups but combines them in new ways, following a different narrative pattern. The least formulaic of all adventure types, the fortune hunter offers the greatest potential for variation. The form is less conventionalized, politically centered, and tied to the standard of heroic conduct. Nonetheless, by the end of their adventure even the fortune hunter comes to believe in traditional adventure values, although that may be expressed more implicitly than in a clear-cut, expository way (*Return of Monte Cristo / Monte Cristo's Revenge*). Another narrative option, similar in its outcome, is to present the hero in a seemingly negative light, then to proceed to vindicate his actions by providing the full context, as in *Wake of the Red Witch* or *Souls at Sea*.

Typical of the differences between the other forms of adventure and the fortune hunter is that it is less tied to the historical setting so necessary to the other types (*Trader Horn* [1931]). There is comparatively little interaction between the fortune hunter and history and the locale ranges from Europe to the exotic Far East, with the areas around Africa and Asia favored. The only initial requirement of the fortune hunter is a willingness to live in rugged terrain, readily sacrificing the comforts of civilization in an often grueling and unsuccessful life (*The African Queen*). Inhabiting such a region, isolated from others of his race or nationality, offers him the opportunity to undergo the transformation and self-discovery that he gropingly seeks (*His Majesty O'Keefe*). Fortune hunters have a virtual monopoly on the South Seas, as in *Ebb Tide*; *Typhoon*; *Son of Fury*; *Fair Wind to Java*; *His Majesty O'Keefe*; and *Lord Jim*. This region has acquired a definite film mythology, even found in *Mutiny on the Bounty* and *Captain Cook*. The greedy, grubby, nerve-ridden white man tries to lose himself among the Polynesians, enchanted by a people with a placid life-style and a more commendable sense of values. Polynesians are shown as innocents, representing the possibility of a non-competitive, almost utopian existence.

Unlike the swashbuckler and empire types, the fortune hunter begins as a self-centered individual without guiding political beliefs or a gentleman's code of honor (*Fair Wind to Java*). Commencing as simply an apathetic nonhero, he is casually disassociated from the world, although not fatalistically so (*Slave Ship*). Often the fortune hunter seems to be a disillusioned romantic, one who has lost interest in life and treats existence as merely an occasion for carefree sport and the acquisition of wealth (*Lloyd's of London*). While not living in defiance of society or its morality like the pirate, the fortune hunter is simply a private person, asocial and unattached (*Watusi; Swordsman of Siena*). Although other adventurers may begin in these ways, the fortune hunter is the most persistent in pursuing mercenary goals and remaining apart (*Santiago*). At this stage he lacks even the commitment of the pirate to his milieu, who at least is willing to defend the alternative society and social order he has helped to create.

Only toward the adventure's conclusion will the fortune hunter recognize his obligations to society. Rather than a change in the political structure, the conversion to new values becomes the central event of the movie, as the fortune hunter discovers forms of conduct and morality that allow life to acquire deeper meaning (*Samar*) (McConnell, 19). The narrative climaxes as the fortune hunter is caught in circumstances that leave him desolate and ready to change (*Legend of the Lost*). Typical precipitating causes include life-threatening encounters or a sudden loss of money or love and the security they have provided. This critical plight may result in violence and confusion, with his few solid friendships betrayed as the fortune hunter discovers the fruitlessness of his desire for gold, as in *The Man Who Would Be King*. The prize often eludes him, or is found only to be lost later, the hero surviving with only memories or at most a few trinkets (*Typhoon*).

As his quest turns sour, the resulting failure reveals the error of the fortune hunter's ways and opens the possibility of new motivations, less tangible and material but more humanist and worthwhile. Altered situations call forth an idealism and patriotism which he did not know existed, allowing the protagonist to achieve respectability and a measure of heroism for a worthy deed. Abandoning his former ambivalent attitude toward existence, the fortune hunter finds a purpose that impels him forward. He may try to make up for the misery his greed has brought about through a heroic, sacrificial gesture, as in *Green Fire*. He discovers that true riches are not in gold but in altruism, travel, romance, and adventure: the capital to be acquired is experience and knowledge (*The Black Rose*). Often this occurs with a discovery, or rediscovery, of romance, so female influence may play a key and beneficial role (*The Fighting O'Flynn*). This at last brings about the hero's willing acceptance of more traditionally lauded values, resulting in his reabsorption into society (*The Southern Star*). Hence, the fortune hunter adventure is fundamentally about an individual's journey to self-realization, an awareness of the impact and benefit his actions may have.

Around the World in 80 Days (especially the 1956 version) centers on a journey begun for profit and glory, depicting a race against time in the age of primitive but rapidly advancing technology. The characters move from single-mindedness to a wider conception of their responsibility to themselves and others, ending in a reconciliation with the traditional code of adventure. Phileas Fogg begins his trip around the world ostensibly as a wager, but in fact it is equally a flight from the minimal human contact he has at the whist table of the Reform Club. However, the journey provides the opposite of his expectation: Fogg's anticipated, well-timed and perfectly scheduled travel runs steadily more afoul of chance and circumstance, until by the end of the trip his mechanical plans have broken down completely. At the outset, Fogg has contempt for everyone who is not English, seeing Americans, Indians, or Asians as equally barbaric and foreign—a perception changed by his experiences. He is brought into the proximity of a wide variety of characters and experiences growing affection for his servant Passepartout and love for the Indian princess Aouda, rescued from death by suttee. They provide Fogg with an appreciation for human comradeship that he had never before known. By the end, the winning of the wager is an accident predicated on Fogg's apparent loss and his new willingness to seek the love of Aouda. The change in his character ends with Passepartout and Aouda invading the sanctity of the Reform Club, signaling the end of the stuffy, aristocratic English snobbery that Fogg formerly reflected.

In the end, the "fortune" is not simply an elusive material wealth but a satisfying life in a free land. While the fortune hunter's initial endeavor is usually a quest for his own material or personal benefit, this is seldom so simple or pure as the age-old search for treasure. For instance, the quest for gold may be part of a plan to facilitate vengeance for his disinheritance; as the hero explains in *The Treasure of the Golden Condor* (a remake of *Son of Fury*), "I have a goal, yes, and I need gold to achieve it, to right a wrong that affects not only my own life, but the lives of many others. That's my goal, not the treasure itself." Learning that there are interests beyond those of the isolated individual, fortune hunters begin to perceive themselves as part of the larger community of humankind; in *High Road to China*, a loner decides to lend his aid to a Chinese rebellion. There may be different types of fortunes; Little Toomai takes the place of his late father to assume the honored family title of Toomai of the Elephants in *Elephant Boy*, and a similar experience occurs in *Call It Courage*. The fortune hunter emerges a changed person, ready to take on wider responsibilities, which may include love and marriage, social and political activities, or new attitudes. As *Anthony Adverse* remarks, "Love and home and a tradition, these things are the very essence of a man's soul, they are his wealth and his power. Without them, he is nothing."

Lord Jim (Peter O'Toole) is typical of fortune hunter adventures using a Far Eastern setting to relate the attempt to redeem a failure to live up to the adventurer's code. Jim is condemned for having shown a lack of courage and honor in abandoning the passengers of the *Patna*. Finally, he realizes he may atone from his disgrace when he arrives in Patusan and discovers that his own new beginning can be tied to a larger endeavor, that of helping to rescue the community. Accepting responsibility for the depredations of Gentleman Brown, whom he has mistakenly trusted, Jim thrusts himself into a situation he cannot escape, facing death fearlessly and proudly. In this way, by finally embracing the adventurer's code, he is able to come to terms with himself and his past actions. Jim's fortune was not a treasure but the self-image of grandeur and glory he searched for, which at last he found in being able successfully to adopt the heroic mold.

Seldom does the fortune hunter become the crusader for social justice that is such a prominent characteristic of the swashbuckler and that causes much of the action in a sea story. The fortune hunter is closer to the empire builder in terms of accepting conditions around him. In *Royal Flash,* the roguish Harry Flashman is buffeted by events, becoming a British hero through a series of accidents and good luck, occasionally acting heroically out of self-preservation but ultimately only peripheral to history. More typical is *The Swordsman* (1947), who does acquire historical significance by ending a bloody clan feud in Scotland. *A Tale of Two Cities* portrays the political injustice of the French Revolution but is primarily concerned with demonstrating the value of the adventurer's chivalric code through the redemptive sacrifice of Sidney Carton. By contrast, *The Man Without a County* only learns the importance of patriotism when exiled from his homeland for his lack of contrition in joining a treasonous plot. Most often, when the quest is achieved, the fortune hunter is content to be integrated as an ordinary member of society, winning approval because of his exploits and rarely extending the fight to the realm around him. In *Prince of Foxes,* Andrea Orsini's commitment to turning back the Borgias is motivated as much by the dangerous position of the woman he loves, a princess threatened by Cesare, as by any particular political beliefs.

Some fortune hunters are motivated less by gain than by a search for revenge, and when it supersedes patriotism as the prime motivation, as in *The Corsican Brothers* and *Black Magic,* the adventure is usually converted into the fortune hunter form. For instance, while Zorro turns family deprivation into a motive for overthrowing the military dictatorship in Spanish California, the Count of Monte Cristo limits himself to personal vengeance on the individuals who imprisoned him, not the governmental establishment they manipulate. Although both use the icons of the swashbuckler, only Zorro fully partakes of its ideological view; the Count of Monte Cristo's actions are too limited and personal, instead qualifying as a fortune hunter. The avenger, more often than other adventurers, views the conflict in more limited terms, as one primarily between individuals. The avenger may also fail to realize the full political ramifications of injustice, seldom attacking the overall nature of the establishment.

In the revenge variation of the fortune hunter, the hero begins full of promise, accepting society's values and eschewing rebelliousness, following the path that supposedly leads to a rewarding life. However, a wrong is committed that cannot be made right through the establishment, forcing the avenger to go outside conventional societal norms, often as an outlaw.[3] The experience of treachery reverses his trusting nature, and full compensation is promised for every moment of misery, to be extracted according to the ethic of "an eye for an eye." In order to convert into the extraordinary person necessary for the task, the avenger develops the intense self-control and ruthlessness this new goal will require. As a result, the avenger frequently adopts a different, more appropriate identity, and the new persona takes on a ferocity and mercilessness not hitherto seen.

Vengeance is initially harsh and unforgiving, but ultimately the hero condemns himself for taking justice into his own hands. Revenge is disquieting, encompassing more than was expected, and only rarely is it carried to its logical completion. Circumstances make its ethical validity less certain, and the hero comes to believe he has gone too far. Unknown family relations may be discovered, or romantic complications intervene (*The Eagle* [1925]); sometimes a woman brings about a moral reawakening. Thus the cause is forsaken that was once followed so assiduously. Although revenge is treated as a sacred, almost exalted motive, it is finally also condemned as ignoble, the genre only sanctioning limited vengeance. Yet the selfless, determined course of the avenger is portrayed in such a way as to evoke admiration. The ultimate regret is more of an afterthought, a corollary to the task's near completion and the maintenance of heroic status. His initial decision to strike back reflects human nature, while the eventual repentance maintains the overall moral superiority over the villain. Unlike the hero of the detective or western genre, the adventurer cannot take remorseless revenge on an enemy while still retaining the audience's approval.

The archetype for revenge adventures is Alexandre Dumas's *The Count of Monte Cristo*, in which the innocent Edmond Dantes is condemned to life imprisonment by a cabal whose various aims he unwittingly threatened. While in the Château d'If, Dantes gains a lifetime of education from the Abbé Faria, realizing how he was wronged and determining to make himself into an avenger. Finally escaping, Dantes gains great wealth through the bequest of his cell mate, becoming a mysterious count by virtue of his fortune. He dedicates this wealth to revenge against those individuals who wronged him by using the money to make himself more powerful, manipulating his enemies into revealing their misdeeds. But Monte Cristo's soulless quest proves bittersweet because of complications brought on by the romantic intertwining of the offspring of two families, one who helped and one who oppressed him. Fearing he has

The adventurer finds benefit even in misfortune: during his imprisonment, Dantes (Robert Donat, right) becomes the student of Abbe Faria (O.P. Heggie) in *The Count of Monte Cristo* (1934).

gone too far, Monte Cristo eventually both offers forgiveness to, and seeks it from, one of his enemies. Overall, the effect of Monte Cristo's actions have done nothing to change the political, economic, and military establishment that his enemies used to imprison him; instead the Count turns the status quo against them by publicly demonstrating the corruption of those who imprisoned him. At the same time, this provides Monte Cristo with another justification; his enemies not only wronged him but violated the standards of society, and it is this villainy he finally uses to bring them down. Only in some versions of *The Count of Monte Cristo* is there a glimmer of the broader context of injustice, demonstrated by Dantes's financial help to Greek rebels.

Scaramouche, Rafael Sabatini's counterpart to Alexandre Dumas's tale, demonstrates how personal revenge may be carried beyond the bounds of apolitical Monte Cristo–style vengeance while still remaining within the fortune hunter form. André Moreau, an unattached drifter without roots or concerns, is radicalized when he sees his friend, a reformist pamphleteer, murdered in public by a member of the nobility who need fear no punishment for such actions. Avenging his friend eventually involves André in joining the rebellion against the aristocrats, although he never becomes a truly political force. His final vengeance, however, is undermined by the discovery that his enemy is, in fact, his father (in Rafael Sabatini's novel and the 1922 picture) or half-brother (1952 version), a fact in both cases concealed by André's illegitimate birth. Nonetheless, André's goals have been achieved, for his principal adversaries have been defeated and disgraced—and in the 1922 version, murdered by the mobs of the French Revolution. Furthermore, he has won the lady he loves, whose affections had been unsuccessfully sought by his relative.

Minor Variations

A few movie serials drew on the elements of regular adventure types and may be loosely classified as belonging to the adventure genre. There were swashbucklers (*Son of the Guardsman / Outlaws of Sherwood Forest* [1946]; *The Adventures of Sir Galahad* [1949]); and the Oriental variation (*The Desert Hawk* [1944]). Republic brought Zorro to the serial screen with a distinctively western flavor in *Zorro Rides Again* (1937); *Zorro's Fighting Legion* (1939); *Zorro's Black Whip* (1944); *Son of Zorro* (1947); and *Ghost of Zorro* (1949). Pirate serials also appeared (*Captain Kidd* [1922]; *Pirates of Panama* [1929]; *Pirate Treasure* [1934]; *The Sea Hound* [1947]; *Pirates of the High Seas* [1950]; *The Great Adventures of Captain Kidd* [1953]), as did fortune hunters (*Around the World in 18 Days*), and empire (*With Stanley in Africa* [1922]). However, out of the hundreds of serials made, comparatively few belong to the adventure genre; the serial form was more amenable to westerns, science fiction, mysteries, and love stories. Frequently, elements of various genres were combined into a melodramatic whole, with adventure as one element in the mixture. A historical setting was anathema to the serial, padded with action and emphasizing thrills, pace, and low budgets over mood, coherence, and atmosphere.

Typical of the strained relations between adventure and serials is the fact that jungles were perhaps their favorite setting. However, jungle films also fall outside the focus of this study. Some film series, such as Tarzan or similar characters like Jungle Jim and Bomba the Jungle Boy, are in a sense adventurous but are also so prolific in their own right as to have a distinctive tradition, with endemic motifs seldom shared with adventure as a whole. Events follow no particular logic, mixing the fanciful and fantastic, without even the minimal adherence to historical probability. Tarzan and his imitators compose an entire genre of jungle films, offering a mythology of inherent danger that ranges from ferocious wild animals to often equally threatening natives and lacking adventure's freedom-fighting motif.

Adventure has occasionally crossed over into the realm of documentary in the movies of adventurers such as Frank Buck (*Bring 'Em Back Alive; Wild Cargo; Fang and Claw; Jungle Cavalcade*), Martin and Osa Johnson, or Thor Heyerdahl (*Kon-Tiki; The Ra Expeditions*). Some of the documentaries of Robert Flaherty could also be located in this context (*Nanook of the North; Moana; Tabu*), along with many lesser, more exploitation-oriented pictures, such as *Ingagi*. While containing an adventurous aspect through the concerns of exploration, living in untamed lands, or survival against a hostile nature, the use of the documentary form and the realist tradition places these films in a category distant from the Hollywood fictional formulas previously outlined.

One way of merging the jungle and documentary traditions into a new adventure form for the post-colonial era has been to shift the foundation to the transcending belief in wildlife conservation, projecting adventure in new eras and circumstances. In such films as *The Roots of Heaven; West of Zanzibar; Ivory Hunter / Where No Vultures Fly; East of Kilimanjaro; Born Free; Living Free;* and most recently in *The Emerald Forest, Gorillas in the Mist,* and *A Far Off Place,* a new ethic of adventure is found. Imperialism has become associated not only with the exploitation of the native but also with the ruination of the land and its ecosystem. Adventurers find a new, postcolonial mission in joining the movement to prevent the loss of animals and their wild habitat. This mission often finds both white and native individuals on each side, with allies and enemies in all races. The menace is now in the ravages of poachers and hunters. The once-heroic figure of the big-game hunter and trapper becomes psychoanalyzed and demystified, with their attributes now considered vices (*Maya*). Conservation allows the clear morality of adventure to be retained, although the law may be on either side of the cause; a heroic figure like Dian Fossey in *Gorillas in the Mist* remains willing to follow his or her conscience, even if that requires going beyond legal or accepted processes. The conflict remains as clear-cut and unambiguous as adventure's struggle's against injustice centuries ago. A colonial hero grows to love the land as his own and defends it from destructive forces. The gamekeeper takes the place of the district commissioner or military authority; through his awareness and commitment to conservation, whites retain justification for a position of authority in foreign lands. Hence, by now seeking to spread enlightenment and appreciation for nature, movies still find a place and a purpose for whites and a new type of colonial mission in developing countries, whether serving in big-game preserves or scientific outposts.

Five distinct types of the historical adventure film have been discussed, along with the relation of several minor variations. The types were examined in a specific order, beginning with the swashbuckler, the best-known and most recognized form, through to the least formulaic variety, the fortune hunter. The genre's politics are the most liberal in swashbucklers and pirate and sea adventures, while empire and fortune hunters move in the direction of conservatism because of the endorsement of colonialism necessitated by their locales. Thus the types are not only separated by narrative patterns, iconography, and locale, but also by the nature of the attitudes to the political issues raised by the activities of their characters.

CHAPTER 3 The Evolution of the Adventure Genre

Not only does the adventure genre have a relation to history, the genre itself has a history which has evolved in a cyclical pattern over the years. Adventure has been impacted by the context in which it has been read or viewed, whether against the backdrop of economic depression or world war—events that caused a flowering, and then a diminishing, of the genre's production. This chapter examines the roots of adventure films in the genre's literature before proceeding to a discussion of the tides of popularity and resistance of adventure's myths on film.

The genres that exist in artistic mediums other than cinema—radio, television, films, literature, poetry, theater—are not necessarily amenable to dissection by the same methods, and there may be little in common between a single genre in different media. In the case of adventure, movies and television vary considerably from the manifestation of the same genre in literature, in ways that extend beyond the obvious differences between the mediums. The swashbuckler, pirate, sea, empire, and fortune hunter have been delineated as applicable to movies and television, but these would not be as appropriate to a literary analysis. Adventure films are relatively unconcerned with the larger issues impacted by adventure as a way of life and a branch of literature. The literary genre of adventure is far more variable, not so codified as its equivalent in the cinema. For instance, empire films typically follow the formula of a group of soldiers subduing an incipient uprising, but the books behind these stories, from *The Lives of a Bengal Lancer* to *Kim* to *King of the Khyber Rifles*, are much more complex. This richness is evident in only a few of the pictures, such as *The Man Who Would Be King*.

The inspiration for adventure movies has come from all forms of literature, whether legends and folklore (*El Cid*, Don Juan and Robin Hood films), poems (*The Highwayman* [1951], *The Midnight Ride of Paul Revere* [1917]), plays (*If I Were King; The Royal Hunt of the Sun*), novels (*Ivanhoe*), autobiography (*The Lives of a Bengal Lancer*), straightforward history (*Khartoum*), or particular fictionalization of a historical incident (*Mutiny on the Bounty; Captain from Castile*). While sometimes movies are faithful in adhering to the outlines of literary plots, inevitably the narrative is compressed, characterizations and theme simplified. For example, Robert Louis Stevenson's novel *The Black Arrow* offers an ambiguous treatment of outlaws, whereas they receive an idyllic depiction in *The Black Arrow / The Black Arrow Strikes* (1948), typical of the celluloid versions of outlaw mythology in the swashbuckler. While Hollywood has taken advantage of the titles of well-known literary works for motion pictures, it is primarily for the prestigious, "presold" status they confer. Roots in classical literature, even if titles refer to specific novels, seldom govern a picture's actual narrative. The source book often becomes merely a springboard for a genre film. Avowed adaptations contain minimal resemblance or are considerably abbreviated, as proved by frequent remakes of classics like *The Count of Monte Cristo*. The adventure movie's debt to classical novels is minimal; the debt is greatest to popular novels of the late nineteenth century and the subsequent pulp stories. Their parameters and narrative conventions come closest to setting the pattern for motion pictures. Even the film of a recent work, such as the 1940 version of *The Sea Hawk*, ignored the Rafael Sabatini novel to instead remake *Fire over England*, a story with more contemporary relevance to Europe in danger (Richards 1974, 108). Adaptations of adventure literature conform less to their sources than to the genre as it already exists in successful films (Thomas Sobchack in Grant 1977, 39). Hollywood prefers works that can be easily made to fit the existing movie formula (*The Charge of the Light Brigade* [1936], *Gunga Din*) or original stories for the screen involving established characters, such as the spin-offs inspired by *The Mark of Zorro, The Three Musketeers,* or *The Count of Monte Cristo.*

Adventure literature is an enormous subject, and only a general overview can be provided here, insofar as it has directly impacted the cinema. A discussion of adventure literature presents some of the same difficulties as defining the genre in film. In one sense adventure is the oldest, most widespread form of storytelling, and a study of this literary form could be carried back to the Middle Ages, or to Homer's *Iliad* and *Odyssey*, even to the beginning of myth-making (Zweig, vii; Gove, 18). However, there is little in common between the historical adventure film and these ancestral types, which usually stray into the realm of fantasy, depicting a world of supernatural forces where the intervention of gods is an accepted occurrence.

The literature of historical adventure, and ultimately the films as well, derive primarily from the romantic tradition. However, this is not to imply "romance" in the sense of its own school, or genre, with its inclusion of fantastic elements; instead, historical adventure films have taken the general thrust and philosophy of the movement (Richards, Summer 1977, 12). In part a sensibility, romanticism includes a historical dimension as well, created from the double impact of the Renaissance and the Reformation. The latter encouraged the importance of individualism and private judgment, while from the Renaissance grew an age of expansion that continued through the nineteenth century. The steady march of progress in terms of trade and technology gave Western civilization an intoxicating sense of power. Social institutions were rethought and improving earthly existence became a more immediate issue as humankind's eyes turned to the idea of progress here on Earth rather than inevitably deferred to the hereafter. The romance hero transcends the world of ordinary experience, emerging free and victorious in an allegory of good over evil (Propp, 8–9). Adventure's romantic sense appears in the narrative tendency to polarize the world into two realms, one innocent and idyllic and the other its opposite, as represented by heroes and villains (Frye, 186–206). The period's popular literature and history were justified in terms of the imaginative emotional appeal of the heroic, adventurous, mystical, and ideal. Romanticism often found its natural articulation through symbolism and myth, initially in stories of knights and chivalrous deeds, before expanding to a broad range of other forms containing love and action. Adventure adopts these themes as the genre becomes a quest uniting people for a better world for themselves and others (Nerlich 1987, 133–34).

Romanticism inspired a look back at the popular history and cultural inheritance of various countries, becoming a force for nationalistic pride. After the French Revolution, the study of history increasingly turned toward investigating how the past shaped the present (Shaw, 26). Politically, this fed revolutionary strains because of the persistence of backward, archaic government despite the advances in learning and the gradual formation of a merchant class. Absolutism, royalty, and the claim of divine authority came to be more and more out of place as the common person became increasingly significant and such instruments of power as knowledge, wealth, and weapons were diffused among a wider group. The outlaw, outcast, and even radical, by their actions the living embodiment of romantic beliefs, became a possible choice for heroic treatment. Fiery rebels or people of mystery, once viewed as antisocial, were now favored. In its philosophical sense, romanticism valued the individual, encouraging the optimistic spirit of revolutionary political reform. To be romantic became almost synonymous with liberalism in the period after Napoleon's fall. In the name of liberty, rebellion against rules and authority, even against conventional religion, was applauded.

There was a yearning for the primitive and remote for its own sake, seeking the far horizons in a desire for the experience and dominion that motivated such explorers of different periods as Drake or Stanley (Allott, 257). Much of this became apparent in the fashion for "Crusoe-ism"; the fascination and absorption with wild, primitive, uncivilized life, and the question of how modern European man would react to such conditions. A parallel factor was the notion of the noble savage, from Friday to its modern culmination in the Tarzan phenomenon. Combined with this fashion was a visionary element that allowed explorers and imperialists to see their endeavors as having civilizing connotations that included nationalism and Christianity. The metaphysical leanings of romanticism, such as the interest in the supernatural, may have further disposed the empire adventurer to be intrigued by the native religions of the colonized areas, especially in the Far East. "I am tormented with an everlasting itch for things remote. I love to sail forbidden seas, and land on barbarous coasts," notes Ishmael in the opening of Melville's *Moby Dick*, expressing the intoxication with an existence far from home and beyond the sea.[1] Just as evaluations of adventure today diverge, contemporaries of romanticism saw it either as a step backward or a rediscovery of beliefs and humanity that feed the mind and spirit.

The principal inspiration for the adventure film was not until much later, as the novel became a popular form of writing. During the 1600s, Cervantes's *Don Quixote* became popular throughout Europe, satirizing the chivalry and class traditions so valorized by folktales and the remnants of courtly adventure. During the eighteenth and nineteenth centuries there was an explosion in the reading and writing of adventure stories (Nerlich 1987, 373). The adventure novel proper may be traced from Daniel Defoe's *Robinson Crusoe*; adventure as it would appear in the cinema commences in the 1800s with Sir Walter Scott, followed by Alexandre Dumas, Victor Hugo, Jules Verne, W. H. G. Kingston, Robert Louis Stevenson, Sir Arthur Conan Doyle, and Baroness Orczy through Sir Edward Bulwer-Lytton, Rudyard Kipling, and H. Rider Haggard (Green 1979, 97–98). A parallel tradition emerged with the novel of nautical adventure. James Fenimore Cooper, although today primarily associated with Leatherstocking western yarns, was equally a progenitor of the sea story, and the tradition was elaborated by Herman Melville, Richard Henry Dana, Captain Marryatt, and Joseph Conrad. The sea story tradition was continued in the twentieth century by Charles Nordhoff and James Norman Hall, of *Bounty* trilogy fame, and most notably, C. S. Forester's Hornblower saga, which began in the same pulp magazines discussed below. This form of naval adventure, primarily set during the Napoleonic era, would be taken up by a number of other writers, and remains one of the most distinctly popular forms of adventure still written today with the work of Patrick O'Brian, Alexander Kent, Bernard Cornwell, and others.

The historical novel, long the object of reviewers' derision, experienced a resurgence upon its amalgamation with adventure, and books such as Stevenson's *Treasure Island* (1883) and Haggard's *King Solo-*

mon's Mines (1885) found popular and critical acclaim that their authors and publishers could not have anticipated (Kiely, 21). The rise in popular literature was attracting a new readership, industrial workers for whom a rising literacy had to offer an appeal to the imagination, an ingredient largely absent in the domestic novels of the educated elite (Zweig, 12). The newly literate middle class demanded a new type of storytelling; no longer was the adventure form dominated by medieval knightly exploits or stories of kings, gods, and nobles but instead had a wide range of character types with more current settings (Nerlich 1987, 186, 298). The tradition of adventure quite naturally allied with an interest in geography and contemporary overseas military activity, sometimes adopting a nearly didactic tone, as in Verne's series of *Extraordinary Journeys*. Literature accented the natural curiosity about the world's far horizons to present life in the colonies as providing whites with the chance to make a name and home for themselves away from the constraints of Europe. A new impetus to adventure writing and the development of the genre occurred with the Sepoy mutiny of 1857. Popular literature, hitherto only incidentally concerned with such lands as India, began to explore the nation and its natives and white rulers more seriously in an effort to understand what had caused the rebellion and how white imperialists could come so close to being defeated by an Eastern nation. Adventure began to increasingly be cast as an experience with a mission, to enlighten and uplift, regardless of the opposition found among various forces in the distant colonial lands. Narratives increasingly dealt with common soldiers, and how their work promoted empire and the missionary spirit, in both its spiritual and civil forms. Soon the explanation of soldiering in the colonies and suppressing native rebellion became a formula throughout the popular literature of the time (Howe, 64–68).

The spirit of Scott and his successors was quickly adapted to the medium preceding film, the stage, where many of the titles that would become staples of the cinema appeared: *Ivanhoe*; *The Cardinal* (Richelieu); *The Three Musketeers*; *Under the Red Robe*; *If I Were King*; *The Vagabond King*; *The Count of Monte Cristo*; *Around the World in 80 Days*; *Michael Strogoff*; *The Prisoner of Zenda*; *Rupert of Hentzau*; *The Scarlet Pimpernel*; and *Brigadier Gerard* (Rahill, 83; Richards 1977, 12). Adventure was stereotyped not only in melodramas but also in boys' periodicals, such as *Boy's Own Paper* in England. The latter celebrated not only the adventurers of the past but also their modern equivalents aiding in the growth of empire, be they engineer, explorer, missionary, sailor or soldier. Boys were often portrayed alongside such heroes, learning moral and political idealism. The values of hero-worship, militarism, nationalism, and imperialism were thus promulgated to several generations of youth. These stories became allied with the historical novel to form an influential stream of adventure images placed in the service of empire for successive generations, adventure becoming the literary expression of the expansion of Western civilization (Bratton, "Of England, home and duty," in McKenzie, 79; Green 1990, 1–2).

The best examples of this type of writing are the nearly one hundred novels authored by George Alfred Henty (1832–1902). Written from 1868, they covered the gamut of adventure, from swashbuckling to empire building, invariably concentrating on military exploits. The books are heavily didactic, almost unbearably so from a modern perspective, with history and biography dominating a slow-moving fictional narrative. Each novel opens with a foreword from Henty, addressed to "My dear lads," urging his readers to manliness and service to country. Henty's stories invariably deal with a boy of modest background who is taken into service by a great general or noble. Growing to manhood, the lad makes good in a dangerous situation by virtue of his courage and daring, proving his worth to his mentor. Beginning as an enthusiastic if unskilled adolescent, he rises through the ranks to become a capable officer, living out a militarized, historical version of the Horatio Alger myth.

A new style of writing gradually emerged by the end of the nineteenth century, more economical and less ponderous and dense, offering an accelerated pace and a greater emphasis on narrative as opposed to description—all ideally suited for adventure (Fisher, 117). Further shifts in adventure literature during the first half of the twentieth century were linked to the rise of serialization in newspapers and especially pulp magazines, which featured the last prolific generation of authors to write classical adventure stories. Such magazines catered to the voracious interest in the world's new frontiers, the distant peoples, places, and traditions that increasingly absorbed modern readers. They also made available adventure fiction to readers who could only afford newspapers and journals, rather than those who patronized the more expensive books.

The best and most notable of these journals was the aptly titled

Adventure, published in issues of about two hundred pages, as often as three times a month, from 1910 until it changed format in the 1950s and finally expired in the early 1970s. Designed for "intelligent readers," *Adventure* was regarded as the most distinguished and literary magazine in its genre and class, attaining a reputation as "The *Atlantic Monthly* of the pulps." The circulation reached up to 300,000 subscribers, including Theodore Roosevelt and "many a lawyer, statesman, physician, [and] college professor."[2] *Adventure* presented fiction but had a practical side as well, sponsoring historical debates, an expedition to Abyssinia, and the founding of the American Legion. The magazine carried the major contemporary authors of the genre, hoping to reconcile action stories with the literary taste for sophistication, realism, and artistic storytelling. *Adventure* had a motto: "If action, however violent, evolves from character there is no higher literary expression."[3] *Adventure* brought together related types, including the western, the historical novel, and occasionally borderline fantasy—although it drew the line at science fiction, horror, and crime stories. This difference in scope can be seen in a similar but more inclusive magazine, *Argosy*, which headlined on its 1930 covers "Action Stories of Every Variety."

Two notable streams as they appeared in such popular fiction can be traced through two important authors in *Adventure*, Talbot Mundy (1879–1940) and Rafael Sabatini (1875–1950). Mundy and Sabatini are among the best adventure writers of their time and embody the basic archetypes of adventure. Unlike authors such as Scott and Alexandre Dumas, Mundy and Sabatini wrote during the peak years of adventure filmmaking, with the knowledge that their stories were always being considered for this medium. Their writing, and those of other authors who appeared in magazines like *Adventure*, exerted a more direct influence on screenwriters than earlier novels. Pulp and popular fiction not only provided a ready source of adaptations but also set conventions and parameters among filmmakers and the general public.

The two men were personal contrasts. Talbot Mundy wrote of contemporary colonial adventure in the exotic lands of Africa, the Middle East, and especially India. Rafael Sabatini wrote of historical European swashbucklers, seafarers and pirates in the manner of Scott, Dumas, and Robert Louis Stevenson. Mundy lived an adventurous youth, and his experiences in the East, cloaked in a cultivated image of mystery, inspired much of his writing. Sabatini's European existence was sedate, researching the past and spinning tales from history. He utilized the genre's conventions and inherent political view without seeking to expand or examine them, preferring an outspoken devotion to historical accuracy. As Sabatini wrote, "To produce historical romance of any value, it is necessary first to engage in researches so exhaustive as to qualify one to write a history of the epoch in which the romance is set."[4] Indeed, he wrote scholarly books on Caesar Borgia and Torquemada, subjects he also fictionalized.

Author of thirty-eight novels over forty-seven years, Sabatini became known as a man born out of his time, "The Alexandre Dumas of Modern Fiction" (Adcock, 288). Plot, style and atmosphere were Sabatini's strengths, and occasionally character as well, as in the revenge novels *Scaramouche* and *The Sea-Hawk*. Sabatini's specialty was the misunderstood hero, a once-respected individual who appears to be a villain when he is wrongfully accused of a crime, and flees in order to later prove his innocence (Fisher, 187). The principal concerns of the Sabatini hero are honor and chivalry. The characters have agile minds; each has a crafty sense of strategy and a ready use of disguise and deception. The Sabatini heroes rely on luck and lady fortune to help him prevail against his enemies; there is little mention of destiny, which is often invoked by Talbot Mundy. The Sabatini hero is a person of high social standing, well educated, a born leader, with a touch of the aristocratic manner. There is nothing gratuitous or sensational in the violence, and the hero ultimately throws himself at the foot of the heroine. "Devotion to a woman is the only religion of a hero," and a love interest eventually brings about the hero's social reconciliation. Sabatini was capable of wit and humor behind the period detail and ornate dialogue; his people, situations, and settings were eminently adaptable to Hollywood (cf. Voorhees, 197). Indeed, Sabatini's rise to literary fame coincided with the cinematic adaptations of his work, and earlier works hitherto unsuccessful in America were republished and became best-sellers.

While Sabatini's outcast heroes are frequently caught up in vengeance, Mundy's less glamorous characters are philosopher-adventurers seeking to understand existence, accidentally stumbling across some fragment of its puzzle that involves them in adventure. Mundy expands on the philosophy of adventure as the key motivational factor, while Sabatini merely utilizes it as necessary. Mundy was almost exclusively concerned with colonial settings, writing of the exploitation of Africa, of the Arab struggles for independence in the wake of World War I, and of the cultural and religious philosophy of the Indian subcontinent. Mundy resented being compared with Kipling, postdating him not only in years but ideas, strongly opposing his imperialist ethic despite their shared British ancestry. Mundy's mind had an unconventional turn not typically found in the genre, one that made him closer to Joseph Conrad than Kipling or H. Rider Haggard.

Only rarely did Mundy give his stories a period setting, usually placing them in a time contemporary to his writing, although he did fuse history and adventure into an innovative trilogy about a sea rover who turns pirate to battle the oppression of Julius Caesar (*Tros of Samothrace; Queen Cleopatra; Purple Pirate*). Mundy also delineated the borders of adventure through a series of fantasies, drawing the line where the latter begins and adventure ends. He began to write in the fantasy genre in the 1920s, looking for a way to shift adventure into new modes that would prevent it from becoming dated. As this became a dominant trend of the 1930s pulp magazines, Mundy wrote in both veins, pure adventure as well as mystical fantasies of the Orient. Mundy's move toward fantasy had an experiential basis; in a manner typical of adventurers, Mundy tried many forms of unconventional philosophical and religious modes of thought, with theosophy his strongest inclination. Consequently, Mundy's fictional adventurers gravitated toward India to explore its philosophical and mystical tradition, with sympathetic interest, investigating apparent magic and the occult (*Full Moon*), and penetrating the monasteries of Tibet (*Om; The Devil's Guard; Old Ugly-Face*). Mundy became an amateur historian and scholar, writing not only fiction but also poetry, essays, and a book of philosophy. This new strain indicates the inadequacy of adventure to address modern concerns; the territory available for a contemporary author in the genre had to be expanded if he or she aspired to a place in literature.

Mundy is a transitional figure, whose achievement was the union and balance of adventure with philosophy, spanning a revisionist like Conrad and sophisticated anti-adventure writers such as Ernest Hemingway and André Malraux. The variations on adventure by

Mundy, and others like him, changed the genre. The time of optimistic works like *Ivanhoe* was over; even Sabatini's contemporary *Captain Blood* seemed more of a throwback than a modern novel. The twentieth-century adventurer becomes a more complex figure in Mundy's work, a fallible person whose dreams are seldom achieved, the genre often becoming the background to support a meditative framework. By 1914, the institutions that for a quarter century had urged adventure into boys' fiction began to reject the genre. Whereas in the years before World War I adventure had such powerful proponents as Theodore Roosevelt, by the early 1920s even Kipling was losing his literary readers. As early as 1911 Sir Arthur Conan Doyle recognized the closing of the overseas frontiers for English empire builders and fortune hunters, placing his explorers of the South American *Lost World* in the science fiction genre (Brantlinger, 249). The generation of writers who fought from 1914 to 1918 would no longer write historical adventure in the classical sense, and a profound shift in critical attitudes toward the genre occurred after the war. The demand for adventure continued from readers and publishers, but it was no longer regarded a viable form for authors with artistic ambitions.[5] In a period that overwhelmed individualism, adventure would turn anachronistic if it maintained an innocent form; it had to become serious and relevant to its time. Literary adventure from the 1920s on, and in subsequent decades films of the genre as well, became increasingly complex. The career of the colonial novel paralleled the rise and fall of western colonialism, reaching its height with Kipling and virtually disappearing as a vital genre after the Second World War (Meyers, vii).

On the other hand, adventure's early identification with boys' periodicals and its later dismissal to the periphery of literature did not diminish but may have enhanced its significance. Such books still form the core of the literature now aimed at the children's audience, and the genre's commercial importance dwarfs the attention it receives from scholars (Green 1991, 42). Indeed, there is a widespread impression that adventure is appreciated either by young minds or those who can still experience their entertainment with the feelings of youth (Fisher, 10). The certification many adventure novels still enjoy as children's classics indicates that for the foreseeable future they will continue to have a certain subliminal impact on the shaping of young minds. While adventure is no longer critically fashionable, it remains as popular as ever; an author such as Kipling, as discredited as his political sentiments have become, has become enthroned in the status of "classic" author.

At the dawn of cinema in the 1890s, adventure was still in its pre–World War I golden age and so was quick to find its way into films. Even before fiction became the dominant movie form, adventure was present in documentary portrayals of contemporary military activities, such as the Boxer Rebellion or Zulu wars (Basinger, 341). However, historical adventure fiction proper soon became a popular genre; the very first fictional contribution to the genre may have been an 1898 British picture of Alexandre Dumas's *The Corsican Brothers*, a story remade at least five more times by 1920 (Cohen, 38–39). This repetition was common; during the first two decades of the twentieth century, first shorts and then feature films regularly adapted and frequently remade such classic adventure novels as *The Four Feathers*; *Under Two Flags*; *Michael Strogoff*; *The Sea Wolf*; *The Count of Monte Cristo*; *Ivanhoe*; *The Prisoner of Zenda*; and *The Three Musketeers*, along with many variations of the Robin Hood legend. Some of the early feature adaptations were stiff and literal, stilted and theatrical, with little action, such as *The Count of Monte Cristo* (1912); *Michael Strogoff* (1914); and *D'Artagnan / The Three Musketeers* (1916) (Everson, 142; Richards, Summer 1977, 13). Or a film such as *The Prisoner of Zenda* (1913) could contain both a stagy, intrigue-filled beginning, together with a rousing concluding half filled with action and romance. The fast-paced, swashbuckling style expected of adventure, with intrigue, romance, and battle against injustice, is clearly evident at least by the feature *Kidnapped* (1917), and even such earlier shorts as *The King's Messenger* (1908) and *The Duke's Plan* (1910). *The Charge of the Light Brigade* (1912), although only lasting one reel, offered a spectacular enactment of the doomed charge, on a scale and with a skill that compares favorably to the more famous one staged by Warner Bros. for the 1936 version of the same title.

From 1920, historical adventure films began to take a definite course, and the genre as we know it can be identified as occurring primarily within four definite cycles. In that year, Douglas Fairbanks starred in the first media adaptation of Johnston McCulley's recent pulp tale of rebellion in Spanish California, *The Mark of Zorro*. The picture was an innovation in the genre; for the first time, a film exhibited the entire archetypal plot and political theme around which most later adventure movies would be constructed. Fairbanks's dashing athletic skill, sense of humor, and panache set a standard that came to be expected of subsequent cinematic adventurers. *The Mark of Zorro* initiated a cycle that continued up to the end of the decade, highlighted by Fairbanks's five subsequent genre productions, *The Three Musketeers* (1921); *Robin Hood* (1922); *Don Q Son of Zorro* (1925); *The Black Pirate* (1926); and *The Iron Mask* (1929). Another similar series of popular and prestigious films was derived from the novels of Rafael Sabatini, including *Scaramouche* (1923); *The Sea Hawk*; *Captain Blood* (both in 1924); and *Bardelys the Magnificent* (1926). All of these pictures helped to set the early parameters of historical adventure movies, particularly the swashbuckler and pirate types. There were also empire adventures, most notably Foreign Legion movies inspired by the success of *Beau Geste* in 1926.

Although Warner Bros. chose a swashbuckler, *Don Juan* (1926), for its first feature with music and sound effects, sound initially brought other genres to prominence. Theatrical adaptations, musicals and gangster films best displayed the virtues of "talkies" to audiences at a time when the careful recording of dialogue or music, often in a stage-bound manner, was regarded as both a popular and a technical necessity. A spate of adventure films had a notable lack of critical and box-office success, including Fairbanks's *The Iron Mask* and director John Ford's *The Black Watch / King of the Khyber Rifles* (both 1929). Adventure became one of the genres whose future seemed questionable, possibly a result of the logistical problems in filming duels and battles in the talkie. Yet, the genre was on its way to a slow but definite recovery. In 1930, M-G-M committed enormous resources to producing of *Trader Horn* on location in Africa, and the movie proved extremely popular upon release the following year. Two jungle adventures were also box- office hits shortly thereafter, *Bring 'Em Back Alive* (1932) and *Tarzan the Ape Man* (1932).[6]

While adventure was slowly becoming fashionable again in the early 1930s, no particular pattern was discernable for several years. Then, a new cycle of adventure filmmaking began with the release of three important films in 1934: *Treasure Island*; *The Lost Patrol*; and *The Count of Monte Cristo*. For the next seven years features in each of the adventure types could be found among the top box-office successes: swashbuckler (*The Adventures of Robin Hood* [1938]), pirate (*Captain Blood* [1935]; *China Seas* [1935]; *The Buccaneer*

[1938]); sea (*Mutiny on the Bounty* [1935]; *Captains Courageous* [1937]; *The Sea Wolf* [1941]), empire (*The Crusades* [1935]; *The Lives of a Bengal Lancer* [1935]; *The Charge of the Light Brigade* [1936]; *Gunga Din* [1939]), and fortune hunter adventures (*A Tale of Two Cities* [1935]; *Anthony Adverse* [1936]; *Lloyd's of London* [1936]). Many won Academy Awards and listings in "ten best" polls, indicating that the second adventure cycle was well on its way to a golden age unique in the genre's history for popularity and critical approval. The genre was equally if not more popular in England with the work of the Korda brothers, from *The Scarlet Pimpernel* (1934) and several sequels and remakes, to such empire adventures as *Sanders of the River* (1935); *Elephant Boy* (1937); *Drums / The Drum* (1938); and *The Four Feathers* (1939), all boasting impressive location photography.

No particular studio dominated adventure; almost all produced such films at one time or another. Adventure only became characteristic of a particular company when an appropriate leading man was under contract: Errol Flynn at Warner Bros., Tyrone Power at 20th Century-Fox, Gary Cooper at Paramount. There was no correlation between a studio's house style and its adventure movies. Paramount, reputedly the most continental of studios, specialized in adventure pictures with an American background, as in *The Buccaneer*; *Souls at Sea*; and *Reap the Wild Wind*—unlike the foreign settings of the adventure movies of most of its rivals. One successful film would inspire imitations by other companies. Paramount's *The Lives of a Bengal Lancer* led to hiring Talbot Mundy in the attempt to draft a worthy successor and also inspired such counterparts as *The Charge of the Light Brigade* at Warner Bros., *Storm over Bengal* (1938) at Republic, *Gunga Din* at RKO, an aborted remake of *King of the Khyber Rifles* at 20th Century-Fox—and *Drums*, from Alexander Korda. The trend was not limited to obvious imitations; *The Lives of a Bengal Lancer* also prompted such similar Gary Cooper vehicles in 1939 as *Beau Geste* and *The Real Glory*, a virtual remake of *Lives* with the locale shifted to the Philippines.

Several factors were important in this second revival. Various genres with a period setting were re-emerging by 1933, and the rigid enforcement of the production code that began the following year may have helped to make historical films a comparatively safe subject. Adventure could offer escape from the problems of the Great Depression, yet despite the period backdrop the genre had a special relevance to its audience (Cohen, 86–87; Davis, 26, 27; Richards

1977, 18). Adventure's assertion of the rights of the people and the obligations of political elites to ensure their welfare became an even more central theme in the depression era than it had been in the 1920s. While the Fairbanks version of *Robin Hood* had been largely a historical spectacle, the 1938 Flynn version clearly cast the story as a conflict between the haves and have-nots of society.

Economically, adventure was also a natural genre for the studio system to invoke. The period of the genre's principal popularity, from 1920 through the late 1950s, coincided with the golden age of Hollywood's studio system. Adventure was perfectly suited to the controlled, carefully organized industrial practices of the studio system and the use of contract talent on both sides of the camera. Emphasis on mass production, typecasting of talent, reliance on formula storytelling, recycling of story properties and sets all made adventure convenient. Adventure films would recycle period sets, costumes, and props, calling on such standard miniatures as ships in battle from the special effects department, as well as utilizing the back lots and ranches for exteriors. The heroes of adventure films tended to be among the leading players in the studio's stable of stars, and support could be effectively drawn from the tier of character players.

Genre criticism frequently discusses movies purely in terms of content, dwelling on thematic, literary aspects, neglecting visual components, but this approach is not such a disadvantage in dealing with the classical era of Hollywood filmmaking, with its subordinate, self-effacing style traditionally at the service of a formulaic narrative (Neale, 31). Adventure fell squarely within the conventions of classical Hollywood filmmaking: straightforward and seamless in its construction, with little that is overtly artistic or pretentious in technique. Outside of the use of sword fights and battles, adventure tends to be impersonal and unstylized, eminently adaptable to the needs of the particular story involved. The use of three-strip technicolor during the 1930s, 1940s, and 1950s, with its enhanced, bright hues, is especially appropriate for the depictions of a mythicized past on which adventure relies. The only flourishes tend to come in performance, although the acting is declamatory with little appeal to deep emotions. However, speech patterns and dialogue may be modulated in an (often inaccurate) attempt to arrive at the "sound" of a certain period, and the athleticism of the stars, especially in the dueling of swashbucklers and pirates, acquires an almost choreographic quality.[7]

The music in the films utilized the full orchestral treatment that contract studio musicians could provide, with symphonic scores created by such notable composers as Alfred Newman, Victor Young, Miklos Rozsa, Max Steiner, Franz Waxman, and Erich Korngold for films such as *Captain from Castile; Around the World in 80 Days; El Cid;* and *Adventures of Don Juan.* The music accompanying adventure is martial in nature, with a stirring, patriotic quality setting the stage for battles, underlining the hero's feats of courage, daring, and physical agility. There are contrasting themes, of quiet love to accompany the heroine, another to emphasize the solidarity of the group of good comrades, often constructed into an semioperatic whole. Bagpipes are a favorite centerpiece of marches, and perhaps the most frequently invoked musical theme is "Rule, Britannia," sometimes becoming the central structuring motif of an entire score, as in Herbert Stothart's music for *Mutiny on the Bounty* (1935). The empire and fortune hunter forms often derived scores from popular folksongs of the period, as in *Flame over India / Northwest Frontier* and *The Man Who Would Be King.* Such music is seldom attempted or equaled in contemporary adventure films, and pictures like *The Mark of Zorro* (1974) and *Zorro—The Gay Blade* (1981) wisely opted to replay original scores from *The Mark of Zorro* (1940) and *Adventures of Don Juan.*

Other facts were important in promoting the genre. Adventure could satisfy a desire for the portrayal of military life without the menace of actual warfare. World War II was still in the future and there was less competition from war pictures since the Great War of 1914–1918 had become an unfashionable cinematic subject. Empire adventures were viable because the era of colonialism was still under way, with much of Europe's colonial system enduring and America's own imperial tendencies still on the rise. Most English-language audiences could share equally in the vicarious thrill of stories of conquest in remote lands.

As well, England had become increasingly important as the primary overseas market for American productions by the late 1930s. Fascist nations such as Italy began to ban American adventure pictures with pro-British sentiment, including *The Lives of a Bengal Lancer; Clive of India; The Charge of the Light Brigade;* and *Lloyd's of London* (Richards 1983, 249). Domestically, thanks to their un-controversial period setting, adventure movies became one avenue for covertly pro-British propaganda. While this was hardly a consis-tent or organized goal of Hollywood, it was an objective of English producers like Alexander Korda (Richards 1973, 4; Richards 1977; 1983). With the growing fascist threat from the Continent, the affin-ity between the United States and England became more pro-nounced. Adventure movies became an avenue for reminding audi-ences of the practical and ideological ties between the two countries, the similarities of language and culture inducing a natu-ral reaction of empathy. With the threat of war, American and Brit-ish films frequently portrayed Englishmen as personifying the very type of Anglo-American morality and virtues—fair play, democracy, equality—that formed the values on which opposition to fascism and a new European war would be fought. For instance, it is not difficult to see a warning of the fascist threat in the unusually harsh depiction of Spanish ambitions in *Fire over England*, a British film of 1937. The same tendency can be seen in the film's unofficial American adaptation, *The Sea Hawk*, although it did not appear until 1940, by which time Europe was already fully embroiled in war. The iconography of fascism even blended with adventure vil-lains; in *Son of Monte Cristo* (1940), George Sanders retains the Prussian hairstyle used in *Confessions of a Nazi Spy* the year before.

Ironically, once war came to America, adventure movies disap-peared almost instantly, ending the adventure cycle that had begun in the mid-1930s (Richards 1973, 4; Sennett, 164). The harsh real-ities of modern combat and of enemies who were all too authentic moved cinema toward increasing realism, making adventure seem excessively escapist and frivolous, irrelevant to the contemporary concern with a worldwide conflict. Empire adventures, especially, became politically unpalatable since colonized countries were often sufficiently reluctant to assist the Allies without importing motion pictures that reminded them of their status. The alliance with Stalinist Russia also seemed unnatural for adventure; a proposed motion picture of *Kim* would have been potentially offensive by exposing czarist plans for India—although the story was finally filmed once the World War II was over and the cold war had taken its place (Richards 1973, 5).

Nonetheless, audiences soon tired of exposure to grim realities and once more embraced the distraction that adventure could provide. Studios were quick to supply such escapism as soon as the close of World War II was within sight, and *Frenchman's Creek* and *The Princess and the Pirate* opened to top box-office business in 1944. Within a year the third cycle (1945–1960) of adventure was underway, one that would last significantly longer and be more prolific than the roughly nine-year spans of the both first (1920–1929) and second (1934–1942) cycles. As with the second cycle, each of the types appeared steadily on the annual lists of top commercial successes from 1945 on. More popular than ever were the swashbucklers (*Bandit of Sherwood Forest* [1946]; *The Three Musketeers* [1948]; *The Flame and the Arrow* [1950]; *Ivanhoe* [1952]; *The Story of Robin Hood* [1952]; *Knights of the Round Table* [1953]; *The Court Jester* [1956]; *El Cid* [1961]), but there also continued to be empire (*Captain from Castile* [1948]; *Kim* [1950]; *Swiss Family Robinson* [1960]; *55 Days in Peking* [1963]), sea (*Two Years before the Mast* [1946]; *Captain Horatio Hornblower* [1951]; *Moby Dick* [1956]; *Mutiny on the Bounty* [1962]), pirate (*The Spanish Main* [1945]; *The Vikings* [1958]), and fortune hunter adventures (*The Black Rose* [1950]; *The African Queen* [1952]; *Bwana Devil* [1952]; *Around the World in 80 Days* [1956]).

The first and second cycles had been a time of comparative innocence that would not be repeated in the genre. The change was reflected in a loss of optimism in the third cycle, making the films distinct from earlier product, displaying a much harsher, more realistic tone. While perhaps the 1920s and the 1930s had been the golden age of adventure films, during the postwar years the genre turned inward to become richer, and more rewarding. The heroes became flawed and less virtuous than they had been in the earlier, more carefree adventures, with narratives placing a greater emphasis on the inner torments of the heroes. Scenes of torture became almost obligatory, and the level of violence increased, while still appearing tame by today's standards. The stars who returned to the genre had visibly aged, especially Errol Flynn and Tyrone Power, and their new adventure vehicles reflected a greater maturity and an absence of the earlier devil-may-care approach. Their new competition included such fresh faces as Cornel Wilde, Burt Lancaster, Stewart Granger, Yul Brynner, and Charlton Heston, while Robert Taylor and Paul Henried shifted from romantic leads to close their careers in the adventure genre. All tended to be more enigmatic, less clean cut and dashing than their predecessors. Similarly, villains became more sneering and underhanded than suave, with Robert Douglas and John Sutton replacing Basil Rathbone and Raymond Massey.

In what was clearly a reflection of the experience of World War II and disillusionment with the Old World, Europe was now often portrayed as a near-barbaric cesspool of depravity and corruption in such films as *The Black Book / Reign of Terror* (1949); *Captain from Castile; Prince of Foxes* (1949); and *The Flame and the Arrow*. Indeed, a new strain emerged that might be labeled the *noir* style of adventure. This was only partially a result of *noir* filmmakers, such as Jacques Tourneur, turning to adventure with *The Flame and the Arrow* and *Anne of the Indies*. Classicists such as Henry King became imbued with the same spirit in *Captain from Castile* and *Prince of Foxes*. A gallery of expressionistic devices was employed, including the stylized use of color, shadow effects, and unusual camera angles, often accompanying convoluted narratives involving brutal villains and heroes with questionable motives.

Just as adventure films continued to be made at all the studios, no individual filmmaker secured a reputation specifically for their work in the form. Commercially speaking, adventure pictures were regarded as only one of several types of action movie, which included westerns, war, crime, and suspense, and there was little recognition of the distinctions among these genres. Nonetheless, a few directors did make numerous and important contributions to the genre. Frank Lloyd made a number of the top adventure pictures at various studios during the first and second cycles, as did Rowland V. Lee in the first, second, and third. Michael Curtiz is associated with Errol Flynn at Warner Bros. during the second cycle, Henry King with Ronald Colman in the first cycle and Tyrone Power at 20th Century-Fox during both the second and third cycles. During the third cycle Richard Thorpe helmed the movies starring Robert Taylor. Henry Hathaway and Raoul Walsh made some contributions to the second and third cycles, although each is known primarily for other action types. Throughout the third cycle, Frederick De Cordova and Rudolf Maté were busily engaged at Universal-International, John Farrow handled sea stories, and Sidney Salkow directed swashbucklers and pirate films. At this time and in subsequent years John Huston made a half-dozen independent productions, while Ken Annakin, John Gilling, Robert Stevenson, and Richard Lester filmed some of the most important adventures to be made in England.

Few producers have taken a strong interest in adventure. Among the exceptions are Pandro Berman, who was active during his tenure at RKO in the second cycle and at M-G-M in the third, where he was principally involved with director Thorpe. Harold Hecht produced the four adventures of the third cycle that starred Burt Lancaster, and Walt Disney was responsible for many of the other leading adventure successes of the same period. At the other end of the commercial spectrum, many of the cheaper adventure films for Columbia at this time were produced by serial veteran Sam Katzman. Samuel Goldwyn produced a number of films in the genre among the many during his long career. Perhaps the most consistent producer of adventure movies was Edward Small, releasing his independent productions through United Artists during the second and third cycles and concentrating on adaptations, often in name only, from Alexandre Dumas. Another independent, in this case a writer-producer, was Joseph Ermolieff, who specialized in empire adventures and collaborated on some of the early international productions, such as *The Soldier and the Lady / Michael Strogoff / The Bandit and the Lady / The Adventures of Michael Strogoff* and *Outpost in Morocco*. The contributions of screenwriters have been most sporadic of all, since credits during the studio period were never wholly reliable. However, among those names who surface frequently are Charles Drayson Adams, Robert Ardrey, Lajos Biro, Oscar Brodney, Harry Joe Brown, Borden Chase, Helen Deutsch, Philip Dunne, Ivan Goff and Ben Roberts, Douglas Heyes, Joseph Hoffman, Talbot Jennings, Robert E. Kent, Noel Langley, Jesse Lasky, Jr., Rowland V. Lee, Alan LeMay, W. P. Lipscomb, Barré Lyndon, Aeneas MacKenzie, Bess Meredyth, Seton I. Miller, Dudley Nichols, Jack Pollexfen, Richard Schayer, Aubrey Wisberg, Arthur Wimperis, Philip Yordan, and George MacDonald Fraser.

The range of stars who have appeared in multiple adventure films is vast. While the list is long, it reveals the extent of adventure production and is worth reciting. In roughly chronological order, the names include Douglas Fairbanks, Alan Hale, Ronald Colman, Victor McLaglen, Gary Cooper, Donald Crisp, C. Aubrey Smith, Errol Flynn, David Niven, Patric Knowles, Tyrone Power, Douglas Fairbanks, Jr., Sir Cedric Hardwicke, Henry Wilcoxon, Akim Tamiroff, Sabu, Louis Hayward, Maureen O'Hara, Robert Newton, Nigel Bruce, Richard Greene, Jon Hall, Paul Henried, Cornel Wilde, Thomas Gomez, Dan O'Herlihy, Orson Welles, Burt Lancaster,

Stewart Granger, Robert Taylor, Tony Curtis, Victor Mature, Alan Ladd, Rock Hudson, Michael Rennie, James Robertson Justice, Jack Hawkins, Torin Thatcher, Harry Andrews, Arnold Moss, John Derek, Ricardo Montalban, Charlton Heston, Christopher Lee, and Peter Finch. Among the reliable villains were Basil Rathbone, Claude Rains, Raymond Massey, George Sanders, Henry Brandon, Robert Douglas, George Macready, James Mason, Walter Slezak, and John Sutton. Many other players made only occasional yet distinguished appearances in the genre; consider Spencer Tracy in *Stanley and Livingstone* (1939) or Robert Donat in *The Count of Monte Cristo* (1934). Curiously, although many of these actors were born in England, none achieved identification with the genre in the British cinema.

During the second cycle, adventure had been identified with elaborate action scenes and period settings that tended to require the resources of a large studio. However, by the third cycle such smaller studios as Universal and Columbia joined in their production. Technicolor was no longer so expensive, allowing films to look extravagant on a relatively modest budget, suggesting that they offered more spectacle than was actually the case. While adventure does not lend itself to hastily assembled low-budget production, a type of B adventure movie blossomed—probably the best was *The Highwayman* (1951)—although the genre was never so adaptable to economical filmmaking as the B western or crime thriller.

Despite the incompatibility with the restrictions of B budgets, conversely, historical adventure is not a genre that may be properly labeled "epic," at least in terms of its content. Adventure heroes exist on a national, rather than universal, scale. They serve primarily as embodiments of political views, and their exploits illustrate a value system. They are not demigods whose deeds command chronicling, as in ancient world–biblical movies (*Ben-Hur* [1959]) and fantasies (*Ulysses* [1955]) that attempt epic stature. The gods, if they can be found at all in adventure, are remote and represented by a priestly order rather than approachable beings by which the epic hero may measure himself. The plots of such pictures as *The Scarlet Pimpernel; Scaramouche; The Adventures of Robin Hood; The Lives of a Bengal Lancer; The Buccaneer;* or *Two Years Before the Mast* are too intimate in terms of characterization, and too often humorous, modest in scale and running time, to deserve the term epic.

Only in considering the adventure genre's style, not its content, can it be regarded as occasionally aspiring to epic status. During the 1950s and early 1960s, a number of genres, among them adventure, became candidates for the new technology of spectacle—with wide screen, color, sound, and increased length all utilized to accentuate the differences between movies and television. However, the use of color and wide screen was appropriate to adventure only insofar as these techniques were useful to the particular story. Historical settings and military events such as battles had always been part of the traditional substance of adventure, so such movies could be treated in a so-called epic style without a need to change generic conventions, as in *The Pride and the Passion*. Most adventure types at some point took advantage of the epic style: the swashbuckler (*El Cid*), the fortune hunter (*Around the World in 80 Days*), and especially empire (*Zulu; Khartoum*). As early as the mid-1950s the limited possibilities for epic treatment of adventure had been discovered, and Hollywood turned primarily to the ancient world–biblical genre, and eventually war pictures—both more amenable to spectacle for its own sake—as more suitable for the epic fashion (Richards 1977, 24). The bulk of the adventure genre was largely unaffected by the epic trend of the 1950s and 1960s, and even where this style was invoked, the narrative conventions remained the same as their smaller scale counterparts. Both expansive and more intimate adventure films were made; a single picture could even have both an epic and a more private quality simultaneously, as in *Captain from Castile*. The television miniseries *Christopher Columbus* (1985) was one of the rare small-screen adventures to acquire an epic aura, due to its six-hour duration and the lengthy period of the hero's life that was covered.

In the 1950s, a far greater impact on the genre than the epic style could be found in the adjustments made to incorporate the possibility of extensive shooting on location. These arrangements did not always have a strong impact on the style or narrative as a whole; for instance, *El Cid* and *Mutiny on the Bounty* (1962) benefitted from the use of locations, although they never came to be a governing factor in the pictures themselves. However, the narratives of a whole series of empire and fortune hunter adventures, including *Around the World in 80 Days; Killers of Kilimanjaro*; and *The Naked Prey*, were largely constructed around the emphasis on pictorial backgrounds of African wildlife and similarly remote locales. In a number of cases, the availability of this background location photography led to the making of separate feature pictures based upon the recycling of such footage, as in the case of *King Solomon's Mines* (1950), which reappeared in M-G-M's *Watusi* (1959); *Drums of Africa* (1963); and *Trader Horn* (1973).

During the third cycle, Hollywood's production of adventure pictures became closely rivaled by competition from such British companies as the Korda Brothers, J. Arthur Rank, and the Hammer studio, providing a commercial and artistic influence. Such pictures were not a uniquely British manifestation of production methods or background. Although the sociopolitical roots of these films were not always identical to those operating in the United States, they derived from many of the same cultural and literary forces. With Anglo-American coproductions and American movies made in England, a true amalgamation took place between the adventure pictures of both countries. There was a ready interchange between the important features of this type in both countries, much more so than between America and the European countries of the continent.

The major weakness faced by the British in making their own distinct cycle of adventure films was the inability to develop an adult star appropriate to the genre; the best individual they found was the young Indian import Sabu (Richards 1973, 86). This was not, at least directly, a result of a loss of talent to Hollywood: no British stars were imported on the basis of their success in adventure movies. Many British adventure pictures, in comparison to their Hollywood counterparts, had a rather pedestrian quality to their action. The importance of fidelity to source material was overemphasized, and a detached, uninvolved perspective informed their storytelling.

Although Britain was the sole foreign country whose domestically made adventure movies had a notable impact on the genre in America, it was not the only country to which Hollywood would later send its production crews. Taking advantage of foreign facilities and studios to use funds frozen outside of the United States, Hollywood sent many of its adventure pictures to locations abroad. The increased use of foreign technicians and talent on both sides of the camera may have eventually hastened the end of Hollywood's era of involvement with the adventure film, as the genre's look became steadily more international rather than American. By the end of the 1950s, what was left of the genre's momentum had shifted to Europe for the production of foreign-language adventure movies (Gow 1972,

40). Italy, Spain, and France made dozens in all types of the genre, favoring especially swashbuckler and pirate tales. Sometimes second-tier Hollywood stars were featured, but the supporting casts and nearly all the crew were foreign in such pictures as *Pirate Warrior / Black Pirate / Rage of the Buccaneers*; *Seven Seas to Calais*; *Morgan the Pirate*; and *The White Warrior*. Many of these productions, in a partially dubbed form, found minor theatrical release in America and, along with many similar but lesser efforts, later appeared on television.

Television has had little direct effect on the genre, primarily offering at various times a home for classical adventure. This was first evident in the 1950s in half-hour dramatic series, a form that necessarily condensed plots to fit the brief running time. Small-scale action elements were amplified, emphasizing formula and repetition at the expense of originality. Such series generally suffered from the same budgetary and narrative difficulties as the B adventure movie, with sets, costumes, and the other historical elements essential to a period genre treated in a perfunctory manner. Although not sufficient in quantity to become a significant movement, the 1950s through the beginning of the 1960s, especially the 1956–58 seasons, saw a number of filmed television series in all the various forms of adventure. There were tales of pirates (*The Buccaneers*; *Adventures of Long John Silver / Return to Treasure Island*; *Tales of the Vikings*), the sea (*Sir Francis Drake*), fortune hunters (*The Count of Monte Cristo*), and empire (*Tales of the 77th Bengal Lancers*; *Captain Gallant of the French Foreign Legion*; *Robinson Crusoe*). As was the case with features of the time, swashbucklers became the most prevalent: *The Adventures of Sir Lancelot*; *The Gay Cavalier* (highwayman Claude Duval); *The Iron Mask*; *Ivanhoe*; *Richard the Lionheart*; *The Scarlet Pimpernel*; *The Sword of Freedom* (set in Italy); *The Three Musketeers*; *The Adventures of William Tell*; and Walt Disney's *Zorro* and *The Swamp Fox* (on Revolutionary War hero Francis Marion). Most popular was *The Adventures of Robin Hood / Adventures in Sherwood Forest*, starring Richard Greene in the title role, which spawned an original feature from the Hammer studios, *Sword of Sherwood Forest*. Occasionally, episodes of television series were edited into movie form and released as features, as with Disney's *The Sign of Zorro* and *Zorro the Avenger* in 1960—and were still in re-release after almost two decades, although shot in black and white. Disney's *Zorro* series (1957–60) became such a phenomenal success that hundreds of toys and tie-ins were made for its youthful audience, and 20th Century-Fox again reissued *The Mark of Zorro* (1940) to theaters.

By the late 1950s, coincident with the decline of the studio system in general, the adventure genre rapidly dwindled once again, and the third cycle drew to a close in both television and theaters. There seemed no discernable pattern in the infrequent adventure box-office successes, and changes in audience taste made the genre appear a thing of the past. However, during the early 1970s, a fourth cycle tentatively emerged. Fewer movies were made than before, but this phase had its own unique aesthetic characteristics. For the first time, the fourth cycle placed adventure under fire by subjecting the genre to parody and revision, reflecting two parallel inclinations of how the genre should be treated in modern times. The fourth cycle was characterized by an emphasis on the unpleasant side of adventure in an attempt to find a new critical respectability for the genre (Fisher, 61).

On the surface there was an effort to recapture the naive, light-hearted tone frequently associated with adventure films of the second cycle. This sometimes resulted in an overemphasis on action over plot, piling on action and incident at the expense of credibility, as in *Nate and Hayes / Savage Islands* (1983) and *Pirates* (1986). In such films the literal choreography of generic elements took precedence over their arrangement in a meaningful way. The resulting style resembled not so much classical Hollywood as the European adventure films made at the end of the third cycle for the international market.

Adventure offered the opportunity to openly burlesque itself, while still functioning within the genre, without becoming primarily comedy—a tradition whose literary ancestry extended back to Cervantes's *Don Quixote*. Humor had always been an important leavening element in adventure plots, deriving from the genre's fundamentally optimistic outlook, since heroes generally succeed in overcoming obstacles. The amount and potential of the humor often increased with the romance and camaraderie in the plot, as in *Gunga Din*; yet even this picture, while commencing in a jocular vein, turns into a serious, grim experience. In a few notable adventure films of the third cycle, humor occasionally became dominant, principally in the swashbuckler (*The Court Jester; Casanova's Big Night*

[1954]) and pirate types (*The Black Swan* [1942]; *The Princess and the Pirate*; *The Crimson Pirate* [1951]). On the other hand, outright comedies merely touching on the adventure style bore only a distant relation to the genre proper, including *We're in the Legion Now / Rest Cure* (1937); *Old Bones of the River* (1938); *Follow that Camel* (1967); Laurel and Hardy in *Beau Hunks* (1931); *Abbott and Costello in the Foreign Legion* (1950), some of the 1960s British *Carry on . . .* series, several Monty Python vehicles, and the 1975 television series *When Things Were Rotten*. Even a brief 1985 television series, *Zorro and Son*, played the story largely for laughs.

Unlike these, an adventure parody does not laugh at adventure, but with it, as the archetypal plot is capably drawn through the motions, only with more emphasis on comedy and a greater realization of the satirical potential. While paying a certain fealty to adventure values, retaining the narrative pattern and characteristics, parody lampoons and mimics many of the genre's conventions and motifs. Because swashbucklers and pirate adventures often included humorous elements, the genre retains viability even as it is parodied, unlike westerns that have been entirely undercut by this approach. The shift had been foreshadowed by *Start the Revolution without Me* in 1970, finding commercial and critical success in 1973 with the production of a new version of *The Three Musketeers* (cf. Richards 1977, 24). This picture commenced the fourth cycle, and for the next several years many successors were inspired by its approach to favor a tongue-in-cheek treatment of the genre.

Much of the impetus toward this move in adventure was the contribution of novelist and screenwriter George MacDonald Fraser. Fraser began his series of Flashman novels in the late 1960s, using the cruel villain of *Tom Brown's School Days* to take a simultaneously parodic and revisionist view of adventure. Fraser imagines an adult Flashman finding himself in a series of dangerous escapades that seem to indicate a courage and altruism he actually lacks, his motives springing entirely from a fortune hunter's instinct for opportunity and self-preservation. The period was depicted with a knowledge of its eccentricities that added both authenticity and additional humor, often through unusual set pieces or incongruous settings. Fraser applied this technique to a series of adventure scripts, including *The Three Musketeers*; *The Four Musketeers* (1974); *Royal Flash* (1975); *Crossed Swords / The Prince and the*

Pauper (1977); *Casanova* (1988); and *The Return of the Musketeers* (1989). Fraser, more than any other single individual, pioneered an approach that revived the adventure form and made it seem fresh, novel, and appropriate to a more cynical age.

Outside of Fraser's work, the trend is perhaps best typified by a parody of one of the most enduring adventure legends, *Zorro—The Gay Blade* (1981). It exploits the inherent idiosyncrasies and conventions of the swashbuckler, in particular the distinctive masked rider of Spanish California (played here by George Hamilton). The film combines elements of *The Mark of Zorro; The Bold Caballero / The Bold Cavalier; Don Q Son of Zorro,* along with *The Scarlet Pimpernel* and *The Corsican Brothers*. Even with amusing caricatures of the stereotypical characters, *Zorro—The Gay Blade* still lives up to the politics of adventure. The movie is loyal to the traditional gentlemanly code of the swashbuckler, despite the modern emphasis on the sexuality of the leading characters. Unlike many other attempts of this period that exceeded parody to ridicule the genre, like *The Last Remake of Beau Geste* (1977) and to a lesser degree *Yellowbeard* (1983), *Zorro—The Gay Blade* remains true to the swashbuckler form, and one reflection of the affection for its antecedents is the effective reprise of a classical adventure musical score.

Only rarely have the underlying politics of the swashbuckler been undercut without the use of parody; one of the few such treatments in the modern tradition was the 1971 version of *Kidnapped*. Expanding the basis from simply the title novel to also include Stevenson's sequel, *David Balfour / Catriona,* Jack Pulman's script concentrates on an adventurer no longer wanted by the people whose cause he would champion. After the last outbreak of Scottish rebellion is crushed, Alan Breck Stewart (Michael Caine) finds that his old friends are not willing to continue the fight. For them the battle is lost, and Alan faces the prospect of dying in lonely exile as he dreams of serving Bonnie Prince Charlie yet again. *Kidnapped* becomes a meditation, not on the failure of heroes, for Alan and David can still be described as such, but their ultimate irrelevance when struggles for freedom change from a battle of brave armies to a case of political expediency. The judge advocate explains to David that Alan's fight is not only against the British but also the Campbells, for it is through this clan that England preserves dominion, and to whom she must bow in local affairs. Finally, realizing that his people are irreparably beaten and his day is through, Alan turns himself in to the police in order to take responsibility for an assassination that he may or may not have committed.

Such an intellectual approach to adventure is more typically found in types other than the swashbuckler. Although the fortune hunter adventure could become a parody, the empire and the sea adventure are both generally humorless forms where defeat, death, and a bittersweet ending are more common. Indeed, the sea story, always the least prolific of adventure forms, has nearly vanished in recent times. The empire builder is challenged by contemporary concerns in a different way than the swashbuckler and pirate, through subjecting imperial politics to revisionist treatment—the second route taken by adventures of the fourth cycle. Although the adventure film in general is seldom a vehicle for social comment, the allegorical aspects of *Son of Monte Cristo; Fire over England;* and *The Sea Hawk* (1940) have been noted. Revisionism is an appropriate term to indicate the genre's reinterpretation of history and the change in attitude that has taken place in adventure's portrayals of colonialism. While imperialism is still practiced through military, economic, and other forms of exploitation of Third World nations, few Western individuals would openly justify such a policy in the manner of, for instance, Victorian England. Imperialism is recognized as evil, and in their own way recent adventure pictures with colonial settings have acknowledged this fact. Even as old-fashioned empire heroes are portrayed, they are placed in a context that undercuts the validity of their beliefs, deliberately questioning colonial politics and the desirability of adventure.

During the first and second cycle, depictions of empire or fortune hunter colonialism had been inclined to accept the Kiplingesque values. However, with the third cycle in post–World War II years, the representation of colonialism gradually shifted: by 1949 *Prince of Foxes* revealed the dark underside of imperialism with a tale of a fortune-hunting agent of Cesare Borgia who reforms after he has experienced liberty. Within a few years the change became more pronounced; *King of the Khyber Rifles* (1954) pinpointed the implicit racist viewpoint underlying the British presence in India, while still using the plot conventions of the genre. Other revisionist adventures carried this idea one step further by making native leaders just as heroic, if not more so, than their European counterparts. Eastern and western philosophies and cultures are explicitly compared in such adventure films as *Genghis Khan* (1965); *The Long Duel* (1967); *The Wind and the Lion* (1975); *Man Friday* (1975); and *Shogun* (1980).

Revisionist adventures take a skeptical attitude toward the politics underlying colonialism and the classes who were served by imperialism. Both receive a thorough indictment, and revisionism only retains respect for the ideal of the true adventurer. This hero seeks the adventurous life as part of his own confused self-development, desiring to experience the exotic as an alternative to the constraints and limitations of occidental life. Even in recent empire films with classical narratives, modern thinking and the change in world conditions cannot be ignored; adventure is regarded in light of contemporary morality even when honored. *Flame over India; Zulu;* and *Khartoum* (1966), although still loyal to the old ways, scarcely demonstrate the triumph of imperialism with the carefree, lighthearted tone of *Drums* or *Gunga Din.* Indeed, revisionism has been prevalent in adventure for a longer period than has parody, permeating nearly all empire pictures after the 1966 remake of *Beau Geste* inverted the heroic lore of the Foreign Legion. There, the brotherhood of the Gestes is found to be the only redeeming quality in a false and brutalizing adventure where everything turns out to be ruthless and unheroic. Even the surviving brother who tells the story falsifies it, knowing that a tale of defense to the last man is expected; instead he had killed the superior officer who caused the death of Beau. In the final irony, the high command decides to abandon the fort as too costly to hold, turning the garrison's valiant defense into a complete waste.

A few "art" movies, some of them foreign made, invoked adventure, including the 1968 version of *The Charge of the Light Brigade* (1968); *Quemada! / Burn!* (1969); *Lancelot du Lac* (1974); *Breaker Morant* (1982); and *Walker* (1987). And yet, there was often a surprising degree of similarity to Hollywood adventure films. *The Royal Hunt of the Sun* (1969) and *Aguirre—The Wrath of God* (1973) depicted events similar to those in *Captain from Castile,* but enlightened by current attitudes, a concept attempted as early as 1955 by 20th Century-Fox in *7 Cities of Gold.* In *The Royal Hunt of the Sun,* the only admirable European is, ironically, the conqueror Pizarro (Robert Shaw), surrounded by fearful troops, barbaric priests, surreal battles, and a self-serving corps of officers and advisors. Although Pizarro is by no means guiltless, he is portrayed as the only one of

The Incas had everything: wealth, beauty, honor and innocence. Pizarro brought them Christianity.

Thus began a drama that is as alive today as it ever was: a spiritual wrestling match between two men, Pizarro, the Spanish conquistador and Atahuallpa, the Inca sun god. A clash of two cultures, two creeds. With no winners!

Robert Shaw Christopher Plummer

"The Royal Hunt of the Sun"

co-starring
Nigel Davenport Michael Craig Andrew Keir William Marlowe
James Donald and Leonard Whiting

Screenplay by Philip Yordan Based Upon the Play "The Royal Hunt of the Sun" [G] Suggested for GENERAL audiences
Written by Peter Shaffer Produced by Eugene Frenke and Philip Yordan
Directed by Irving Lerner Technicolor® A Cinema Center Films Presentation A National General Pictures Release

Revisionism undercuts the earlier ideological underpinnings of adventure, as in this advertisement for *The Royal Hunt of the Sun* (1969).

the Spanish leaders who consciously agonizes over what he is doing, an attitude he shares only with a scribe, a representative of modern education and enlightenment. Compelled to participate in the murder of the Inca king, Pizarro becomes fascinated with native beliefs, perceiving them to be no less bizarre than the Christianity he has known.

Fortune hunter adventures using a colonial background also reflect revisionist inclinations. *The Man Who Would Be King* (1975) undermines standard empire politics with a portrayal of how it leads two ambitious men not to riches but to death and a reversion to the barbarism of the land they regarded as ripe for conquest. Two former British soldiers in India, dissatisfied with army life, determine to become imperialists for themselves, reaching a distant, unexplored land that they take over with ease. One of them, Dravot (Sean Connery), acquires a reputation as immortal and, entranced with this new region and taking advantage of an ancient prophecy, he sets himself up as king. However, his dreams extend beyond his reach, and the priests execute Dravot and send his friend (Michael Caine), tortured and insane, back to India with nothing to show for the adventure but the decaying, severed head of his companion. Unlike the standard fortune hunter narrative, the final realization of their errors comes too late for a reawakened morality.

Largely abandoned as a television genre for over a dozen years, historical adventure returned to the small screen in the mid-1970s. First came the production of feature-length adventure pictures specifically for television, followed by miniseries. Adventure truly found a comfortable home on television, and despite a few exceptions the narratives remained largely straightforward, unlike the predominance of parody and revisionism in the theatrical side of the fourth cycle. The almost annual titles included *The Man Without a Country* (1973); *The Mark of Zorro* (1974); *Swiss Family Robinson* (1975); *The Count of Monte Cristo* (1976); *The Four Feathers* (1977); *Mayflower: The Pilgrims' Adventure* (1979); *Ivanhoe* (1982); *The Scarlet Pimpernel* (1982); *Cook and Peary: The Race to the Pole* (1983); *The Master of Ballantrae* (1984); *Kim* (1984); *The Zany Adventures of Robin Hood* (1984); *The Corsican Brothers* (1985); *Casanova* (1988); *The Lady and the Highwayman* (1989); *Treasure Island* (1990); and *Robin Hood* (1991).The construction of these pictures as an entertainment for a single evening and the fact that many were of high quality and released as feature movies overseas indicate their similarity to theatrical movies and demonstrate the possibility of a productive film-television interchange in the genre. One advantage of American television showings was the option of scheduling in a three-hour time period, allowing far greater detail, plot complexity, and character development than many an adventure movie shown in theaters.

The rise of cable television, and its increased specialization permitted adventure to return, both in series and in more frequent showings of the uncut old classics. Possibly the most accomplished half-hour adventure series ever made, *Zorro*, emerged on cable, commencing with a pilot feature, *Zorro—The Legend Begins* (1989). In the television miniseries format, worthy work in the genre honoring the old conventions was presented during the 1980s—*Shogun* (1980); *Marco Polo* (1982); *Christopher Columbus* (1985); *Around the World in 80 Days* (1989); *Captain Cook* (1989)—with *Shogun* also being edited into feature length. A few limited-duration miniseries appeared primarily on British television, including *John Silver's Return to Treasure Island* (1986) and *Dick Turpin* (1979–1982). The 1972–1973 British series, *Arthur of the Britains*, presented a new interpretation of Arthur as a sixth-century Welsh king trying to unite his island, and several segments were condensed into a feature, *King Arthur—The Young Warlord* (1973). Public Broadcasting showed such British miniseries as *Drake's Voyage* (1985) and *The Last Place on Earth* (1985), along with others predominantly historical or scientific but having a measure of adventure, such as *Poldark* (1975–77) and *By the Sword Divided* (1988), or *The Search for the Nile* (1972) and *The Voyage of Charles Darwin* (1980).

Curiously, considering the usual preconception that television aims for the most readily entertaining forms, revisionism has appeared far more frequently than parody in small screen adventure. The BBC miniseries *The Last Place on Earth* demythologically portrays the polar trek of Robert Falcon Scott as a legend manufactured for public consumption. Rather than the schoolbook story of courage doomed by fate, as in the 1948 British feature *Scott of the Antarctic*, the expedition is exposed as undermined by English arrogance and the unsuitability of its leader, unfavorably compared with the cool and pragmatic Roald Amundsen. The miniseries *Captain Cook* is strongly revisionist but lacks the harsh, insistent tone of *The Last Place on Earth*. Instead, *Captain Cook* offers a more complex portrait, a man who must overcome the British class system and is driven to succeed. Cook (Keith Michell) is also a kind and faithful husband and father, with enormous sympathy for his men—that is, for white men, not for the Pacific islanders. In reaching the goals of his voyage, Cook is simultaneously heroic and also the worst sort of conqueror, becoming a paradigm of the imperialism to come: refusing to understand native culture, repaying hospitality with militarism. Cook becomes vain and overbearing, leaving his family behind for a fateful third voyage, but even in his final moments displaying the courage and charisma that made him a heroic role model.

The revisionist tendency can also be found in various other related pictures. In an adventure-love story such as *Out of Africa* (1985), the principal character is a heroine whose concern is not simply with establishing her own colonial fiefdom but with appreciating rather than exploiting the land, its people and wildlife. The Russo-Italian adventure *The Red Tent* (1971), which crosses into fantasy briefly to demonstrate the hero's torment in reenacting a tragic chapter in polar exploration, is dramatized in light of ambiguous motivations that render an imperial endeavor disastrous.

A whole new generation of adventure performers emerged in the fourth cycle. Most first appeared in notable roles in *The Three Musketeers* and *The Four Musketeers*, followed by a reunion in *The Return of the Musketeers*: Richard Chamberlain (*The Count of Monte Cristo; Shogun; Cook and Peary: The Race to the Pole; Casanova*), Simon Ward (*The Four Feathers; Zulu Dawn* [1979]), Michael York (*The Last Remake of Beau Geste; The Master of Ballantrae*) and Oliver Reed, who had appeared in five 1960s adventure pictures from the British Hammer studios before going on to *Royal Flash; Crossed Swords;* and *The Black Arrow* (1984). The other top adventure actors were finally united in *The Man Who Would Be King* after earlier appearances in the genre: Sean Connery (*The Red Tent; The Wind and the Lion; Robin and Marian* [1976]) and Michael Caine (*Zulu; Kidnapped*). Talented practitioners behind the camera have also come forward, and the television remakes of *The Count of Monte Cristo* (1976) and *The Scarlet Pimpernel* (1982) are easily the equal to if not superior of their cinema predecessors. The spectacle and action of such theatrical adventure movies as *The Wind and the Lion* or *Zulu Dawn* exceed the standards of the studio era, with the modern advantages of location shooting and wide screen fully compensating for the lack of the contract musicians, art directors, and costume designers who were once regularly available.

By the 1980s, genres with a period setting, including the Old West, World War II, or the ancient world, seemed to be losing popularity among younger and more cynical viewers. Producers responded with stories about contemporary or wholly imaginary life, and tales that might have once been treated as adventure were transformed into other genres, although the revisionist tendency often persisted. *Robin Hood / Robin of Sherwood / Robin Hood—The Legend* (1984–86), a British series shown in America on cable and PBS, concentrated on medieval magic and wizards, although occasional episodes stayed within the confines of history. The network television series *Tales of the Gold Monkey* (1982–83) again chose to emphasize supernatural connotations, while *Bring 'Em Back Alive* (1982–83) transformed animal hunter Frank Buck into a secret agent battling pre–World War II Japanese espionage. In features, one response has been to attempt to amalgamate adventure with other genres in a manner calculated to better assure commercial success. Merging adventure with the love story was utilized in *Robin and Marian* and *Out of Africa*, while adventure and the religious film were combined in *The Mission* (1986) in a manner similar to 7 *Cities of Gold* and, and, to a lesser degree, *The Crusades* (1935) and *Stanley and Livingstone*. The appeal of geographically remote and exotic locales has been renewed as an element in suspense (*Romancing the Stone* [1984]) and fantasy (*Excalibur* [1981]; *Raiders of the Lost Ark* [1982]) to such a degree that they are often mistaken for adventure.

The altered narrative priorities of the post–world War II era undercut the apparent viability of the genre in the marketplace for modern audiences. This was especially apparent during the 1960s, 1970s, and 1980s. Adventure pictures seemed to have a certain sentimental charm, like the outgrown relics of childhood, an embarrassing reminder of what our attitudes once were. The adventure genre declined, not only with changes in the nature of the movie industry caused by the end of the studio system but also because of the shift away from reliance on formulas. In adventure, plot is nearly always foremost, with character secondary and growing out of incidents. The genre is predominantly about deeds, and often the people in its milieu are portrayed with little attempt at depth or verisimilitude

(Meyers, vii). Adventurers were presented as idealized role models or as figures who moved toward such a status, not as thoroughly flawed antiheroes. This tradition goes against postclassical filmmaking, which during the 1960s saw a change from reliance on stories to movies principally about characters, with only a background consideration of plot. Such an emphasis has not been conducive to adventure, except where revisionism is applied. Another of the appeals and limitations of adventure is the old-fashioned clarity of its ethics, and seldom is there any acknowledgment that they may be outmoded or inadequate to deal with the world (*Billy Budd*). When ambiguity is the accepted watchword, a narrative that states its views so unequivocally, in such striking moral relief, seems out of fashion. The low cultural estimation of adventure became evident in the lampoons of the comic strips "Crock" and "Hagar the Horrible," dealing with the Foreign Legion and Vikings, respectively. Even "Peanuts" features Snoopy imagining he is leading his band of bird friends to Fort Zinderneuf of *Beau Geste* fame. Among comics "Prince Valiant" opposes these with the proud tradition of classical adventure. In a similar fashion, such "rides" as the *Swiss Family Robinson* treehouse and the Pirates of the Caribbean give adventure a presence at Disney theme parks.

The return toward more traditional forms of storytelling from the mid-1970s was slow to include historical adventure. While the move toward parody and revision in the fourth cycle changed adventure, the cycle lost its vitality in the 1980s. The commercial failure of *The Return of the Musketeers* revealed that the satirical vein seems to have been fully mined. The most recent adventure films and television programs eliminated the contemporary edge by reverting to a more classical form, including the television series *Zorro* and 1992's *The Young Indiana Jones Chronicles* and *Covington Cross*. The same is true of 1991's *Shipwrecked*; *Robin Hood*; and *Robin Hood—Prince of Thieves*; and 1992's two celebrations of the Columbus quincentenary, *Christopher Columbus—The Discovery* and *1492—Conquest of Paradise*. Only *Mountains of the Moon* (1990) included a strongly revisionist element, but even there it was no longer dominant and seemed a remnant of the 1960s, a movie made after a fashion that had become outdated decades ago. The revival of adventure, as a possible fifth cycle takes shape, appears to be comfortable with the myth, lacking the need to justify the genre's invocation that was so apparent during the fourth cycle. As in *1492—*

Conquest of Paradise, a return to the *noir* style adventure of the post–World War II decade, the spirit of adventure is celebrated once more, along with the men and women who practiced it. While the often regrettable consequences of their actions are recognized, they are placed in the context of their times and the adventurer's intentions. An adventurer like Columbus is looked upon as a visionary dwarfing those around him, whose dream ultimately helped to open up both the New World and begin the process of freeing the Old World from the dark, confined thinking of the Inquisition.

While the genre has evolved, it has in a sense returned to its original roots, and the outcome of seventy years of development has been very little change. A comparison of Douglas Fairbanks's *Robin Hood* (1922) with *Robin Hood—Prince of Thieves* (1991), starring Kevin Costner, reveals astonishing plot congruity, from the beginnings in the crusades to the choice of a more serious tone. Adventure has returned as a genre that now appears to be almost a novelty after its long hiatus. Yet other than this freshness, the timing of the revival lacks any overt justification. Or does it? Perhaps the reason for adventure's return is the same as the reason for its long hibernation—the cold war. Just as adventure previously disappeared during the world wars, and tended to decline as the cold war heated up, so the genre has returned with the end of the nuclear threat. Whereas once adventure seemed excessively escapist and naive when the world was threatened with global conflict, the genre can resume absorbing some of the interest in military life now that an era of peace seems at hand. Beyond escapism, adventure films from *Son of Ali Baba* to *The Charge of the Light Brigade* (1936) offer an opportunity to depict military life in a detached context, with all the excitement of victory but none of the reality of fighting. Adventure follows a pattern, declining when war seems imminent or is taking place, while reappearing as a commercially viable form during more pacific times—why the genre was most popular during the 1920s, the mid- to late-1930s, and the post–World War II decade (cf. Basinger, 118). Ironically, peaceful eras seem to demand the need for the type of stylized violence adventure can supply—while the end of communism has made adventure's winning struggle against tyranny appear no longer unbelievable or passé.

CHAPTER 4 **The Era of Adventure**

The foremost element that distinguishes each of the five types of historical adventure films is the role of history, which is as important as any theme or character type. Adventure movies are notable for their removal, not only from the geographical areas most familiar to their audiences, but from their time as well. The events of the plot need not be incredible, merely distant from the experiences the audience is likely to have had, as in the comparatively mundane sea adventure *Captains Courageous*. Other action-oriented genres, such as the crime or suspense film, take place predominantly in the present, but adventure requires a setting remote in time and place, although not the entirely imagined world of science fiction or fantasy. Adventure is distinguished by its reliance upon events of the past, yet at the same time its own period of history is distinct from the setting typical of other such historical genres as the western, the ancient world–biblical epic, or the world wars of the war film.

After noting how the genre uses history, this chapter will move to a more detailed examination of adventure's interaction with specific eras.

Why the need for history in adventure films? The past, as presented in adventure films, provides an escape from the frustrations and limitations of twentieth-century existence. History opens a door into a romanticized and more exotic life, where individuals are still their own masters. Watching people who live by a code of chivalry seems to offer the possibility of emulating the behavior of heroes with impeccable manners and motives. The genre forecloses despair; life is worthwhile, and in performing formidable tasks, the hero overcomes both his own and society's problems. Adventure offers an exotic world of half-fulfilled dreams, an alluring, imaginative golden age more secure and honorable than our own (Frye, 186). Although the temporal settings are in many cases their own best and worst of times, they offer a clear contrast between good and evil, with the most intelligent, courageous, and moral emerging victorious. Justice is a matter of simple right and wrong; ambiguity is rare. By "living in the past," adventure's unequivocal standards are less susceptible to audience skepticism (Slotkin, 5).

As well as the promise of escape, the thematic values of adventure resonate with a greater significance because of their setting: we learn from the past. History sets the context for the adventure, and adventure is one of the principal ways in which history has been dramatized. A few authentic details set against notable events will tend to grant a story greater credibility, helping the audience to suspend disbelief more easily in the fictional part of the narrative (Cohen, 37). The use of history itself, with the settings, costumes, and real persons, underlines the importance of the film's subject. Highlighting the mingling of believable fictional characters with real individuals validates the genre, and fictional subplots are dramatically charged by mixing them with specific incidents in actual lives. Often films include a brief glimpse of a historical figure, such as the ritual appearance of King Richard the Lion-Hearted at the end of Robin Hood tales, validating Robin's actions while ending his outlawry.

However, adventure movies are less likely to document the past than to use it as a colorful background (Landers, 23; Vivian Sobchack, 28). Despite the importance of setting, authenticity is almost invariably sacrificed in favor of myth, as epitomized by pirate or empire adventures. While possessing an affection for history, adventure movies spend little time filling in factual details, instead relying primarily on fictional components. Even more pressing is the motion picture's limited duration, usually not more than three hours and often an hour and a half or less. Dramatization often transposes or combines events, and even a movie that treats history with respect must unify the plot, often personalizing and simplifying motivations, forces, and politics to make them cohere. While *The Buccaneer* is based on Jean Laffite's actual role in the Battle of New Orleans, the picture exaggerates both his contribution to the victory and his commitment to the United States. History is reduced to mutually opposing personalities, away from complex, ambiguous socioeconomic forces and political systems, substituting such dramatically appealing motivations as a despot's tyrannical desire for riches and power. Frequently these representations are inaccurate, especially in empire adventures such as *Captain from Castile*. Many less conscientious pictures feature costumes, settings, and mores taken out of context; speech patterns are stilted or redolent of contemporary America. Seldom does adventure's historic specificity extend beyond a single opening graphic announcing the year or period and locale in general terms, perhaps offering an indication of some of the forthcoming conflicts. This is as much a claim to authenticity as is made; rarely is there a corresponding admission of distortion.

Among period genres, adventure is conventionally conceded a wide degree of poetic license (Neale, 37). For instance, a typical swashbuckling drama of secret royal intrigue such as *The Three Musketeers* is hardly held to the historical standards expected of a biography of King Louis XIV. Adventure utilizes rather than reproduces the past, turning the setting into a springboard for generic, predictable stories. While a form of historical fiction, adventure is distinct from the historical picture per se (Fisher, 9). Adventure is seldom constructed as a deliberate effort to represent history, willingly suspending narrative excitement in the interest of accuracy, in the manner of *A Man for All Seasons*; *Juarez*; *The Private Lives of Elizabeth and Essex*; *Marie Antoinette*; or *The Last Emperor*. Instead, the principal concern is to create a satisfying fictional narrative that provides greater enjoyment and inspiration than straightforward history would allow (Manzoni, 63, 36, 126; Matthews, 21).

Adventure is expected to divert rather than to enlighten, unless the film manifests clear pretensions otherwise, as in the case of biographies such as *Scott of the Antarctic* and *Christopher Columbus*. Even adventure films that concentrate on an actual life usually emphasize the adventurous aspects of the protagonist's career, such as those dealing with Marco Polo, Father Junipero Serra (7 *Cities of Gold*), or *Stanley and Livingstone*. Or else their lives are fictionalized to associate the individual's ideals with those of adventure, as with Jean Laffite in *The Buccaneer; Anne of the Indies; King Richard and the Crusaders;* and François Villon in *If I Were King*. By interweaving historical material into the story's texture to create an illusion of historicity, fact and fiction frequently become indistinguishable. History and fiction combine so thoroughly that it becomes difficult to discern where the one begins and the other ends.

Since adventure is primarily genre entertainment rather than historical reconstruction, attempting to assess the proportion of fact to fiction is not only pointless but also misguided. For the historian, any fictional film of past events, particularly in the adventure genre, will naturally prove disappointing. However, such a specialized perspective is not shared by the general audience; historical fiction always permits more imagination than the historian is allowed (cf. Sheppard, 15). The "history" in adventure is far from a social science, instead basing itself in popular history, emphasizing great and heroic deeds that helped to create the world we know. The narrative style adopted by historical adventure movies is similar to the standard nineteenth-century presentations of schoolbook history. Not only was there an emphasis on history of an adventurous nature but history itself was also in many cases transformed into an adventure—commemorating the lives of memorable men and the advance of freedom through the centuries. By participating in a cause with historical significance, adventure heroes endow themselves with a sense of meaning and purpose, becoming catalysts, instruments of history who influences the course of events. This approach to history uses adventure's emphasis on personality, the genre's pictures showing "the grand sweep of events" affected by an individual life; without the hero's participation the outcome would not have been the same (Rosenzweig, 51). For instance, *Robin Hood* (1922) begins by noting, "History—in its ideal state—is a compound of legend and chronicle and from out of both we offer you this impression of the Middle Ages." History itself becomes both an escape and a source of knowledge about adventure and the past, demanding an appreciation for days gone by and a feeling of kinship with earlier generations (Lascelles, 2).

The past is explained in such a way that the adventurer is situated at the center of this struggle. Usually adventure pictures tell of a crisis, gaining both suspense and significance by depicting history at the crossroads, placing our own heritage momentarily in the balance to reveal how the tide turned and the basis of the values we hold today are first discernable (Slotkin, 18; Lascelles, 114). Intuitively aware that they are riding a wave of destiny, adventurers become the instrument of history by daring to take control over events. The mythic portrait of Cortés in *Captain from Castile* embodies this belief as he burns his ships behind him, announcing, "Either this will go down in history as a monument to our determination, or history will forget us." Authentic historical situations, often ones previously utilized by adventure novels and even poems, are made legendary, such as the defeat of the Spanish Armada (*Fire over England*; *The Sea Hawk* [1940]), the fight against the Barbary pirates (*Old Ironsides*; *The Wind and the Lion*), the Sepoy Mutiny (*King of the Khyber Rifles*; *Bengal Brigade / Bengal Rifles*), the charge of the Light Brigade, the battle of Rorke's Drift (*Zulu*; *Zulu Dawn*), or the voyage of the *Bounty*. Through adventure, history is transformed into legend, not in the sense of a fable or deliberate falsehood, but as a tale designed to explain how civilization arrived at a certain point (McConnell, 7, 87, 6, 12, 8). Adventure's history is based on facts that have been mythologized to reveal a pattern, purpose, and progress in mankind's endeavors—a movement along the road toward freedom for all people.

Two very different films illustrate the divergent manner in which adventure can utilize history. *Khartoum* (1966) is a meticulously constructed re-creation covering the final struggle of an empire builder. The story of Gen. Charles Gordon's last battle is told as a lesson from the past, how one adventurer dramatically affects military and political events. By contrast, *The Exile* (1947) is a frankly fictionalized account of a private chapter in the final months before King Charles II is restored to the British monarchy. At no point in *The Exile* are famous events or additional actual characters summoned, providing only enough background for a perfunctory sense of historicity that keeps the central characterization from becoming entirely fictional. Typically, in *The Exile* the genre is less concerned with the facts than with simply using the milieu of the past to validate its values. Swashbuckler conventions provide the framework, the Roundhead-Cavalier conflict becoming a backdrop for a love story of the man who must lose his heart to assume his royal duties. By contrast, *Khartoum* avoids its hero's private life, instead underlining its accuracy through a strictly historical account that surrounds Gordon with other well-known figures, who played both major (Prime Minister Gladstone) and minor (the young General Kitchener) parts in the event. The events of the siege and fall of Khartoum unfold in an ordered sequence, keeping speculation and invention to a minimum, developing a logical buildup to Gordon's inevitable fate. The visuals, including the opening, emphasize the outdoors and location photography, going beyond second-unit backdrops for a wide sweep and scope that create an epic sense. This use of location footage, period detail, a careful narrative development, and multiple famous characters does much to enhance the overall impression of authenticity.

The film's writer, Robert Ardrey, who also wrote the screenplays of *The Three Musketeers* (1948) and *Quentin Durward / The Adventures of Quentin Durward*, emphasizes the essential complexity of Gordon and the events and background of the saga. *Khartoum* uses actors who are not genre players but are associated with prestige productions, including Laurence Olivier (the Mahdi) and Ralph Richardson (as Gladstone). Only Charlton Heston (Gordon) has a significant background in adventure, starring in *El Cid* and playing Andrew Jackson in *The Buccaneer* (1958), yet his reputation is thoroughly grounded in other historical pictures. *Khartoum* is one of the most complex adventure films, presenting a simultaneously military and psychological account of the battle. The movie also depicts Gordon's nemesis, the Mahdi, a Moslem fanatic who believes himself chosen to smite the city's unbelievers in the name of Islam. Like the Mahdi, Gordon is a man of the Orient, a mystic who embodies numerous ambiguities and an understanding of Eastern thought. However, he is also imbued with the adventurer's sense of duty, in this case to save Khartoum from a religious massacre. Although driven to seek his destiny, Gordon combines the best of both East and West, eagerly departing England on a patently hopeless mission because of his love of the land and the Sudanese people he resolves to protect.

The tragedy of *Khartoum* is unavoidable, but Gordon willingly

CHARLTON HESTON   LAURENCE OLIVIER   RICHARD JOHNSON
RALPH RICHARDSON

in A JULIAN BLAUSTEIN PRODUCTION

Filmed in ULTRA PANAVISION   Copyright © 1966   United Artists Corporation.   Printed in U.S.A.   TECHNICOLOR   Released thru UNITED ARTISTS

While Gen. Gordon (Charlton Heston) leaves London virtually unnoticed, he is warmly cheered upon his arrival in Khartoum, and his fellowship with the residents is symbolized when he carries a lonely child with him.

becomes a martyr to remind his homeland of its responsibility to the empire. Gladstone has sent Gordon alone, without troop support, and expects him merely to evacuate the white residents. However, Gordon easily chooses between his obligation to those local people who have sought refuge in the city and the orders of the prime minister. Remaining in Khartoum, Gordon refuses to abandon the natives to the Mahdi, hoping by force of his example to shame the British government into lending aid. Gladstone, the politician, cannot understand the adventurer who is unafraid to sacrifice his life on principle rather than to find an expedient way to save himself. Empire adventures frequently laud the military over civilian authority, but the genre also goes to great care to provide important reasons. Ironically, it is Gordon the imperialist, not the anti-interventionist Gladstone, whose actions are free of racial bias. In the end, because of public opinion a rescue expedition is sent, but it is undersized and deliberately delayed so that it arrives too late.

The unprepossessing Charles is a man of the people, who comfortably adopts peasant disguise to escort a royal imposter (Robert Coote) in *The Exile*.

Gordon is killed as Khartoum falls, and years will pass and many more lives be lost before peace is restored to the Sudan. Yet divine power seemingly intervenes ahead of the British, and the Mahdi dies shortly after his victory over Gordon.

Whereas *Khartoum* focuses on empire, a series of battles, and a military character, in *The Exile* historical details are subordinated to the fictional aspects. There is no attempt to tell a documented story, and the tradition of such adventure movies as *The Exile* has established that the genre's use of a biographical incident is largely for its own mythmaking ends. The story could have happened but probably did not, with a plot constructed according to the dictates of genre, not historical fact; *The Exile* would never be mistaken as a realistic attempt at biography. Considering the representation of Charles II and the situations that involve him, he could almost be an imaginary character. The story is meant to provide a showcase for a swashbuckler and a hero personifying the political tenets of adventure. (By contrast, a historical picture that is not an adventure, *Cromwell*

[1970], depicts the same era but thoroughly subordinates action to period detail by centering on the rebel as politician and accenting parliamentary over military maneuvers.)

The Exile concentrates on Charles's action-filled exploits, mythologizing the history by personalizing the narrative and minimizing the political and historical content. Douglas Fairbanks, Jr., who also wrote and produced the movie, portrays Charles as a lighthearted, seemingly carefree man, stealing food and living by his wits. Most of *The Exile* is set around an isolated Dutch inn where Charles finds employment in his effort to remain undercover. All of his haunts are similarly proletarian: an open-air market, a river, a mill, a farm. He gladly undertakes the work of a farmhand; there is nothing aristocratic or pretentious about his life-style, despite the eventual fate his lineage will demand.

Charles vividly illustrates the adventure convention that a legitimate ruler should be a man of the people, the same belief embodied by Robin Hood. Charles's democratic inclinations are contrasted with the dour, elitist, unsympathetic Roundheads who try to assassinate him. Despite his royal blood, Charles has become a freedom-loving rebel, the last potential leader of a new (counter) revolution. Neither a liberal nor a reactionary, Charles simply symbolizes change from an undesirable status quo. His suitability for kingship is underlined by his love for a commoner, a Dutch farm girl at the inn, and his contrast with an imposter who pretends to be Charles in order to live idly and high handedly off of the innkeeper's combined good will and fear. Despite the happiness and love Charles has found in his life in exile, patriotism compels him to depart and assume the burdens of his royal birth. Like Gordon, history demands a sacrifice of Charles: when England calls, he must leave behind the sweetheart and life that he clearly loved to assume the throne—an ending similar to that of *The Prisoner of Zenda*.

Both *Khartoum* and *The Exile* are representative of the era favored by adventure. The genre's stories are derived from the history, legends, and values of the time when European civilization established and preserved world dominance. Adventure commences with the Middle Ages through the enlightenment's struggle for freedom. The era continues until the onset of the modern industrial world and the breakdown of moral and patriotic certainty in 1914 and the rise of fascism and communism, which became the enemies in the war picture. The adversaries opposed by the adventurer are men such as

The moral superiority of the hero, in this case Charles II (Douglas Fairbanks, Jr.) is shown by his sense of humor when standing alone against roundhead foes in *The Exile* (1947).

Prince John, Cardinal Richelieu, and the Mahdi, not Hitler or Stalin and their uniquely twentieth-century barbarity.

Since the direct intervention of gods into the lives of mortals is not suitable to the genre, adventure stories take place when an increasing concern with secular life replaced the religious and supernatural concerns that dominated history through the Roman Empire. Unlike adventure, ancient world–biblical epics typically overlook the common man to emphasize spectacle and the beginnings of Christianity: *The Egyptian*; *The Ten Commandments*; *Ben-Hur*; *The Sign of the Cross*; *Quo Vadis*. Even such pictures as *Julius Caesar* and *Cleopatra*, while containing moments of adventure, such as battles, focus on the issues of government and politics in fundamentally different ways. Only occasionally does a film such as *Spartacus* or *The 300 Spartans* share the same ideological bent as adventure, but the setting casts the struggle for freedom in a time when it is doomed to defeat.

Despite the genre's wide range of historical time periods, spanning well over a thousand years, adventure films display relatively little change in the themes, characterization, or even decor (George MacDonald Fraser, 104–5). For instance, nearly every European country appears, almost interchangeably, sharing both narrative patterns and atmosphere. Many other settings are Europeanized, such as Zorro's early nineteenth-century Spanish California or pirates in the recently Americanized New Orleans (Richards 1977, 1). Within the various time periods, and to a lesser degree despite differences of locale, there are few except general iconic differences in adventure. The thematic uniformity offered by the genre allows the lack of period accuracy to be a less debilitating factor than it otherwise might be. While some plots do have actual historical antecedents and places, many do not, following the Ruritanian pattern, named for the imaginary central European country and situation of royal intrigue imagined by Anthony Hope in his novels *The Prisoner of Zenda* and *Rupert of Hentzau*. The characteristic concerns in such a mythic instance are no different from those having a nonfictional basis.

Nonetheless, a certain temporal evolution is evident. In depictions of times prior to the 1800s, adventure formulas may be recited with a sprightly, idealistic tone. Only in portrayals of the nineteenth century does more complexity appear; not until the Napoleonic conflicts does war lose some of its glamour and adventure begin its decline. Situations and emotions grow more difficult, and duty less clear. This is evident in the temptation toward divided loyalty in *King of the Khyber Rifles*, the pointless quarrel over honor in *The Duellists*, and the valorizing of both British and African bravery in *Zulu* and *Zulu Dawn*. The same problems are also illustrated by the impossibility of achieving a romantic union between the queen and the royal imposter in *The Prisoner of Zenda* or the difficulty for a pirate to become a patriot and to gain a wife and country in *The Buccaneer*. While nineteenth-century adventurers regularly face such challenges, with less hope for a happy ending, characters from earlier eras, such as Robin Hood, rarely encounter these difficulties.

Certainly adventure is not the only genre to utilize these centuries for a historical setting. Some other types even have a direct iconic resemblance to adventure. For instance, a swashbuckler cannot be simply defined by the mere presence of a sword fight, a standard that would include such prestigious literary adaptations as *Hamlet; Henry V; Barry Lyndon;* and *War and Peace,* or the love stories *Cyrano de Bergerac* and *Romeo and Juliet.* Many movies set in periods from the Middle Ages through the end of the nineteenth century that emphasize military or political leaders will tend to have a relation to adventure, or contain moments of it, while belonging to their own generic categories. Among these are love stories (*The Howards of Virginia* and *Casanova* [1927]) or the Napoleonic romances *Conquest* (1936) and *Desiree*, melodrama (*Blanche Fury; Saraband for Dead Lovers; The Wicked Lady*), children's movies (*Wee Willie Winkie*), comedies (*Monsieur Beaucaire*), biographies (*Voltaire*), and political pictures (*The Leopard* [1963]). Similarly, distant colonial lands have also been a setting for many Hollywood genres besides adventure, from love stories and melodramas to biographies and political pictures. For instance, a biography such as the 1929 George Arliss film, *Disraeli*, may be tangentially related to adventure because of his status as an empire builder. Unlike adventure, biographical dramas of British monarchs such as *The Private Lives of Elizabeth and Essex* depict lives and eras, adventure only impinging as it was a part of the times, not as a force motivating their actions. *Fire over England, The Sea Hawk* (1940), and *Seven Seas to Calais* are exceptions because Queen Elizabeth becomes a supporting character to adventurers whose exploits are the centerpiece of the narrative. In only a few cases do disparate genres amalgamate in a way that is directly related to adventure; for instance, *Lorna Doone* and *China Seas* are both "women's" films—love stories, but they are also a swashbuckler and a pirate adventure, respectively.

Many horror films have a setting and certain iconic similarities to swashbucklers, but they are far too morbid and violent to be considered with adventure. Although adventure may contain scenes of torture, such scenes are not emphasized in the manner of horror pictures but included only to indicate the enormity of a villain's evil before quickly passing on to the next event. *The Man in the Iron Mask* (1939) is such a horrific version of the Alexandre Dumas novel that it does not properly belong in a discussion of adventure, although other adaptations, especially *The Fifth Musketeer / Behind the Iron Mask*, minimize the terrifying concept inherent in the title. There are a few musicals with a setting and narrative motifs similar to adventure, but the adventure elements are secondary or on a largely iconic, visual level, rather than thematic. The song-and-dance format, not adventure or history, dominates such films as

The Dancing Pirate; The Firefly; New Moon; Man of La Mancha; The Pirate (1948); *Rose of the Rancho; Rose of the Rio Grande;* and *The Vagabond King.* Only *Camelot,* using the Arthur-Guinevere-Lancelot story so often told in the traditional swashbuckler format, resonates directly with adventure. More typical are the 1929 and 1953 versions of *The Desert Song,* which do not take the Arabs' fight for freedom seriously, while the more politicized 1943 adaptation has Nazi villains, relating it to the war film rather than to adventure. Similarly, the spy film *Action in Arabia* places an Arab revolt in the context of an Allied-Nazi confrontation, not as a colonial revolt.

Much of adventure's commitment to a largely fictionalized historical past is evident in the genre's treatment of violence, which is far different from most other action forms. The chivalrous adventurer rarely experiences disillusionment or relishes the reckless killing indulged in by more modern hard-boiled detectives, vigilante cops, the western gun-for-hire, or the war movie's brutalized, weary troops. Adventure is only "fantastic" in the innocence of its violence and the nearly inevitable death of the villain and vanquishing of his forces, even if victory has been at the cost of the hero's own life. Although revolutions and battles proliferate in adventure, fighting is usually slick and almost bloodless, presented in an innocent and often playful manner. Often the hero proves capable of dueling with multiple adversaries at the same time, his sword fending off a number of attackers; indeed, the hero may prefer fighting this way, as in *The Black Pirate* (1926) or *The Fighting Guardsman.* Stylized violence takes on a make-believe quality, precluding a gruesomeness that would destroy the aura of unreality that makes a battle enjoyable as a metaphor of good triumphing over evil. Fighting becomes an idealistic, honorable struggle between individuals, not nameless, reluctant masses. The distinguishing nature of the on-screen violence in adventure is indicated by the genre's close identification with the sword, a weapon associated with the speed and skill of personalized, hand-to-hand combat; the sword is neat and controlled in comparison to firearms or artillery

With only the most minimal means at his disposal, the hero often duels as much with his rapier wit as with the blade. Frequently the preferred weapons, better even than the sabre, are tricks, acrobatic stunts, physical blows, and the like. Throughout *The World in His Arms,* the heroes rely on nothing more than fists, clubs, and sailing

The fight against oppression is carried on despite inferior weapons; in *The Flame and the Arrow* (1950), the hero, Dardo (Burt Lancaster), uses a torch to fight off the palace guard, armed with pikes.

ships, to repel their opponent's cannon, swords, and steamers. Without advanced weapons, adventurers use their imaginations to improvise. No picture more extensively exploits this convention than *The Crimson Pirate,* incorporating balloons, bombs, firecrackers, mines, even a primitive submarine. The genre implicitly argues that, although such weapons are simple and homemade, they are more powerful, having justice on their side.

Unlike most characters in action genres, the cinema's adventurer is fundamentally peaceful; as in *Captain Blood,* he often makes a point of trying to renounce violence. The adventurer is never inherently violent, a characteristic defining the villain. The hero only takes up the sword in self-defense after every other method of overcoming the enemy has been exhausted. Despite a devotion to peace, at the same time the adventurer is an expert fighter who will bring down his enemies (Shanks, 76; Green 1979, 56). In adventure, evil must be subdued in a manner that does not taint the hero's conscience, preserving the amenities of civilization. The enemy, no matter how numerous, must be defeated with as little killing as possible. In the end, the adventurer will only execute his nemesis in a scrupulously fair duel. Invariably the hero displays simultaneous moral superiority and fencing skill when, disarming the villain, he orders him to retrieve his sword. The villain, disarmed and at the hero's mercy, fails to understand the chivalry that allows him one more chance and returns to the fray with redoubled fury, only to die fighting. The willingness of the hero finally to bring about the death of an adversary becomes a measure of the seriousness of the film's portrayal of the struggle, and explicit, close-up killing is reserved for the worst of villains.

Similarly, battles follow a predictable pattern, beginning in a series of skirmishes, with music tracing how the episode unfolds. The successful attack comes at the height of the villain's arrogance and weakness, a fatal strategic error opening the way for the more patient hero. The adventurer and the villain personify their forces, even in a large-scale clash of armies. With the emphasis on the thrill, not the terror, of battle, the audience feels confident the hero will be victorious but must watch him and his cause brought to the brink of defeat (Rosenzweig, 56–57). This is equally true of a sword fight or of the public trial Stanley endures from the Royal Geographical Society on claiming to have found Livingstone in *Stanley and Livingstone*. The ensuing scenes of climactic victory frequently serve as lead-ins to romantic unions.

There are some thematic similarities between the empire adventure and the war movie, with their stress on the military unit, depicting the performance of duty through the interaction of men welded hierarchically into a fighting unit (Grant 1986, 118). The heroes of both war and empire frequently discover the pressure of separation from the main body of troops, fighting in small groups or making sorties against their opponents, with incidents of torture and many Asian enemies. However, beyond the joint use of military structures or settings, there are more crucial differences between adventure and the war movie, even beyond the obvious temporal and iconic contrasts. Adventurers often discuss their politics, exhorting their followers at length and with self-conscious eloquence, seldom preferring the laconic taciturnity of traditional soldiers. Adventure offers a more realistic opportunity for episodes of romantic love to be fulfilled than in wartime, and the position of women is more variable. In contrast to the typical war story, the adventurer's superiors seldom ask him to perform tasks he would otherwise regret or that violate his conscience. There is often explicit criticism of the disadvantages of the military, especially where officers seem to command primarily by seniority, while younger men closer to the field are more attuned to events. Frequently those who are younger have a greater understanding than their more experienced elders, who are often stodgy and short sighted, placing excessive emphasis on the conformity to regimental routines. In *The Charge of the Light Brigade* (1936), Colonel Campbell places Fort Jakoti in the hands of Surat Khan against the advice of Capt. Geoffrey Vickers, resulting in a massacre of defenseless men, women, and children.

War, in fact, disrupts adventure, rather than producing it; for the adventurer, war is only a reluctant necessity to preserve liberty. In war there is only room for those qualities most essential to existence, while in adventure, much of the chivalrous refinement of civilization is present even in the harshest environment, such as the respect between adversaries of different cultures in *King Richard and the Crusaders* and *The Long Duel* (cf. McConnell, 37). The adventurer has a code of honor and a sense of noblesse oblige. His exploits have a positive tone leading to a better future, whereas the war hero fights ingloriously against a dehumanized rather than individualized enemy. The adventure genre, as opposed to the war picture, celebrates not the rigors of combat, but instead the joy of freedom and the willingness to defend it. Unlike war heroes, most adventurers and their followers generally survive their combat, rather than die in battle.

In the twentieth century, fighting implies a technological warfare that cannot be invoked in the romantic fashion of adventure. Visions of war have changed in this century to become far more graphic and horrifying, beginning in 1914: the trench warfare, poison gas, and aerial combat of World War I present a stark contrast to adventure. Weapons are no longer carefully crafted swords permitting a demonstration of fighting skills, but mass-produced armaments of an industrial society. Fighting has gone beyond a question of honor between two people; in the twentieth century it is only vicariously possible to emulate or to identify with an individual in an enviable battle that will end evil's reign. Unlike the positive outcome of adventure, the action in war films frequently reveals a futile or regressive effect.

The genre peaked when real adventure was not quite so impossible and could still be recalled in the living, collective memory of audiences. Although adventure stories continue to be told, today's films in the genre must be set farther in the past as the era of adventure grows ever more remote, steadily more removed from each generation. Only in the first years of filmmaking could a contemporary adventure movie be made without a period setting. Perhaps the last conflict to be made into an adventure is the Spanish-American War, as in *A Message to Garcia.* Almost simultaneously, the Boer War marked the turn of world opinion against imperialism and warfare to achieve political ends; films like *Breaker Morant* reflect the disillusion it caused. The setting of such a movie determines its attitude toward adventure. By World War I, the loss of faith in militarism and war was complete; no longer could such a brutal, searing conflict be imagined as an adventure. A conflict so utterly destitute of justice, chivalry, or purpose shattered old illusions about the beneficent effects of adventure and fighting (Paul Girouard in Fisher, 78). The loss of innocence and the nature of warfare in such films as *The Big Parade* and *All Quiet on the Western Front* indicate the different manner of generic presentation brought about by the conflict.

Lawrence of Arabia (1962) portrays the transition, the time when adventure ended and the modern era began, represented by another genre, the war movie. Following the lure of an exotic land, T. E. Lawrence dares the impossible in his early guerrilla raids, proving that an individual's heroism and leadership could make a difference even as events in Europe were proving otherwise. A glorious adventure seems briefly possible, but Lawrence is soon defeated by the overwhelming conditions of World War I—mechanized combat, global politics and his own hubris. He is at the mercy of flaws within himself as well as powers outside his control, from scheming politicians to the bloodiness of contemporary warfare. Lawrence discovers the impossibility of compelling idealism in himself or others, resulting in a failure that would be inadmissable in the optimistic adventure genre. As the biography of a modern warrior, *Lawrence of Arabia* validates its skepticism by negating the potential for adventure.

Few pictures set during World War I diverged from *Lawrence of Arabia* by focusing on the geographical fringes of the conflict to still find a possibility for adventure. Only by isolating the characters in a situation redolent of an earlier era do such movies as *The African Queen; Royal African Rifles / Storm over Africa;* and *Trader Horn* (1973), all set in the jungles of Africa, offer adventure during World War I. *The Lost Patrol* (1934) is in a realm so far from events associated with World War I as to seem in another time entirely. This saga of a small British military group stranded by snipers at a Mesopotamian oasis is, by contrast, more similar to the temporal netherworld of the castaway's struggle for survival on a desert island, or in this case, in a desert.

A brief lapse occurred for the 1920s and 1930s, a window where adventure was still found in areas remote from the modern, Western world, as in the contemporary portrait of colonial India in *Drums* or the French Foreign Legion of *Outpost in Morocco* or *Ten Tall Men*. Making a few concessions, the narrative and iconography match similar tales of an earlier period. Yet such films were exceptions; even contemporary adventure filmmakers found it steadily more necessary to invoke increasingly remote periods. *Flame over India / Northwest Frontier*, a movie made twenty years after *Drums / The Drum* and with a similar plot, had to be set around 1900. Variations were tried; for instance, two 1930s tales of newsreel cameramen, *I Cover the War* and *Too Hot to Handle*, tell of rough-and-tumble reportage of tribal conflicts in Arabia and Africa, but these films are more emblematic of a short-lived subgenre that hardly qualifies as an adventure trend.

After World War II, the last bastions of imperialism fade, and even the most remote areas become developing nations rather than colonies. Movies set in the locales that formerly belonged to adventure illustrate how it has become increasingly problematic in the twentieth century. A contemporary post–World War II adventure must depict its milieu as a throwback to an earlier time, as in *Fort Algiers* or *Legion of the Doomed*. The old formula could even be adapted to make an anti-Communist film, as in *Savage Drums* (1951), where the insurgents are Russo-Chinese representatives of "people's" governments. More typical was the spy film *Rogues' Regiment*, in which the post–World War II French Foreign Legion is demythologized through revealing its infiltration by escaped Nazis serving on behalf of French imperialism in Indo-China.

With the social, psychological, industrial, and military tensions of the cold war, adventure was precluded in almost any environment. A number of "neo-adventure" pictures were adapted from Ernest

Hemingway: *The Macomber Affair; The Snows of Kilimanjaro; The Sun Also Rises.* Here men aspire to find adventure, but their pitiful efforts are either futile or destructive in a cynical, modern world. Would-be adventurers are no longer colonizers, promoting their homeland, but members of a lost generation. Unable to live up to adventure's ideals, the myths it has engendered turn sour, even when a measure of redemption is achieved, as in *The Snows of Kilimanjaro.* Neo-adventure pictures such as *The Desert Song* (1943); *Thunder in the East;* and *Beloved Enemy* explore situations similar to empire adventures, but by their lack of a period setting introduce fundamentally new elements, such as making a colonial rebellion signal a legitimate desire for independence. Movies set in postcolonial lands are distinctly outside of adventure's tradition, and, ironically, many are even less progressive in depicting natives, such as the cycle inspired by the Mau-Mau revolts, including *Simba; Something of Value; Safari* (1956); and *Dark of the Sun.*

The dilemma of the adventurer in history is accurately summed up by the medieval title character in *Quentin Durward;* screenwriter Robert Ardrey turns the Sir Walter Scott novel into an early meditation on the anachronistic aspect of adventure. As Durward tells a lady he must guard: "I have been described as a slightly obsolete figure. I was raised for the knighthood. I was trained to the lance and the bow and the sword. I was taught to be proud, to praise God, to defend the weak, to respect womanhood, to be loyal to my family, and to be true to my word above all things. . . . That's about all. I was born perhaps a few minutes too late." Historical adventure presents its ideas grandly, admitting little hesitation or compromise. Adventure in the old style becomes a curiosity in the modern age—unnecessary, antiquated, and out of step with today's world, where a loss of idealism renders the adventurous life problematic. The word *adventurer* conjures someone with reckless, immature, and dangerously outmoded views about life; swashbuckling has become a derogatory label. Adventure is a contradiction in the modern age, even an anachronism—at best irrelevant, at worst archaic—or else exalted to a specialist's job, whether as astronaut or a deep-sea navigator. Even the exploration of the world's remote regions becomes largely the province of scientists, persons of a far different character than the dedicated amateurs of adventure. If there is adventure in this century, it is of a fundamentally different kind, suited to an age of questioning the nobility of so-called heroic motives.

CHAPTER 5 **Characters and**
Their Traits

One of the distinguishing facets of historical adventure movies is the nature of the characters portrayed. While sharing with other action genres such traits as courage and determination, adventurers also possess qualities unique to the themes developed by the genre. The characters in all forms of adventure consist of a number of instantly recognizable types arranged around the poles of good and evil. There is a hero and a villain, a heroine and/or villainess, with followers and supporters of each. Women are respected and treated in a dignified fashion that is absent from many other action genres. This chapter discusses the types and traits of adventurers, their relationships with one another, and the role of gender.

The adventurer hero is usually attractive, endowed with personal magnetism, ardent in romance, a natural leader with worthy goals and a sense of duty to a country or cause (Cohen, 58). While enjoying existence to the fullest, the adventurous life is also serious. The hero is politically motivated and patriotic, selflessly dedicated to justice.

Epitomizing altruism, the hero is pure of purpose, brave in war, honorable, fair, and chivalrous, behaving as a gentleman and recognizing a code of conduct (detailed in the next chapter). Peace loving at heart, the adventurer only kills the most dangerous of villains, often in highly stylized duels.

The adventurer is also a lively figure, whose life-style indicates his politics and moral stand. Character is expressed through both speech and deed; introspection must be matched by experience, rhetoric by action—what a person thinks is measured by what he does. Never remaining passive, the adventurer's view of the world is enunciated in his deeds, and he is often at his best in the midst of history in the making. His essential nature is revealed, finally, in the moment when he must act in the midst of danger. The ability to accomplish good both defines and fulfills existence, imbuing it with a positive exhilaration. By actions, the hero asserts his importance in a world where individual effort is found to make a difference. Through the hero's determined embodiment of adventure ideals, his activities bring about desired goals.

The adventurer is typically honest and blunt about what he stands for, a person who sees his ideals under attack and defends them. With righteousness on his side, his beliefs remain constant, although tested by various ordeals (V.F. Perkins in Cameron, 123; Nottridge, 9). There may be room for maturation and growth; a hero like d'Artagnan in *The Three Musketeers*, helped by his trio of friends, develops from youth to manhood during his adventure, a transformation less physical than thematic and metaphorical (Richards 1973, 92). The age of such an individual is usually between twenty and the early thirties; films featuring younger heroes, especially if they are in their teens, often require older, parental or mentor figures. These range from *Swiss Family Robinson* to the companionship of a more dashing, dynamic, romantic fellow adventurer, such as Alan Breck Stewart in *Kidnapped* (Fisher, 30, 112). An adventurer may be apprenticed to an understanding mentor who recognizes the potential beneath the veneer of inexperience, as in *Prince Valiant*, or learn by emulating an avuncular figure, such as Roger Byam from Fletcher Christian in *Mutiny on the Bounty* (1935) (John Fraser, 18). The process occurs without consideration of age or race, such as *Kim* from the Tibetan Lama and the native horse trader Mahbub Ali. As a consequence, through all of adventure runs the theme of boys striving for manhood and men who wish they were

Two adventurers may team up, the younger one finding a mentor. Kim (Dean Stockwell) becomes the student of a wise Tibetan Lama (Paul Lukas), joining him on a Holy quest in India in *Kim* (1950).

still boys. A similar pattern is reflected in the frequent pairing of two authentic heroes who compliment one another, such as Jean Lafitte and Andrew Jackson in *The Buccaneer* (1958). In some cases, the lives of two heroes become parallel, as in *Stanley and Livingstone*—the new hero learning from the older one—or in providing a fictional hero in a similar position whose career corresponds to another authentic historical figure. In *Lloyd's of London*, fictional Jonathan Blake turns into an adventurer by assisting his boyhood friend, Admiral Nelson, who remains an oft-discussed but largely unseen presence throughout the movie.

Another archetype, although less common, portrays a slightly older figure, who is less innocent, glamorous, or aristocratic. Often beginning as an outsider, living apart in rugged surroundings with a devil-may-care demeanor, such an adventurer has learned to survive through experience. Although partly disillusioned, his dormant ideals are still intact, as in *King Solomon's Mines* (1950); *Fair Wind to Java*; and *The Black Swan*. These soldiers of fortune shift from cynicism to altruism as the adventure makes them aware of higher values, such as Gil de Berault in *Under the Red Robe*.[1] A change in nature, from disillusioned greed to political commitment motivated by love, is undergone by Andrea Orsini in *Prince of Foxes*, altering him from a selfish pragmatist and tool of the Borgias to an adventure hero defending an endangered noblewoman. The adventurer is generous, always sharing his possessions with his fellows or those less fortunate. Even though he may have some of the instincts of the fortune hunter, he joins his quest to some laudable endeavor; a person whose only concern is plunder is by definition a villain.

The adventurer is a "whole" person, an ideal in all respects, with courage, strength, and altruism, rather than mere brute strength. The hero is not necessarily the strongest physically, with the villain often announced as the premier swordsman (cf. Anderson, 32, 196–97). Athletic ability is only an obvious surface characteristic necessary for a life requiring the ability to overcome enemies of man and nature. Courage alone is not enough but must be linked to a sense of responsibility and a capacity for truth (Noyce, 58). As the hero confronts perilous situations in a distant period, adventure portrays a mental as well as a physical endeavor (Fisher, 182). Although there is a tendency to simply expect heroism, rather than account for it, the genre also offers reflection as well as action, with occasional psychological portraits (Fisher, 19, 181, 113). Some notable individuals subject their thoughts to an unflinching self-examination, most often as a result of a wrenching ordeal, including Gordon of *Khartoum*, Fletcher Christian in *Mutiny on the Bounty*, and Pedro de Vargas in *Captain from Castile*. Such adventurers as Columbus, Livingstone, Gordon, and Saladin have a genuine scholarly bent, and whereas many genres (like gangster or western films) regard intellectualism with suspicion, in adventure it is a mark of leadership, as in *John Paul Jones* and *Omar Khayyam*. Nonetheless, while the adventurer is capable and articulate, instinct plays a more significant part than analysis in choosing the appropriate side of a conflict. The adventurer's views are almost spontaneously conceived, rather than the product of intense reflection (Katz, 69). There is little agonizing before the moment of decision or after its result. A hero like *Captain Horatio Hornblower* has done his best and feels no regret, learning from mistakes but seldom brooding before moving on to the next crisis.

Indeed, a quick-thinking, nimble, and sometimes wily cleverness is often required to triumph. The adventurer shrewdly but swiftly weighs his chances, considers hazards, and takes precautions, predicating action on a wise strategy (Anderson, 238, 26, 49). When placing themselves in danger, adventurers usually know or find a way out, rapidly devising ingenious schemes and solutions, seizing opportunities and acting with resolute dispatch (Rowse, 56; Simmel, 248–49). There is enormous self-confidence in the ability to improvise and adapt successfully on a moment's notice, a belief amply justified. Although occasionally the hero may seem immature or hotheaded, he usually finds resources that others would fail to notice, taking advantage of circumstances rather than becoming discouraged. For instance, the imprisoned Edmund Dantes acquires his education and ultimately escapes thanks to the Abbé Faria in *The Count of Monte Cristo*. Unlike the cowboy in the western genre, the adventurer may also be a trickster and still remain a hero. Captain Blood's pirate crew, about to be outgunned, surrenders its ship and surreptitiously swims to the other vessel to seize her while the apparent victor is distracted—an incident in the film and Rafael Sabatini story of *The Fortunes of Captain Blood*.

The adventurer effectively utilizes disguise, a course that adds the suspense of potential unmasking to his dangerous existence. For men, confidence in their own manliness allows them to be unafraid to sometimes take refuge behind stylish dress and play the dandy or fop. Using this mask to fool enemies and penetrate their defenses, as in *The Scarlet Pimpernel* and *The Eagle* (1925), the adventurer may simultaneously prove a capable actor in his own right, like *Scaramouche* on stage or Dantes manipulating his enemies in *The Return of Monte Cristo / Monte Cristo's Revenge*. Disguise may be more than a way to hide identity; Zorro's costume is transformed into a political symbol. The hero may even enter the world of espionage, being transformed into a spy in the camp of the enemy, as with *Kim* and Kenneth of Huntington in *King Richard and the Crusaders*. However, such efforts, unlike the spy genre, remain only one experience among many (*Rogue's March*). Disguise also serves as a great equalizer, bringing together those of different social levels. Even the king may feel compelled to adopt the appearance of a commoner under special circumstances, whether Richard in *The Adventures of Robin Hood* or Umbopa in *King Solomon's Mines* (cf. Frye, 188). This situation frequently utilizes the idea of twins, dual heroes who are sometimes related (*The Corsican Brothers*; *The Man in the Iron Mask*; *Start the Revolution without Me*), sometimes not

(*The Prince and the Pauper; A Tale of Two Cities; Royal Flash*), or only distantly so (*The Prisoner of Zenda*). The existence of doubles almost inevitably results in intrigue, royal substitutions, and political machinations at the highest level.

While adventurers may have some exceptional strength or skill, they are fallible and restrained by human limitations (Cawelti, 40; Shanks, 76). *The Beloved Rogue* (1927) introduces its hero with just such a contrast: "François Villon—poet, pickpocket, patriot—loving France earnestly, Frenchwomen excessively, French wine exclusively." There is no completely virtuous or faultless adventurer: most of the hero's various distinguishing traits are admirable, although some are contradictory. The adventurer may be unsure of his course and delay action or be uncertain in love and unable to communicate his true emotions, as in *Don Juan; Under the Red Robe; The Spanish Main; Captain Horatio Hornblower;* and *Clive of India.* While ready to defend a lady's honor, he may be a rogue with the instincts of a Don Juan, who must make up for the frivolous, fun-loving side of his nature with a concern for social justice. The hero may be naive (*The Black Shield of Falworth*) or vain (*Khartoum; The Pride and the Passion*), too trusting (*The Fighting Prince of Donegal; The Buccaneer*), or stubborn (*The Crimson Pirate*), excessively confident (*The Adventures of Robin Hood*), or too ready to disobey an order (*The Lives of a Bengal Lancer*). Any one of these flaws may result in a setback or even capture. The hero's challenge is to summon all his resources, channeling them in a disciplined way toward his goal; the adventurer only seems stronger than most because of the distinctive courage, fortitude, determination and self-discipline guiding his energy (Anderson, 36, 197; Cawelti, 40).

Although the hero is in the position of a role model, his mistakes permit him to be a more sympathetic character, not excessively idealized. The adventurer is an otherwise unremarkable individual who finds himself in extraordinary conditions that requires him to draw on certain innate abilities. He almost invariably has typical human failings and may begin inauspiciously as a bumbler (*The Black Shield of Falworth,* d'Artagnan in *The Three Musketeers*) or a carefree person without political concerns (*The Fighting O'Flynn*); only through the adventure does he come to represent an ideal. The potential to become an adventurer is presented as within anyone's reach, whether a practiced soldier or a novice to fighting, as demonstrated by the British officers who must take command of a seemingly indefensible position and succeed in saving Rorke's Drift in *Zulu*. Adventure universalizes the theme for all, since, through persistence and unwavering courage, even the most ordinary person can become a hero. The genre's very viability is in the degree to which it seems open and possible for anyone. There is nothing about the adventurer's character that seems too difficult to duplicate by anyone willing to apply himself, making the genre democratic rather than elitist in nature (Anderson, 197; Cameron, 41). Indeed, adventure most readily succeeds in becoming believable wish fulfillment to the extent that spectators are able to place themselves in the position of a hero (Basinger, 248–49). Part of the genre's lure is the accessibility of the hero; he may resemble what the viewer would hope to be had he or she lived in the same period under similar conditions. What the adventurer achieves only appeared impossible; the success proves the goal was obtainable all along (Campbell, 207).

Adventurers who do seem beyond ordinary mortals, larger than life, are often historical figures presented for hero worship, whether *El Cid* or *Scott of the Antarctic*. The past is presented as a time that produced such venerable individuals, providing examples of behavior and ideals that transcend their own era and are valuable today. This tradition goes beyond biography toward the heroic standard to which the genre is prone, teaching that by emulating others who are found admirable, one's own best instincts can be summoned forth. Lessons are taught by analogy to the audience, examples to follow and carry back into daily life; courage, daring, and self-denial are portrayed as traits that can be imitated. The adventurer is not a superhero or godlike individual exhibiting extraordinary, even divine qualities, but falls into the category Northrop Frye has labeled "high mimetic": "the hero is by *degree* superior to the [audience] *but not* to the laws of nature" (Northrop Frye in Todorov, 11).

Captain from Castile (1948) offers a range of character types, and each of these individuals will be examined in turn to exemplify the various possibilities inherent in the genre. *Captain from Castile* tells a near-epic story, beginning in the terrorized Spain of the Inquisition before traveling to Mexico and relating the early days of Cortés's toppling of the Aztec empire. The hero who eventually becomes the *Captain from Castile*, Pedro de Vargas (Tyrone Power), begins as a naive young innocent who suddenly realizes that the world is hardly the pacific place he imagined but one where torture and injustice flourish. In the opening scene, Pedro willingly joins a slave hunt but

The family of Pedro de Vargas (Tyrone Power, right) is imprisoned under the inquisition by order of Diego de Silva (John Sutton); moments later, Pedro's younger sister will die under torture.

learns that the pursued is an Indian friend, Coatl (Jay Silverheels). Pedro sympathetically gives Coatl money to aid him on his way, but the slaveholder who pursued Coatl uses the Inquisition to imprison Pedro's family. Taking them to the dungeons, Pedro's little sister dies on the rack. Pedro becomes a fugitive, escaping to the New World as the only future open to him, where he will again encounter Coatl.

To compensate for his absent parents, Pedro acquires two mentors, one religious and one secular: Father Bartolome (Thomas Gomez), the expedition's priest, and Hernando Cortés (Cesar Romero). Like many adventure films, *Captain from Castile* foregrounds contradictory convictions regarding religion; Pedro and his family have experienced its worst excesses through the Inquisition, and Cortés alternately also invokes and ignores Christianity for his own ends. However, Bartolome, who saved Pedro from deportation to Spain, is truly a holy man, allowing Pedro once again to find solace in the Christianity he was ready to discard. As Pedro interacts with important events, he proudly begins to emulate Cortés, and this omnipresent historical character initiates the fictional neophyte into greatness. Cortés's actual nature is replaced by an idealized, heroic model of the empire builder, disposing of historical truth in favor of a fictional narrative that better serves the conventions of the genre. Rather than attempt to justify the invasion of Mexico, *Captain from Castile* mythologizes it, portraying Cortés as a charismatic visionary. Royally sanctioned at first, Cortés must rely almost wholly on wit and clever strategy, seldom resorting to violence, instead overcoming challenges through personality and persuasion. His extraordinary wiles unite contending Spaniards and dissident Indians under his banner, exhorting and inspiring his followers to new feats with a humorous bluster and swagger. Cortés's ultimate loyalty is to neither church nor crown, but to conquest, defending himself not only from the Aztecs but also from dissent within his expedition and those who would undercut him in Cuba and Spain.

The adventure hero may be provided with personal support in three different ways: friendship, military service, and love, relationships that encompass those other protagonists to whom the adventurer may turn for immediate assistance and comradeship. Among friends, the hero often has a sidekick, a companion to provide a contrast, complementing his nature: James Durie and Colonel Burke in *The Master of Ballantrae* (1953), Harvey and Manuel in *Captains Courageous*. One of the hero's friends frequently serves a humorous role to provide comic relief. These individuals maintain a buddy relationship to the hero, joining him during hours of relaxation as well as adventurous exploits; the acting team of Alan Hale and Errol Flynn epitomized this combination in *The Adventures of Robin Hood*, *The Sea Hawk*, and *Adventures of Don Juan*. Occasionally, other distinct types fill this capacity, drawn to the hero's kindly nature: a midget (*Adventures of Don Juan*), a hunchback (*Captain from Castile*), a child (*The Four Feathers* [1929]; *The Real Glory*; *The Buccaneer* [1958]; *Raiders of the Seven Seas*), even a pet (*The Sea Hawk* [1940]). The commands of a leader like *Captain Horatio Hornblower* are followed on faith and out of respect, even if momentarily their purpose is not understood. The adventurer may remain apart from his followers, at the very least first among equals (*Captain Blood*). Frequently the leader's position in battles is not in the midst of his group but to one side, dueling with the villain or conducting a raid behind enemy lines, as in *Ivanhoe* or *Omar Khayyam*.

In *Captain from Castile*, not only does Pedro acquire a mentor in Cortés, he also meets new companions. The de Vargas family is rescued from prison, not by their aristocratic friends but by fresh acquaintances: Catana Perez (Jean Peters), and Juan Garcia (Lee J. Cobb). Pedro follows them to the New World, gradually becoming more egalitarian, and the trio discovers how much they share in common despite prior social barriers. They suffered from similar traumas in Spain; Pedro learns that Juan strangled his mother at her own wish rather than allow her to be burned at the stake by the Inquisition. In some respects, Juan's fate parallels that of Pedro, both finding freedom and equality in the New World, though Juan does not have the destiny that will be Pedro's or the love of a woman like Catana. Pedro proves so loyal that he allows friendship to endanger his position with Cortés by abandoning his post when Juan becomes deadly drunk. A fourth companion provides humor, the expedition's quack physician, "Humpback" Botello (Alan Mowbray). After operating on Pedro, he assumes his patient is dead and is about to roll the dice for Pedro's possessions. Then it is discovered that his patient is still breathing, and Botello announces that "in the practice of true science, God often lends a hand."

Beyond the hero and his followers are several other types of characters endemic to adventure. Rather than providing "support," they may oppose or uniquely supplement the hero and are in a secondary position to the plot's principal concerns. These types are villains, natives, women, and the family; two are often combined (native characters are discussed in Chapter 8, on colonialism and adventure). Supporting characters are often further intertwined, as the villain may control a woman the hero loves or his family, further personalizing the conflict. In *The Black Arrow / The Black Arrow Strikes* (1948), Joanna Sedley, the object of Richard Shelton's love, is the ward of the ruthless Sir Daniel Brackley, who has killed Richard's father and consequently will suffer Richard's vengeance. Politically, Brackley has not only deprived Shelton of his inheritance but also has betrayed both sides in the War of the Roses.

Villainy is defined more by certain traits than by any status in relation to government or societal position, since in many cases the hero is the outlaw while the villain has temporarily usurped a position of authority (Cohen, 48; Richards 1977, 5). The villain disrupts peaceful lives, causes war, and forces others to violence. Neither fantastic nor excessively realistic, the villain tends to be fanciful, incarnating the oppression the hero must fight. Sometimes a blackguard is even the most interesting character, dominating a story, as does Long John Silver in the many versions of *Treasure Island* (Pickering, 104; Richards 1977, 5). Overall, the villain often possesses the adventurer's skills, activity, and decisiveness but lacks the virtues that give him value, the void thereby becoming an instrument of evil (Nerlich 1987, 62). The hero personifies the culture's mythology, and the villain its failings. As Talbot Mundy wrote, "Our heroes are the men whom in our hearts we would rather resemble; our villains illustrate those failings we are striving to avoid."[2]

Villains flaunt the hero's qualities, replacing unflinching honesty with treachery, cunning with a lack of scruples, and true love with lust. The villain's threats and attempts to lure the hero toward evil inevitably fail, although sometimes snaring lesser men. The villain is as suave as the hero, but that characteristic becomes a thin, obvious veneer, excessively smooth, exposing his cruelty, crudeness, and gaucherie (*Captain Kidd*). While perhaps once handsome, indulgences have made him a travesty of the hero's pure or at least more restrained appearance. Whatever race or sex, the adventure villain is flawed by excessive pride, avarice, and ambition, traits that bring about his downfall. Dazzled by his own skill, the villain is obsessed with delusions of grandeur, becoming overconfident, a weakness for the hero's ingenuity to exploit (Lindsay, 15, 24; Hirsch, 105). Although the villain may be as tenacious, resourceful, courageous, and physically dexterous as the hero, he usually does not have the hero's humor, wit, and secure self-confidence (*The Prisoner of Zenda; The Scarlet Pimpernel; The Mark of Zorro*). In actuality in *The Scarlet Pimpernel*, Sir Percy Blakeney uses the veneer of a fop to compose doggerel both to amplify the Pimpernel's myth and to taunt his opponents.

> They seek him here, they seek him there
> Those Frenchies seek him everywhere.
>   Is he in heaven, or is he—in hell?
> That d'mned, elusive, Pimpernel.

Villains are conscious of the evil they do, usually enjoying it, minimizing any possible sympathy for them; yet they are also bad losers

(Rosenzweig, 36–37). Only occasionally are villains cast ambiguously, torn between two warring sides of their nature, such as Bois-Gilbert in *Ivanhoe*.

Diego de Silva (John Sutton) is clearly marked as the villain from the outset of *Captain from Castile*, when he leads the pursuit of the slave Coatl, who had escaped after a savage beating. Suspecting Pedro of assisting him, de Silva maliciously charges the members of the de Vargas family with heresy. Vowing revenge, Pedro apparently kills de Silva, turning his hypocritical piety back upon him by forcing him to renounce God before stabbing him. By the time Pedro repents, de Silva reappears, having recovered and come to Mexico to spread the Inquisition's terror. However, his evil career is brought to an end in the land of the Aztecs by Coatl, another man who has suffered at de Silva's hands and has no need to practice Christian charity.

A third type of adventurer, beyond the hero and his followers, is provided by a romantic companion. This is generally a woman, or, in the rare cases of a female adventurer, her male consort. Although adventure tends to position women in an unenlightened way, women are significant, as are romantic attachments and the family structure generally.

While the traits and activities of the adventurer are possible for members of any race and either sex, the principal characters are nonetheless nearly always men. Adventure is, like most Hollywood action forms, largely a male genre, traditionally focusing on men and their exploits (Cameron, 137; Cohen, 84; Green 1991, 3, 58). The concentration is on deeds predominantly associated in movies with men, whether military, revolutionary, or political. Amplifying this is the fact that the period of adventure films was clearly patriarchal and dominated by male figures. The position women occupy on the sidelines is at least partly dictated by history and geography, the result of their long exile from the military and political centers of decision making. To achieve a certain measure of believability in its setting, the genre is almost obligated to place women in the typical background positions they occupied at the time. During exploration or at sea, women were—and are in films—largely absent. Yet given these historical constraints, women are considerably more active and numerous in the genre than accuracy would warrant. While a few films avoid feminine influence, escaping to a world of men and male dominance where women may be for the most part absent, such examples are rare. The hero may flee from a woman on occasion, but a misogynistic streak is almost never apparent, since a new female companions is found in pictures as diverse as *Son of Fury* and *King Arthur—The Young Warlord*.

The primacy of the family and male centrality are never questioned in adventure films. Children of both sexes believe in patriarchy. Even when they are orphans, they strive to emulate an idealized father figure. The hero maintains enormous esteem for his family as a microcosm of the larger community-nation he is eager to serve. Parental figures are always respected, and the adventurer seeks approval for his actions, especially from his father. Otherwise anguish is experienced, as when Zorro must upset his family by adopting the guise of a fop. In many instances the son takes on his father's cause, just as Stanley will carry on in the footsteps of his mentor Livingstone in *Stanley and Livingstone*. The only tension in the family structure occurs when the hero fights to restore family position and reputation, as in *The Black Shield of Falworth*. Familial conflicts that do occur are most often between siblings rather than generations, brothers or half-brothers turning into rivals, a perilous situation inducing guilt on the hero's part, as in *The Master of Ballantrae; Omar Khayyam; The Vikings; All the Brothers Were Valiant; The Conqueror;* and *The Corsican Brothers*.

There is no attempt within adventure to explore realistically the relationship between the sexes; the genre's concerns are elsewhere. Whereas the adventurer experiences the outside world, women are usually limited to serving as observers—mothers, wives, mistresses, and camp followers in a domestic realm where men are the only means of contact with historical events (Nottridge, 11). Women are consorts who do not challenge the hero's centrality, while still deflecting attention from the predominantly male environment. No matter how important she may be to the hero's life, a woman is usually a support or at best a partner, assisting or measuring the hero's progress. Women are essential in adventure as inspiration and love interests, but the hero's relationships with them are depicted primarily insofar as they impact a man's life, adopting his viewpoint, not that of the woman, as in *The War Lord*. Yet the love interest is also more important to adventure films than to such other action genres as westerns, war, or crime films. Love forms a subplot that parallels the main themes, placing the woman in a perilous situation that provides the hero with the opportunity he seeks to prove his nobility, chivalry, courage, and altruism. The resolution of the love interest reflects the political settlement, reinstituting the proper relation of peasants, nobles, and monarchy in *The Adventures of Robin Hood* or the union of nobility and peasantry in *The Flame and the Arrow*.

Chivalric behavior is shown as involving a deference and protectiveness that places women in subservient, dependent positions; in *The World in His Arms*, the adventurer comes to love the woman he must rescue from a forced marriage to a tyrant she loathes. Occasionally, the adventurer must seem less than gentlemanly, even selfish, while saving a woman from a danger she does not perceive, although she ultimately recognizes its necessity, as in *The Black Swan*. Or else the woman is a queen to be served, whether Elizabeth in the time of the Spanish Armada (*Fire over England*; *The Sea Hawk*; *Seven Seas to Calais*) or to be loved at a distance, as in *The Prisoner of Zenda* or *Adventures of Don Juan*.

A woman's exalted, adored social position is nonetheless far from powerless; it allows her to manipulate the hero. Despite remaining comparatively inactive, such women may govern the hero's actions, expecting to be pursued with determination by a hero who will courageously overcome any obstacle, dare to perform any mission, to secure her approval and respect (Rahill, 76; John Fraser, 76; Campbell, 344). Love is so important to the adventurer that he is willing to attempt valiant deeds to secure romance. Swearing loyalty, it is often to satisfy her injunctions and to prove himself worthy of the lady's hand that the hero must undertake a dangerous, violent endeavor (*Down to the Sea in Ships* [1922]) (Zweig, 68, 64). The hero's words of wooing may also be turned back into a task for him to perform, as in the words of François Villon in *If I Were King* (1938).

> Beneath your feet what treasures I would fling
> The stars should be your pearls upon a string,
> The world a ruby for your finger ring,
>   And you should have the sun and moon to wear
> If I were king.

And indeed, Villon's spontaneous wooing of the princess ultimately leads the king to give him royal power in a moment of national crisis. In *The Four Feathers*, it is the condemnation of Feversham's fiancée, not his comrades, that provides the strongest motive for his search for redemption. Expecting to be obeyed, such a woman withholds her favor until the man has successfully completed his task, whether Constance for D'Artagnan in *The Three Musketeers* or similar couples in *Fire over England; The Crimson Pirate; Under the Red Robe; Prince of Foxes;* and *The Fighting O'Flynn*. The woman becomes almost a reward as part of his victory over adversaries; only when he has proven his ability is she willing to accept and return his love. Yet the quests of knights also make their ladies become interdependent with the success of its outcome; the combatants in a joust often wear their kerchiefs, and the woman's position depends on having chosen the victorious party.

Frequently, the lack of a true love leaves a hero unfulfilled or he has been disillusioned in love, such as Athos in *The Three Musketeers*. The hero may ignore women until meeting the one who wins his heart, with love often found as part of the dangerous situation in distant lands. Or romance may be at first a way to pass idle moments, used as a means to another adventurous end—a minor lady love may convey messages for the hero or provide information. The tendency to be a "ladies' man" becomes one of the adventurer's traits; the rake's roving, uncommitted spirit is part of his keen wit, rebellious nature, and physical agility. This unattached, "Don Juan" aspect is depicted as irresistible to women, perhaps because such a character seems more likely to approve of an assertive woman who can take care of herself and is a useful ally (Rahill, 77). As a romantic partner, the hero is magnetic, never crude or coarse; even those who are shy and inexperienced find a charm of their own, such as *Prince Valiant* (Anderson, 33). In any event, the hero's treatment of women is a sharp contrast with the villain, whose attitude is mercenary and perfunctory, pursuing her with the same fanatical ardor he brings to his political dealings. Often the villain's pursuit of love proves his undoing, and he is unprepared for the possibility that a woman might resist his lure (Lindsay, 31).

Movies do not concentrate on the hero's wooing but on the dramatic moment when at last he finds true love. Often he falls for the one woman who is not immediately seduced by his charm; she is hostile to the untraditional person who courts her, and the two make an unlikely pair. The adventurer is almost invariably smitten

Even *Don Juan* (1926) concentrates on the events that befall the adventurer (John Barrymore) from the moment he meets his one true love (Mary Astor).

at first sight, and his emotion deepens and matures with time until all his actions are planned around her. He discovers the sentimental side of his nature; the older and more world weary he has become, the stronger is love's appeal. Even *Don Juan* (1926) concentrates on the legendary lover's abandonment of his old ways in the face of a single love and his subsequent involvement with politics. In some cases, villainous machinations endanger the couple, forcing them to become closer and more involved, as in *The Adventures of Robin Hood*. By the conclusion, it is the adventure hero, not the woman, who is "tamed," preferring the favor of the woman he loves to the others he has known.

Although the hero may seem scarcely monogamous at first, as in *Shadow of the Eagle* (1950) and *The Flame and the Arrow*, by the narrative's conclusion he is almost inevitably committed to a monogamous relationship that will likely end further roguish capers. When the hero's feminine interests are narrowed to a single woman, his intentions become honorable. Only if he is ineligible to marry her will he reluctantly forsake her in the face of social obligation; *Captain Horatio Hornblower* maintains a formality toward his new love until he is widowed. Rebellious heroes may encounter a cultural chasm, as is experienced by Jean Lafitte and Annette Claiborne, the daughter of the governor of New Orleans, in *The Buccaneer* (1958). For those of royal blood, true love may be frustrated, position and responsibilities precluding personal happiness: *The Prisoner of Zenda; Adventures of Don Juan; The Exile; Sword of Lancelot / Lancelot and Guinevere*. To serve their country, noble women are willing to marry an unloved man or give up the affections of the hero.

To win his lady, the hero must often conduct his last and greatest adventure before renouncing this life-style forever. Marriage implies a sublimation of the adventurous instinct, the hero joining the new establishment as the narrative's conclusion indicates that the need for adventure is now over. When a new king has ascended to the British thrown, *Captain Blood* is made governor of Jamaica, replacing his enemy and marrying his predecessor's sympathetic daughter. The adventurous life is rarely permanent; the circumstances that motivate or make it possible, from bachelorhood to political oppression, are alleviated by the outcome of the story, with its establishment of liberty, justice, and a romantic union.

As in *The Eagle* (1925), political triumph is tied to romantic fulfillment, the adventure frequently culminating with a marriage between a rebel and a representative of the establishment he has opposed. The essential justice of the hero's cause is often demonstrated by converting a woman who was neutral or opposed to his goals. Often she is even a member of the social elite the hero is fighting (*Captain Blood*) or the daughter of an antagonist (*El Cid*) (Davis, 30). Misunderstandings plague her early relationship with the hero (*The Crusades*), and she may not understand his commitment to social justice (*The Scarlet Pimpernel; The Mark of Zorro*). However, she comes to realize that those she has supported are in the wrong, her sympathies and love going to the hero as a fighter for the downtrodden. The success or failure of the romance is partially measured by the democratizing experience adventure has on the woman. This is the corollary of the change love creates in the hero; just as he becomes domesticated, his way of living brings her an appreciation for the common man and woman. The future holds domesticity for the hero, a personal reflection of the renewed social compact between the people and their rulers that has resulted from the rebellion (Sobchack, 49). Their romance becomes liberating, releasing the constraints of class consciousness that governed her life. As she discovers the righteousness of her suitor's cause and joins him against his opponents, she becomes a moderating influence on the conflict. In the end the woman may instigate the hero's rescue, regardless of her original opinion of him and the differences that remain, as in *The Wind and the Lion*. Through her involvement with the hero, she adopts many of the traits of the adventurer: fighting injustice, even when it means turning against her own class and accepting an active, outdoor life away from the comfort of high society.

The same point is made by providing two women who are romantic possibilities for the hero, one of high birth, the other socially less desirable. By selecting the latter (*The Prince Who Was a Thief; Captain from Castile; Son of Fury*), even if this choice occurs after he is forsaken by another love (*China Seas*), the democratic inclinations of adventure are accented. The same sentiment occurs if an aristocratic woman chooses the commoner (*If I Were King* and Oriental swashbucklers) or the man of the people (*Son of Monte Cristo*). In some cases the adventurer is not a born aristocrat but of lowly birth, rising through position and ranks finally to marry above him (*King of the Khyber Rifles*). Even if that hero is later discovered to be the long lost son of nobility, courtship takes place before this is known, the aristocrat falling in love with someone who seemed to be a member of the lower classes (*Scaramouche; The Black Shield of Falworth*). Class equality has been asserted; love is supreme over the position into which one is born. When such views cannot be fulfilled, the social system is criticized; as Colonel Sapt tells the ineligible Rudolf Rassendyll in *The Prisoner of Zenda* (1937 and 1952), "Heaven doesn't always make the right men kings."

The conversion of a woman to the hero's cause is not a matter of her becoming a member of the hero's group of comrades. She does not turn into "one of the boys" but is a unique part of the organization supporting the hero's endeavor. Seldom does the adventure indicate that the hero prefers fighting or male comradeship over the company of women, only that this has been a temporary expedient to serve a political purpose. Although fighting at one point may seem more fun, ultimately it is romance that is the greatest delight, and when his task is accomplished, the hero gladly returns to his lady (*Don Q Son of Zorro*). Comradeship and friendship among one's own sex is not preferred over, nor does it interfere with, love between the sexes; male friends almost never discourage the hero's romance, and friendship, adventure, and love often merge, as in *Captain from Castile*. The best and truest fellowship is achieved between a man and woman who join not only in heart but in dedication to a cause, such as that experienced in *Son of Monte Cristo* and *Adventures of Don Juan*. Changing from an object of desire to an active participant, she shares risks, proving to be a bold and gifted adventurer when the need arises, as in *Captain Scarlett* or *Sea Devils* (1953).

Women play basically two different types of roles in adventure (Fisher, 233). Most often, especially in the swashbuckler, the woman is the attractive but meek recipient of romantic attentions. She is usually an aristocrat in manners and beliefs: Marian in *The Adventures of Robin Hood*; Anne in *The Flame and the Arrow*; Rowena in *Ivanhoe*; Marguerite in *The Scarlet Pimpernel*. While not helpless, such a woman is submissive, respectable, and unthreatening, a passive adjunct to the hero, a sexual opposite who is seldom of assistance; it is the Jewess Rebecca, not Ivanhoe's love Rowena, who cures his illness. Performers associated with these ornamental roles include Olivia De Havilland, Joan Fontaine, Barbara Britton, Virginia Mayo, Janet Leigh, Arlene Dahl, Debra Paget, and Jane Seymour. Even the most recent incarnation of Marian (played by Mary Elizabeth Mastrantonio) in *Robin Hood—Prince of Thieves* offers a woman who begins as a strong swordsmen, only to turn helpless once Robin is available to protect her.

Some women in the genre are more practical, ready to help guide the adventurer's life, such as Aouda in *Around the World in 80 Days*. Female characters may also evolve, especially when thrown into an adventurous situation where love is not initially present, including the women who hire the hero to lead a safari in *King Solomon's Mines* (1950) and *Killers of Kilimanjaro*. Another variation on this type is described by one of the genre's favorite terms, the wench, one who cynically relies on her looks (*Botany Bay*) for survival. Seldom truly a prostitute, she is a woman with spunk, whose lowly birth has precluded marriage and necessitated living by her wits, often working in a tavern. She proves ready to sacrifice herself to save the hero's life, such as Huguette in *If I Were King* and Cigarette in *Under Two Flags*. The opposite of such a character is the evildoer's accomplice, the villainous temptress and seductress, like the Countess Milady de Winter in *The Three Musketeers*. Occasionally, such a woman may be redeemed through sacrifice by attempting to aid the hero or his supporters, such as Sangarre in *The Soldier and the Lady / Michael Strogoff / The Bandit and the Lady / The Adventures of Michael Strogoff*. Although women are often isolated in a subordinate status, those who are brave may become heroes in their own right. Enjoying the same life-style, these female counterparts break through feminine stereotypes to prove their own courage and daring. Such characters are often the equal of men in the swashbuckler (*At Sword's Point / Sons of the Musketeers*; *Son of Ali Baba*) and pirate types (*Against All Flags*; Anne Bonney in *The Spanish Main* and *Anne of the Indies*). Active rather than passive, she may take the initiative or become the hero's sidekick (*Frenchman's Creek*; *The Southern Star*). These strong women may even be preferred by the hero, proving as much an asset to the cause as male associates, and heroes are fond of saying "I like a girl with spirit." Such women have been generally played by Yvonne De Carlo, Susan Hayward, Margaret Lockwood, Patricia Medina, Maria Montez, and Maureen O'Hara.

With the less civilized, more distant settings of empire, the sea, and fortune hunter adventures, there are fewer openings for traditional feminine participation. The heroes of colonies and the sea tend to be isolated, lonely characters; the loss of feminine companionship may force them to pursue patriotic service in a strictly masculine way. Empire builders generally do not prefer an all-male environment but have little alternative, and they pursue opportunities for romance regardless of how wise or accepted such a course may be (*The Lives of a Bengal Lancer*; *Adventures of Marco Polo*; *Outpost in Morocco*; *King of the Khyber Rifles*). Despite remote and rugged locales, in movies a commander's daughter or wife frequently resides with the garrison at outposts along rebellious frontiers (*The Charge of the Light Brigade* [1936]; *The Real Glory*; *The Long Duel*). While women in empire are rarer, they are independent individuals, frequently born or married into military families (cf. Richards 1973, 166). When danger threatens, they may be urged to leave for a less dangerous area but insist on fearlessly staying, such as Marjorie Carruthers, wife of the British resident in *Drums / The Drum*. The preference for this environment over returning to Europe indicates that these women are as spirited as their brothers, fathers, or husbands.

Catana (Jean Peters) decides on her own initiative to join the expedition led by Cortez (Cesar Romero), as Juan (Lee J. Cobb, left) and Pedro (Tyrone Power) look on.

Pedro's behavior toward women reveals both the chivalric expectations as well as his changing attitude toward class difference. Shortly after the opening of *Captain from Castile,* Pedro encounters two of de Silva's men setting their hounds on Catana, a local tavern girl. Rescuing her, Pedro ignores social barriers and preserves gentlemanly standards by giving her a ride on his horse to the inn. Catana recognizes and accepts the difference in their status, a realization that allows her to endure the trials that will be necessary before they are united as a couple. Pedro had courted the daughter of his father's best friend, who refused to help the family in its hour of need. Ironically, while Pedro continues to esteem Louisa de Carvajal (Barbara Lawrence), she and her aunt pray for Pedro's escape, not because of love but fearing that he will be caught with her kerchief. Unlike the selfish purity of the shielded stay-at-home Louisa, Catana is a strong, independent woman, devoted and self-sacrificing. Catana arranges for Pedro's rescue from the dungeon and later disobeys him to become an adventurer herself, boldly entering Cortés's headquarters to sign her name to the rolls of the expedition. She takes destiny

Against All Flags (1952) begins with the heroine (Maureen O'Hara) dominant over the hero (Errol Flynn), saving his life when he is taken prisoner, but by the conclusion his secret mission has outwitted her.

into her own hands, and when Pedro is blamed for de Silva's death, she tries to kill her lover mercifully rather than allow him to be executed. Although remaining secondary to Pedro, her hopes come to fruition as their romance parallels the thematic movement of the narrative, with the new society freed of the customs of the Old World that barred Pedro's love for Catana.

Despite the frequency with which strong women are found in the genre, rarely do they move to the forefront of the action. A number of so-called female swashbucklers and pirate adventures, far from leaving men in the background, are little different from the more typical films. Many of the women who take up the sword surrender it during an even more than usually demeaning courtship. An adventuresome woman may be outwitted by an adversary who becomes her lover, such as the naval officers who betray *Anne of the Indies* and "Spitfire" Stevens in *Against All Flags*. A common soldier tracks down a female descendant of the legendary count who has taken up the familial *Sword of Monte Cristo*. *The Son of Robin Hood* is really his tomboy daughter, but she allows another noble-

Robin's daughter (June Laverick) unites the aging members of her late father's men in *The Son of Robin Hood* (1959).

man to adopt her identity, the better to stop the usurper. In fact, the nobleman performs most of the heroics, and by the end marries the now thoroughly feminized daughter.

Less objectionable are such films as *Quebec* and *Swordsman of Siena*, in which women support revolts while masquerading as members of the governing elite. Some movies position women as both full-fledged adventurers and as romantic objects; in *At Sword's Point / Sons of the Musketeers*, one of the "sons" is the daughter of Athos—who eventually marries the son of d'Artagnan. In *Flame over India / Northwest Frontier*, the governess Catherine Wyatt (Lauren Bacall) proves to be the heroic and resourceful equal of the British officer (Kenneth More). Together, they lead a small, mixed-race group to safety during a religious uprising, and she even remains elusive from the hero's overtures at the movie's conclusion. The *Flame of Calcutta* is the daughter of a French consul who was killed when a treacherous native faction took power, and to gain revenge she is now leading the rebels. In love with a British officer, they fight and plot together to depose their rivals during the time of Lord Clive.

At Sword's Point (1952) features the exploits of the sons—and daughter—of the original three musketeers, and the daughter (Maureen O'Hara) proves herself fully the equal of the sons in wielding the sword.

Buccaneer's Girl (1950) follows the implication of its title, prioritizing the woman rather than the male pirate. Deborah McCoy (Yvonne De Carlo) thoroughly overshadows in skill and daring her romantic partner, who has far less screen time and is played by the lackluster Philip Friend. *Beverly of Graustrak* (1916) places a female adventurer in a Ruritanian situation where she is mistaken for a princess. Finding herself at the center of an attempted coup d'état, she handles the situation with aplomb and skillfully adapts to new circumstances by manipulating events. Perhaps the most progressive portrait of a female adventurer is, surprisingly, found in *Princess of the Nile* (1954). The ruler's attractive and dynamic daughter, Shalimar (Debra Paget), leads a double life as a dancer at the bazaars and chief of the rebels seeking to remove the evil influence of her father's shaman. Finally, the usurper is overthrown, along with a man who tried to blackmail her into marriage. Throughout, the medieval princess is the catalyst, the dominant, central force. Her ally, a visiting caliph, is a romantic partner but definitely secondary, although no less manly for it. An ideal feminist union is depicted in the unlikely setting of a purely imaginary Oriental swashbuckler, juvenile though enjoyable.

None of these pictures was the box-office or critical success that might have spurred imitations or changed the genre's overall conventions. Women have fared better in generic combinations of adventure–love stories, such as *Lorna Doone*; *China Seas*; *Untamed* (1955), and *Out of Africa*. In *Untamed*, the Irish Katie (Susan Hayward) pursues Paul van Rieback (Tyrone Power) to the new colony of South Africa, becoming an adventurer herself. However, as he constantly departs to lead commandoes to make the land safe for white settlers, Hayward dominates the narrative, raising a family, building homes and a life in his absence, taking advantage of other men who love her more devotedly. Although the heroes of adventure are nearly always men, a sufficient number of other examples exist to prove that there is no inherent reason within the genre's narrative structure for the hero to be male. While casting women in the primary role may be counter to audience expectations, the genre is eminently adaptable to such a change, whether a swashbuckler, pirate, or empire adventure. The most recent television series of *Zorro* has transformed the outlaw's love interest into an independent career woman, a tavern owner and political leader of early Los Angeles. The 1992 swashbuckling television series, *Covington Cross*, featured a teen-aged tomboy who is an expert with the crossbow and prefers male pursuits to those expected of her gender in the medieval setting. Together, these examples may point toward a future direction of the genre, one where women take their place as full-fledged adventurers.

CHAPTER 6   **The Code of Adventure**

Underlining the plot conventions and basic character traits of the hero are a series of patterns of prescribed behavior—a code of conduct—that the genre offers as a model. The code of adventure is comprised of the ideals and concepts underlying the adventurers' motivations, and from this unifying core of attitudes, the genre's narratives produce their meaning, providing coherence, cohesiveness, and depth. The result of the code is to place less emphasis on the action itself than on the behavior and motives surrounding it. The code has many different aspects—a code of honor, of behavior, of chivalry, of comradeship, of faith, of patriotism, of politics, all ultimately interrelated. Each of these aspects will be examined in turn, building on this foundation to note how the code serves as the springboard for the genre's political inclinations in the next chapter.

The code underlies the expectations formed of the type of action the hero will undertake, becoming a force to steer him or her in productive and altruistic ways that adhere to honorable means as well as goals. The hero finds causes worth serving, becoming in- volved in important movements or moments that are significant in the course of human events. The adventurer finds self-fulfillment in an arduous dedication to an integrated social and spiritual ideal—a milieu best created in the period setting used in adventure. Whereas many genres are known primarily by certain formulas, adventure is defined not only through particular types of activity (sword fights, exploration, imperialism, battles) but also through a thematic com- mitment to certain beliefs. Unlike the protagonists of many other genres, such as the cowboy or the hard-boiled detective, adventure has strict limits on the methods its hero may use; it is these stan- dards, obeyed or transgressed, that distinguish between the hero and villain.

The code and adventure's distant temporal settings are both em- blematic of the genre's illusions. The adventurer's code is a trans- forming device, re-creating history, individuals, and motivations in ideal terms. While the conventional dictionary definition of *swash- buckler* describes a braggart, ruffian, or daredevil, films expunge these faults. Highwaymen, sailors, pirates, crusaders, empire build- ers, fortune hunters, and big-game hunters become admirable fig- ures. Adventure films transform and valorize actual persons, regard- less of their true historical character. Christopher Columbus, King Richard the Lion-Hearted, Hernándo Cortés, Don Juan, Casanova, Jean Lafitte, *Anne of the Indies,* and *Scott of the Antarctic* become courageous, commendable figures because their cinematic por- trayals follow a strict code of conduct.

This heroism derives from adherence to a sense of honor reflect- ing the legendary chivalric virtues of the medieval knights and their descendants (Richards in MacKenzie, 158; Richards 1977, 4). The adventurer is required to be valorous and humane, reliably gallant, and merciful toward those who are weaker (Rowse, 57). With a gener- ous, kindly disposition, an adventurer should cheerfully admit er- rors; as *Don Q Son of Zorro* announces, "My father always said, when you are in the right, fight. When you are in the wrong, ac- knowledge it." The code requires the hero to be a gentleman at heart, although his outward manner reflects his station in life. A pirate, for instance, will naturally seem coarse when compared with a member of the nobility; among his own type he will appear a pleasing exception, a dichotomy noticeable in *Frenchman's Creek* and *A High Wind in Jamaica.* In adventure, it is assumed that instinctual behavior is cultured, as epitomized by the myth of Tarzan adopting "civilized" virtues amidst the wilds. The myth of the French Foreign Legion embodies the genre's belief in inherent, intuitive morality, that natural life is innately civilized, and an adventure provides the opportunity for anyone to fulfill this potential. Adventurers of all classes, occupations, and periods are held to fundamentally the same standard governing conduct and goals that are laudable, from *King Arthur—The Young Warlord* to Father Junipero Serra in *7 Cities of Gold*.

According to the code, victory is always possible, no matter the odds. While the adventurer's enterprises often bring him glory, fame, or promotion, such personal gains are not his primary aim; instead, they are a by-product of his fidelity to the code (Noyce, 34; Nerlich 1987, 272–73). Preserving honor and consciously fulfilling the obligations of duty and selflessness become a goal in and of itself (Fisher, 109). This may demand the readiness to accept a sacrifice, even death, rather than violate a pledge or the hero's commitment (Welsh, 219). The importance of observing these tenets is foregrounded in such films as *Beau Geste*; *The Prisoner of Zenda*; *The Buccaneer*; *The Exile* (1947); and *The Long Duel*. Fidelity becomes its own "success," fealty resulting in victory that is inevitable although not necessarily easy. Victory and martyrdom may be achieved despite death and momentary failure if the code has been obeyed, an apotheosis achieved by *El Cid*; *Scott of the Antarctic*; and Sidney Carton in *A Tale of Two Cities* (Durgnat, 17). The 1936 version of *The Charge of the Light Brigade* even reverses both the Tennyson poem and historical fact to accommodate this convention. The only concession is that Geoffrey Vickers (Errol Flynn) dies, gloriously leading his regiment against the enemies who had perpetrated a massacre. Since he reversed official orders, the hero's forthcoming death is necessary compensation.

The adventurer's strength and position derives from fealty to the ideals of the code, no matter the temporary disadvantage it may cause. For instance, one's word of honor is upheld even if it was extracted by trickery or under duress and will benefit the villain, a trait exploited by Long John Silver in *Treasure Island* (Pickering, 103–4). Indeed, the hero's moral scruples often create difficult situations. A villain, who cannot comprehend such standards, despises the hero, dismissing the code as mere weakness, as illustrated by the relationship between the cultured Humphrey Van Weyden and the brutal Larsen in *The Sea Wolf*. Although minor indulgences are allowed—drinking, gambling, debts, even a touch of the Don Juan nature—compensation must be made for such flaws, whether by upholding justice, such as Alan Breck Stewart in *Kidnapped*, or saving the queen, in *Adventures of Don Juan*.

Seldom is a hero allowed to violate these standards, and those who do find themselves in dire consequences as a result of their error, whether *Souls at Sea; Prince of Foxes; The Man Who Would Be King; Under the Red Robe; Knights of the Round Table; Sword of Lancelot / Lancelot and Guinevere;* or *The War Lord*. Sometimes, the personal trauma of an ambivalent hero eventually erupts in extreme acts, and a few such figures become avengers, losing much of their possible heroic stature. Generally heedless of the cost in innocent lives unrelated to the original crime, the avenger may never be fully reconciled but demonstrates some contrition in the knowledge his path leads to certain death. In *Moby Dick* (1956), Ahab leaves his protesting mate on the *Pequod*, and in *The Charge of the Light Brigade*, Geoffrey Vickers saves his brother from the forthcoming battle for his fiancée's sake. Both Vickers and Ahab then find redemption in leading their eager men in a courageous attack upon the enemy. However, villains wholly fail to achieve any such compensation. Captain Bligh, upon his return to Tahiti in pursuit of the mutineers in *Mutiny on the Bounty* (1935), is reprimanded; Wolf Larsen, in his crazed search for his brother in *The Sea Wolf*, dies. In *Genghis Khan*, the enemy's final defeat also brings about the hero's death. The code of adventure only sanctions the limited vengeance achieved in *The Sea Hawk* (1924); *The Light at the Edge of the World;* and *Nate and Hayes / Savage Islands*.

Avengers are typical among adventurers in finding a larger order in a sense of predestination. The adventurer is attuned to the moment, boldly, and with a touch of fatalism, risking all, banking on luck and instinct to point out the road to be followed. The adventurer may not plan every detail of his mission in advance, confidently placing destiny in the hands of fate. For instance, when one of the crew raises an objection to the stated plan in *The Fortunes of Captain Blood*, Blood replies: "I'll leave that to Lady Chance. She's obliged me more than once. Perhaps she'll oblige me again. I've great faith in the lady." Adventurers frequently believe they are the tool of forces larger and more powerful than themselves. While rarely fully understanding this destiny, they believe its summons must be instinctively obeyed, placing their trust in the service of a higher calling, whether *Anthony Adverse; The Count of Monte Cristo; The Conqueror; Genghis Khan;* or biographies of Christopher Columbus. Both *El Cid* and Gordon of *Khartoum* are at the mercy of a fate that grants them the strength and selflessness to sacrifice themselves and become national myths rallying their countrymen.

Adventure itself may take on the dimensions of a creed, a secular or civil religion, especially in empire stories; indeed, Christianity is most valued when tempered to support the adventurer's code. Just as fantasy and the supernatural are out of place in adventure, the celluloid adventurer often distrusts worship or demonstrations of faith in a god. To the adventurer—especially an avenger—providence cannot be trusted to correct injustice and punish villains; existence is too important to be left in the hands of any god. The hero's god, if he has one, demands self-reliance; it is the active and resourceful who will endure. Only after human resources have been exhausted do adventurers turn to religion. Even then, the god invoked is bound together with patriotism, sanctioning nationalism and its goals, providing the hero with a facade of holy justification. In *Outpost in Morocco* one of the Legionnaires goes so far as to conflate the military and religious icons together on the barracks wall; for many swashbucklers, especially knights, a sword is not only an instrument for war but doubles as a cross. In the swashbuckler the church itself is often on the side of the tyrant or usurper or part of the unjust establishment that adventurers rebel against. Just as France is shown with a ruthless Catholic cardinal and Spain its inquisition, so do their Eastern counterparts lead uprisings in the colonies. Even when a spiritual quest is ostensibly crucial, as with pictures centering on the Crusades, the spiritual side is inevitably subordinate to patriotic endeavors. The sea story dismisses spirituality as irrelevant, captains indifferently reciting a prayer as the body of another sailor slides into the sea. The genre's preferred religious figures are missionaries or priests who have a touch of the adventurer in their soul, whether Dr. David Livingstone, Father Junipero Serra, or the friars who assist Robin Hood and Zorro. They leave cloistered security behind to work for a better life on earth, rather than merely preparing for the afterlife. Practicing a type of social gospel, their concept of religious calling often make them dissenters from the church hierarchy.

Just as spirituality becomes part of the code, even sports has its

The seemingly opposite symbols of religion and soldiery merge for two
members of the French Foreign Legion (George Raft, right, and Akim Tamiroff) in *Outpost in Morocco* (1948).

place, not as games, but in order to engender the sporting instinct, a
training ground for the skills that will be needed. Beyond encompassing a demonstration of precision and skill, such as the archery
of Robin Hood, sports shift from a playful contest to become useful
in the battle against tyranny. As an adventurer, *Scaramouche* learns
fencing in order to be able to gain revenge, and in *Adventures of Don
Juan* the royal fencing academy prepares the queen's supporters to
fight in her defense. Archery, sword play, and jousting contests often
become a trial by combat, the hero's agility and skill ultimately
proving victorious, no matter how hard pressed and bloodied
Ivanhoe or *El Cid* may have been. Sports serve a larger purpose,
becoming a paradigm of the challenges the adventurer must overcome, from the determination to prepare and train to serve a cause,
to summoning the courage to face danger, to a life-and-death confrontation with an enemy.

As a consequence of the task the adventurer sets out to perform
and his willingness to face danger, he frequently faces an ordeal, a

test of willpower (Fisher, 216).[1] For instance, a cruel villain may capture him and subject him to grueling torture. However, these encounters are usually brief, depicted more metaphorically than graphically, and often off screen, with the hero instantly recovering, ready to resume fighting. Survival in such incidents does not rely on base, competitive instincts or simple muscular strength, which are associated with the villain's brutality. Instead, the hero endures through a wily mental fitness. He does not simply stay alive, he preserves the code's gentlemanly standards and belief in altruistic goals. Through such a trial, the adventurer experiences self-discovery, tapping unsuspected resources and willpower to achieve a new, nearly spiritual, threshold (Campbell, 190; Green 1990, 200; Fisher, 268). The adventurer in these circumstances represents humanity, an everyperson figure, who gains control of the world around him by mastering his own personal resources, becoming stronger and wiser (Nerlich 409 n. 59). The entire adventure may come to resemble a rite of passage, an initiation that celebrates a progression to "manhood," whether for men, women, or children, such as in *Swiss Family Robinson*.

For instance, in the versions of *Michael Strogoff*, the czar's courier is sentenced by the Tartars to be blinded, but almost miraculously he does not lose his sight and goes on to complete his mission. Often, the hero seems defeated and for a moment is ready to yield to despair after an ordeal when a friend or lover, in this case Nadia, comes to raise Michael's spirits to fight again. The adventurer usually experiences such episodes alone, but when more than one character is included, they cement the ties of comradeship (Campbell, 384; John Sutherland in Fisher, 19). An ordeal is usually presented as a subordinate aspect of a plot that centers on a lengthy siege or its equivalent that isolates the hero (*Beau Geste*; *55 Days in Peking*; *Khartoum*). Only in a few pictures does survival become the dominant theme (*The Lost Patrol*; *Zulu*; *The Naked Prey*; *The Light at the Edge of the World*), usually in desert, island, polar, and other similarly barren or remote locales, including *Robinson Crusoe*; *Man Friday*; *Ebb Tide*; *Swiss Family Robinson*; *Strange Holiday* (1969); *Scott of the Antarctic*; and *The White Dawn*. As a result, with the obstacles either natural or man-made, adventure may become not only a predominantly historical and political genre but also one with psychological and almost metaphysical implications.

The ordeal may turn into a direct, serious confrontation in which

Michael Strogoff (Anton Walbrook) is about to face Tartar-style blinding through a white-hot saber placed over his eyes, as his mother (Fay Bainter) and Nadia (Elizabeth Allan) look on, in *The Soldier and the Lady / Michael Strogoff / The Bandit and the Lady / The Adventures of Michael Strogoff* (1937).

adventurers discover evil and must find the resources to face fear and death with equanimity. Life is regarded as a form of warfare, with a courageous and voluntary willingness to face danger the most essential of virtues (Nerlich 1987, 281). When adventurers are ready to put their lives on the line for a cause in which they believe, they often find that the possibility of the final sacrifice is the most effective. As General Gordon discovers in *Khartoum*, "A man's most valuable weapon is his own life. If he is afraid to lose that life, to face death, he loses that weapon." To the adventurer, death is humankind's inevitable fate, so he should overcome this natural fear and use this ultimate end for a purpose. This attitude allows adventurers to position themselves to take advantage of whatever opportunities fate may offer, and if victory is beyond their grasp, they may prefer to die as a defeated martyr, as in *Lord Jim*. The adventurer still succeeds, and the conventions of the genre are preserved (Fisher, 379).

The code not only governs how action is to be taken but also the types of behavior among those who join together in a cause. The widespread recognition given the code among adventurers is indicated by the readiness with which a network is formed, utilizing fellowship and teamwork toward a collectively agreed-upon goal (Noyce, 79). Compatibility and respect arise from shared ideals, and through the willingness to sacrifice for these ideals, close-knit friendship may evolve into something higher, comradeship (McConnell, 40). The hero may not be so much a single individual as a group, whether strangers, friends, or relations brought together in a mission, as in *At Sword's Point / Sons of the Musketeers; The Man Who Would Be King;* and *Swiss Family Robinson.* Alexandre Dumas set the archetypal pattern in *The Three Musketeers,* and the interaction between d'Artagnan, Athos, Porthos, and Aramis has been widely imitated, from P. C. Wren's *Beau Geste* to *The Lives of a Bengal Lancer* and *Gunga Din* (Ward 1984, 26; Green 1991, 70–71).

The adventurer is often outnumbered, acting alone or as the leader of a small band who must overcome tremendous odds. However, he prefers it this way, and these apparent disadvantages often work in his favor (Rowse, 57). As a leader, the adventurer tends to be best with an independent command, not as part of a large enterprise outside the grasp of one person (Anderson, 57). When involved in a military situation, the exploits of irregulars are more likely to be the focus, concentrating on a solitary hero, or a duo, trio, or foursome (Green 1979, 211). This is true of both an amateur organization such as Robin Hood's merry men or the naval expedition against the Barbary Pirates by *Old Ironsides.*

Actively seeking those who share similar views, the adventurer is never exclusive, elitist, or sexist. In groups ranging from the French Foreign Legion to a pirate crew, when newcomers attempt to join, they are almost always accepted, even when there are doubts about them. The friends do not require extravagant displays of courage and are only disappointed if the recruit fails to live up to their expectations. This trusting nature may be taken advantage of, by Long John Silver in *Treasure Island* or Fix in *Around the World in 80 Days,* and a traitor may have to be killed to rectify the error, as with Levasseur in *Captain Blood.* The openness of this aspect of adventure is captured in Arthur Sullivant Hoffman's oft-reprinted introduction to "The Camp-Fire, A Meeting Place for Readers, Writers and Adventurers," the letter section of *Adventure* magazine.

Many have gathered about . . . and they are of all classes and degrees, high and low, rich and poor, adventurers and stay-at-homes, and from all parts of the earth. . . .

We are drawn together by a common liking for the strong, clean things of out-of-doors, for word from the earth's far places, for man in action instead of caged by circumstance. The *spirit* of adventure lives in all men; the rest is chance. . . .

If you are come to our Camp-Fire for the first time and find you like the things we like, join us and find yourself very welcome. There is no obligation except ordinary manliness, no forms or ceremonies, no dues, no officers, no anything except men and women gathered for interest and friendliness. Your desire to join makes you a member.[2]

The regiment or its equivalent, such as the more informal band headed by the swashbuckler or pirate, is lauded in the genre for promoting a social mix among the ranks. The closest companions accept advice, even criticism, from each other, and while there is less fraternization and a greater reserve toward subordinates, there is also mutual respect and devotion, regardless of social position (Rosenzweig, 48–49). Diverse levels of society are brought together in an idealistic cause against a common enemy, with differences of class and caste forgotten. Each individual must prove himself worthy, regardless of station, birth, or wealth, and the only distinctions are based on ability. No one is given preferential treatment, and even Robin Hood must prove superior skill over Friar Tuck and Little John before they acknowledge his leadership.

As a result, adventure acquires a collective side, with individuals often united in military endeavors that take place on a large scale (*The Pride and the Passion*). The ability to meld themselves into a single unit gives adventurers not only their power but something more. In the words of Talbot Mundy: "A regiment is not a congeries of men who have been drilled: it is the embodiment of an ideal, and men have the honor to belong to it. It is nearly as deathless as a religion, and is almost as independent of individuals. Men join it and are taught the spirit of it . . . the regiment goes on forever."[3] The group's aims may be internalized by the individual heroes; *The Three Musketeers* make the quarrel of the king's musketeers with the cardinal's guards their own vendetta. The adventurer is privileged to share in the respect of his comrades and the recognition earned by the group, whether they are the associates accompanying Scott to the Antarctic or the regiment that will make the charge of the Light Brigade. Rather than simply serving out of a sense of patriotic obligation, soldiery becomes part of the adventurer's life, an attitude from which he may never retire (*Khartoum*; *The Real Glory*).

Yet comradeship is always tenuous and uncertain, and frequently of short duration. It is cherished precisely because of its rarity and often pivotal role in accomplishing a deed, such as Alan Breck Stewart helping David Balfour to secure his inheritance in *Kidnapped*. Frequently, camaraderie becomes secondary to discovering the limits of one's own capabilities in advancing the cause. Some of the adventurous experience can never be fully shared and must be undertaken alone, facing danger and adversity in self-sufficient isolation (Peter Fleming in Noyce, 81; Anderson, 32; Bolitho, xvi). Much of the greatest satisfaction comes in solitary exploits conducted away from their comrades and outside the normal military life. Self-esteem becomes the greatest reward; isolated on a mission, the adventurer must act on his own, exceeding orders and exercising personal judgment. Narratives offer a repeated pattern of the individual and the group separating and re-merging, each having his own separate tasks and strengths; for instance, the hero accomplishes a deed that could only be performed alone, then returns to his comrades for assistance in completing the task, as in *Gunga Din* and *The Black Arrow / The Black Arrow Strikes* (1948). This allows a sense of interdependence while retaining an emphasis on the heroic potential of the individual. Even the group heroics of the Three Musketeers serve primarily as a background to highlight the exploits of d'Artagnan; the most difficult adventures, such as the rescue of the queen's diamonds, are completed by d'Artagnan. Crucial to the development of the story is this ultimate test of d'Artagnan's abilities, which comes, not when aided by his fellows, but while he is alone. Only under these circumstances does he fully prove himself; the title characters are actually of secondary significance, with d'Artagnan only becoming truly close to the troubled Athos.

Loyalty is prized, and adventurers are willing to sacrifice for a comrade, invariably trying to save another in a fight, in some cases risking their lives (Cohen, 13). While an attempt will always be made to rescue a friend, the adventurer will not rush blindly to a comrade's help, instead proceeding in the most effective way possible, as in Lafitte's bargain to save his crew in *The Buccaneer* (Anderson, 31–32). Allowing emotion to govern a decision inevitably leads

Comradeship with the three musketeers (background) does not interfere with d'Artagnan (Douglas Fairbanks) proving his individual heroism, in *The Three Musketeers* (1921).

to a debacle, complicating the hero's ultimate task, as in the failed undercover rescue of young Donald in *The Lives of a Bengal Lancer*. Loyalty dictates that the highest fealty is owed to honor and the ideals that first united the group, and personal concerns must never be allowed to endanger the cause.

While the adventurer displays many of the characteristics of the born soldier, obeying orders is not a ritual of the code. Discipline is inculcated by instinct and example; when overt, external force is present, it is usually a sign of elitism, the sort of class differentiation that is resented and may provoke rebellion. Adventurers never subordinate themselves completely, retaining their wanderlust and love of freedom and independence, thriving on the challenge of promoting its advance in a way that is fundamentally incompatible with regimentation. The hero retains individuality and a sense of responsibility through a willingness to disobey orders when the need arises, and the military structure is only valued for facilitating the adventurer's goals (a sharp contrast with the war movie). In *Beau Geste*, becoming part of the French Foreign Legion occurs because of both a boyhood dream and the desire to conceal the loss of a family jewel. The Geste brothers have no interest in French military goals, remaining loyal only to each other, abandoning the legion as soon as its usefulness and circumstances permit. Joining is a means rather than an end, utilized when it seems to promote the adventurer's endeavor.

In the adventurer's code, duty has a definite hierarchy, with wealth and companionship variable but secondary goals. First comes responsibility to country and the larger cause of justice and liberty; second to the community, family, and friends; and only third to personal considerations, including romantic love. Patriotism is always chief among these duties; it is the loftiest and most prized value of the genre, the prerequisite for security, respect, happiness, and love. Devotion to homeland comes before all, and the obligations it imposes must be fulfilled before a romantic interest is enjoyed. In effect it is necessary for the adventurer to father a country before he is eligible to marry and begin a family, as in *Untamed* (1955). Because of the paramount importance of fidelity to the cause, many adventurers remain romantically unattached or unfulfilled for at least part of the picture; *El Cid* even abandons wife and family when patriotism calls (Anderson, 32). The difficulties for *The Master of Ballantrae* begin when he places family before nation and loses the esteem of friends and countrymen. The myth of the romantic triangle between Lancelot, Guinevere, and Arthur reveals the danger of allowing passion to open a political pandora's box of civil war and dissension, as shown in *Knights of the Round Table* and *Sword of Lancelot / Lancelot and Guinevere*. All three agonize over their duty to each other as friend, lover, and patriot, and their sworn obligation to uphold the law. Despite Lancelot's valiant service at the king's side before and after the scandal, neither can forget the affair with Guinevere; just such a scandal is averted when Flavia and Rassendyll follow the code to renounce their own love and preserve the kingdom in *The Prisoner of Zenda*.

Regardless of whether the hero is an irregular, soldier, or missionary, patriotism and love of country are always strong motivations. A lapse in patriotism is never forgiven, and there is no worse disgrace and misery than to lose or be deprived of homeland, as Philip Nolan discovers in *The Man without a Country*. Heroes forced from their homeland suffer great anguish, whether *Captain Blood* or Fletcher Christian in *Mutiny on the Bounty* (Davis, 26). In *The Buccaneer*,

Jean Lafitte wishes to join a land that espouses ideals he can support, such as the American Declaration of Independence. To be able to serve one's country is essential to well-being and a satisfying life; only under these circumstances is the adventurer content (cf. Anderson, 322). A country's mistreatment or ingratitude may only increase the desire to serve; Lafitte and his pirates fight alongside the Americans after their initial offer of aid has been answered with an attack on their base. *John Paul Jones* continues his naval war for the Continental Congress even when it repeatedly fails to heed his advice and becomes dominated by captains chosen because of influence rather than ability. Only for the fortune hunter is the unifying theme of nationalistic devotion sometimes relegated to the background.

However, adventure patriotism is more complex than the ethic of "my country, right or wrong" generally espoused by the war film. The adventurer's ultimate loyalty is to his conscience, and he feels free to question dictates given in the name of the national interest. A more accurate paraphrase of the slogan for adventure would be, "My country, may she always be in the right, and if not, I'll follow my own judgment." Adventurers acknowledge the possibility that their homeland may be wrong and work to correct its inequities (Cohen, 59). Adventure patriotism is mature, almost modern in advocating thoughtful decisions rather than reflex action. Patriotic adventurers may serve their country as they see fit. They fulfill a patriotic obligation in a way that seems best to them, the code simply requiring a willingness to serve, in the appropriate manner, whatever cause is chosen. The genre's view of a patriot's duty and how it should be fulfilled may place them in opposition to an authority whose legitimacy they doubt or whose policies they oppose. Adventurous patriotism is not identified with unthinking obedience but with an unwillingness to see dissent and disagreement as equally respectable manifestations of a love of country. This brings us to the topic of the adventurer's politics, which will be the subject of the next chapter.

A. E. W. Mason's 1901 novel *The Four Feathers* is one of the most oft-filmed adventure stories, and its progression of screen versions delineates not only the adventure code but also, from today's viewpoint, its fatal flaws. In the first five versions of *The Four Feathers* (1915, 1921, 1929, 1939, and 1956—the latter under the title *Storm over the Nile*), the code is depicted as the backbone of empire, a force

Harry Feversham (John Clements) receives the final feather from his fiancée, Ethne (June Duprez), as her father (C. Aubrey Smith) looks on in *The Four Feathers* (1939).

that shames men to serve lest they be branded as cowards. The code becomes reductive and constraining, forcing men to live a Prussian-style military life, with women enforcing the warlike, patriarchal order through the choice of a husband.

Harry Feversham, scion of an old army family, has been reared from infancy to be a soldier. His childhood memories and nightmares are of his father's stories of men who discovered they were cowards and so did the only decent thing: commit suicide. As a result Harry becomes intimidated by his lineage, afraid not of war but of living up to expectations—afraid he will be afraid. On reaching adulthood, he tries to establish his own identity, leaving the army to become a civilian. However, just as he plans to depart the service, England mobilizes for war in the Sudan. In not reconsidering his resignation, Harry's three regimental friends and fiancée Ethne believe he is shirking his duty, and each gives him a feather to signify the accusation. Harry is not certain that they are wrong, and determines to prove the contrary. He quietly leaves for the Sudan to fight undercover by posing as a native.

The irony of the story is that while the picture centers on the return of the feathers, this is of relative insignificance. More important is Harry's odyssey, as he is driven by a combination of reasons that primarily involve exploring his own nature. Like many adventurers, Harry finds his own way to serve his country outside of the conventional military order, and he is ultimately celebrated more for these actions than his friends who simply followed the more traditional path. This is especially true of Durrance, who goes blind in the desert and must ultimately lose to Harry the affections of Ethne despite Harry's initial disgrace.

This fundamental incompatibility between what is actually depicted in *The Four Feathers* and what it pretends to teach was evident even in the early versions of the first and second cycle. A different emphasis is found in each movie of *The Four Feathers*. The 1929 version accents the loss of innocent fellowship between Harry (Richard Arlen) and his fellow soldiers. With Ethne he feels disloyal to his buddies and the venerated regiment even before the Sudanese war began. After leaving the service, Harry's dying father gives his son a pistol to use on himself and prevent disgrace. However, once in the Sudan, Harry's feats become almost superhuman, the return of the feathers taking on a revengeful hue that fails to restore friendship, his father's life, or even the innocent love he once had for Ethne. A soldier's daughter, she had only wanted a soldier for a husband, and Harry finally is molded to her desire.

The internal inconsistencies are even more obvious in the 1939 version of *The Four Feathers*. While ostensibly preaching classical nineteenth-century patriotism, the narrative makes apparent many of the contradictions and failures inherent in the ideology as practiced. Young Harry leads a terrified childhood in a home where threats and warnings are substituted for love. On discovering his blindness, Durrance attempts suicide, already pronounced as the "coward's" way out. Ethne's father repeatedly tells of his service in the Crimean War, falsifying the story to eliminate the fact it was not he, but his horse, who charged impulsively into battle. Even Harry's mentor advises him that his comrades's feathers should be treated with contempt if the accusation is unfounded.

Storm over the Nile, while a very close remake, was made seventeen years later and is less harsh in its treatment of Harry. While Harry's childhood is abbreviated, and his intention of quitting the service less clear, he still seems far from a coward. Besides Durrance, his other two comrades are unimpressive. A year after his father's death, Harry is just beginning to put together a life of his own and preparing for marriage. Harry had believed he and his fiancée understood one another, but her first reaction is to serve as the most rigid enforcer of the military code. "Oh yes, we've talked and dreamed about things we'd do if we were free. Some people are born free, and they can do as they like, but you weren't born free, Harry, nor was I. We were born into a tradition, a code—a code that we must obey even if we don't believe in it. We must obey, Harry, because the pride and happiness of those nearest to us depends on our obedience." Although initially failing to comprehend his action, she later tries to make up for it. While this scene closely resembles the 1939 film, a subsequent scene provides a contrast. Harry's mentor understands both the motive and its result, and tells Harry: "You're a man of ideals and great imagination, perhaps too great, and you've paid a terrible price for your father's lack of understanding. But you're not a coward. Right or wrong, you refused to live by a code you couldn't believe in . . . That wasn't the act of a coward, but a very brave man." Yet Harry proceeds to feel the same need to prove his courage, even going so far as apparently to turn the tide for the British in the battle for Omdurman. The remake also relies on the same location footage as the preceding version, limiting the range of narrative possibility. Curiously, in both of these versions, produced by Alexander Korda, the singularly colorless performance of the leading men (John Clements in 1939 and Anthony Steele in 1956) robs Harry of much of his possible depth of character, heightening the emphasis on the code by making him primarily a vessel to fulfill its requirements.

The 1977 remake of *The Four Feathers* creates an entirely new mythology and hero, epitomized by the opening credits over an army of toy soldiers. The film emphasizes the psychology of a man who must overcome his fear not only of being afraid but also of not living up to the model of imperial service so ruthlessly adopted by the military class. To do so, Harry (Beau Bridges) must discover the values truly worth supporting through experiences far from home, presented through a story clearly framed in terms of the Vietnam era's questioning of patriarchal, nationalistic authority and the tradition of fighting for one's country. While less spectacular than its 1929 and 1939 predecessors, the 1977 narrative more capably accounts for the hero's actions, emphasizing the drama's interior side. This revision shows a thorough awareness of the absurdities in the plot twists of the original, instead acknowledging and puncturing the false myths that were its underpinnings. Unlike the 1939 version, Harry triumphs over the others with their antiquated world views, rather than acting to redeem himself in their eyes. His travels are made credible through an alliance with an Arab pursuing private vengeance against the Mahdi.

Upon receipt of the feathers Harry initially attempts suicide, then decides to save his friends and return the feathers, as much to avenge their having dared to question his motives as to discover his own courage. In the Sudan he observes each of his former comrades react with weakness to moments of crisis that had demanded strength, just as he did in burning the regimental summons— although unlike them, he now recognizes this vice in himself. Durrance, knowing it is Harry who rescued him, even lies to Ethne by saying that he never heard of him while in the Sudan, so that he may court her in Harry's absence. Each of the comrades, along with Harry's father and his fiancée Ethne, realize it is actually they who have failed Harry.

Especially notable is the humiliation Harry's father (Harry Andrews) must undergo for having raised his son like a soldier, terrorizing but never loving him, finally humbly asking for Harry's forgiveness. As Ethne warns, "Doesn't a father also have a code?" At the end Harry declares his own individuality, knowing he is no longer afraid of his father, nor his dark home with its imposing rows of portraits of decorated Fevershams from wars past. The love subplot is also in a more modern mode, with an emotional and independent Ethne (Jane Seymour) who regrets and repudiates the beliefs that had caused her to reject Harry. Instead she wishes she had helped him through his crisis—an attitude far removed from the Ethne of the 1929 *Four Feathers*, demanding Harry conform to the model of the military hero.

The treatment of the code is necessarily one of the more problematic aspects of modern adventure films. During the fourth cycle of adventure, the code was ripe for revision and satire. A film such as *The Duellists* (1978) found the code's idea of honor to be wholly absurd, on the surface causing a seemingly endless quarrel. Yet it is the code's abuse that distinguished villain from hero, and only the proper invocation of the true code can finally allow right to prevail. Without the historical context and the suspension of disbelief that it implies, the genre's assertion of the code's various notions seems outdated in the contemporary world (Fisher, 77). While much of the code's behavior seems simplistic today, such as its emphasis on masculinity and comradeship, other aspects retain their validity, such as the spiritual side and its emphasis on the solitary human being. Only through misconceptions regarding the code's patriotic obligations has it seemed archaic and militaristic in a post-Vietnam America. Perhaps this is understood, considering the decline of satire and revisionism in the genre. The return of adventure in the late 1980s and 1990s seems to have brought back the code in its entirety; it is still in effect, although the emphasis on certain aspects may be slighter or greater than in previous years.

CHAPTER 7 **The Politics of Adventure**

The ethics of the adventurer's code and its relationship to the true meaning of patriotism and chivalry support the genre's political beliefs. While adventure novels are wide-ranging in their subject matter, movies have concentrated on the adventurer's interaction with government, laws, and authority.[1] The decision to support a cause is dictated by how well it serves the adventurer's code. The hero is the one who most fully embodies its precepts, whether a ruler (incumbent or aspirant), a ship's captain, an imperial power, or an outlaw bandit. From the outset, the principal conflict and motivation are political, revolving around oppression and injustice as the hero battles to attain and preserve social ideals that match the standards of the code. Emphasizing the union of the people with the national interest, adventure demands a just society where individual rights are respected and class differences are minimized.

Although politics is a motif, it is never a generic "given," an accepted formula that need only be mentioned rather than explained, in the sense that Indian-as-villain became standard in the western. Adventure films are full of the rhetoric and romanticism of justice, honor, and liberation, the hero instinctively enunciating a view that becomes the film's rallying cry. Since the genre is organized around the issue of political legitimacy, authority must constantly demonstrate its value (Green 1979, 274). The political nature of tyranny is meticulously depicted and given a historical background and justification so that the adventurer's response becomes morally necessary and positive. The eagerness to portray the overthrow of authority frequently moves beyond conflicts that are partly personal or involve vengeance to encompass an entire movement that derives from the clash of social forces over issues of class and economic justice. To be accepted, rebellion must be justified on an intellectual, political basis, offering not only an end to injustice but a positive alternative for the future.

While adventure films have a definite perspective on political issues, the starting point is the adventure hero, who is not only the narrative centerpiece but also enunciates the film's political views (Roddick, 236). In the populist view of the genre, the inherent traits of the adventurer—following the standards of the code—provide the moral compass. Goals are achieved through a hero who embodies the beliefs of the code, personal and political events becoming intertwined and inseparable. The genre's ideology emanates from the adventurer's strenuous life-style and moral stand; the hero shaping society, rather than being conformed to it (Campbell, 391; McConnell, 86). Because the adventurer's mindset values risking the unknown, there is a belief in the efficacy of change, accepting revolution as the sphere from which new order will emerge (Nerlich 1987, xxi; Nerlich 1986, 16). Tradition is revered, but only as part of a glorious past, implying a willingness to grow with the times. The hero is a fundamentally constructive person, maintaining or building for the future, capable of both a social vision and the practical ability to implement it; the dream of freedom and justice is never an intangible utopia. Indeed, the adventurer's life is incomplete unless it extends beyond the personal to encompass larger interests, maintaining a social responsibility and a romantic, optimistic view that a better future is within reach. Whether based on authentic individuals or not, the life and thinking of the heroes represent and personalize historical forces, moral conflicts, and significant movements. The adventurer becomes a "great" individual because his goals coin-

The democratic nature of the adventurer's conception of politics allows him to duel within the palace walls to defend his honor and that of the king. Here, Louis XIII (Arthur Lubin) interrupts a confrontation between the treacherous noble Chatellerault and the heroic courtier Bardelys (John Gilbert) in *Bardelys the Magnificent* (1926).

cide with these historical movements, expressing and becoming the standard-bearer of the popular will. Such heroes appear at the moment when a crisis is facing the nation and its population, providing the spark for the rebellion (Georg Lukács in Brombert, 203, 206, 208).

The code provides the hero with a basic groundwork that is evident in his political beliefs. This spirit is manifested in the code's belief in fluid class relations, ignoring or minimizing social barriers. The hero never hesitates literally to leap into the palace, bypassing guards and the social barriers they represent, to provide a warning or provoke a confrontation with the king. Frequently heroes are descended from noble blood, but their families may have lost their position, and the heroes struggle to restore their former prestige (*Ali Baba and the Forty Thieves*). Consequently, adventurers have empathy for those less fortunate; their primary concern is always for the lower classes, chivalrously caring for the weak and defenseless. The character of the hero both illustrates the obligations of the upper class and makes clear that the people's needs are just. Elitism has no place in the behavior of the adventure hero, who prefers to associate with common folk for friendship, companionship, and sometimes love, the political movement creating unity across all social strata. This is often reflected in a romantic involvement between the hero and a woman who is from an endangered group—either a commoner or a threatened but caring aristocrat (*The Crimson Pirate*; *Prince of Foxes*). The true aristocracy in adventure is less a matter of titles and estates than of intelligence, courage, and caring. Even a minor court philosopher such as *Omar Khayyam* is allowed to marry the widow of the shah. Although the view of human rights expressed in the genre includes property along with liberty, property may be forfeited by its abuse, as in Robin Hood's actions to redistribute wealth by taking from the rich to give to the poor. Members of the landed gentry rebel against the excesses of their class, fighting for the rights of the bourgeoisie as well as of the common people, often at their own expense. *The Mark of Zorro* explicitly brings military authorities into conflict with beneficent landowners, who are inspired by the initiative of an unknown individual avenging wrongs committed against the poor.

Since patriotism is expected and assumed as a motive, the hero is free to serve the legitimate needs of the state in the way he believes best. True loyalty and the obligations it imposes are owed less to a person than to a country, promoting the ideal of the kind of nation it should be and how the needs of its people should be met (McConnell, 110). In *If I Were King* (1938), François Villon, under sentence of death but temporarily granted royal power, opens the king's storehouses to the starving people, defining a country by its inhabitants, not by those few who govern. In adventure, the clarion call of king and country may often involve, even require, subversion. D'Artagnan and Miles Hendon remain patriots by following their conception of who is the rightful king, even when he is temporarily removed from power in *The Fifth Musketeer / Behind the Iron Mask* and *The Prince and the Pauper*, respectively.

Patriotism, a generally conservative belief, is transformed by the adventure genre into a rationale for leading insurgencies against an unjust government. The breaking of laws that are unjust, oppressive, or inhumane is sanctioned by the code, and the adventurer is lauded for disobeying directives that violate it, especially if issued by someone who has mishandled power or acquired it illegitimately. In fact it is the code that is the ultimate, true law, which the adventurer invariably upholds against subversion or a usurper (Roddick, 236–37; Bolitho, xvii). Hence the true patriots in adventure are often precisely those individuals who are frequently regarded as a traitor or outlaw, and either label is almost inherently part of the adventurer's existence (Green 1991, 29). Indeed, a ruler may be so capricious that the hero is shifted from knight to outlaw in a moment's whim. The outlaw hero, unlike the villain he opposes, remains a gentleman by continuing to observe the tenets of the code; temporary outcast status does not change his behavior. If his activities become "criminal," it is in name only, in the sense that it may be called criminal to help the unfortunate and fight those who manipulate power and position for their own ends (*The Mark of Zorro*) (Cohen, 33; Richards 1977, 8). *Kidnapped* (1917) introduces Alan Breck Stewart with an intertitle proclaiming him "an adventurer, an outlaw, and a gentleman," establishing the compatibility of all three characteristics. Unlike most genres, in adventure these labels carry no inherent condemnation. Such an outcome is usually the result of a breakdown in the political establishment, requiring the hero rectify the flaws in the system by going outside its norms (*Captain Blood*).

One of the adventurer's key ideals, stemming from the code, is that a fundamental covenant between the people and those who lead them binds the fabric of society together. The people and their rulers are united in mutual respect, the rulers accepting the rights of their subjects while the people demand the highest principles from their leaders. When the motivations and goals of a government or leader are humane and above reproach, they are upheld (*Captain Horatio Hornblower*). If the people's trust or expectations are betrayed, any obligation vanishes. They are not only entitled but also obligated to depose the incumbent and choose a new leader who will remain true (*Under the Red Robe; Two Years before the Mast*). This compact is almost a contract, promoting order and the rule of law, while guaranteeing freedom, since the discipline is provided from within the conscience of each member of society, rather than externally by force of arms (Welsh, 214–15). A ruler may earn loyalty by dispensing justice, but fealty is never simply pledged because of power or royal blood. An existing regime is not justified on the basis of incumbency, and the pragmatic support of anyone who might hold power is condemned as opportunistic. Empire and sea adventures, in particular, seriously trace the development of the talent for heroic leadership that makes some men ready to follow others (*Billy Budd; The Lost Patrol; The Crusades; El Cid; Zulu*).

Narratives follow a progression that carries the hero from idleness and sometimes apathy to political commitment. The hero is searching for personal and social freedom, a quest that may lead to such remote areas as the outposts of empire. Yet even on the margins of society, this life-style proves tenuous and threatened by a tyrant, whether it is Robin Hood or the threesome of *Gunga Din* breaking regulations to thwart a Thuggee uprising. While the adventurer is no coward or pacifist, he resists involvement at first. He presents a facade of cynicism or indifference to his milieu, either as a comparative innocent, unexposed to the evils of the world; as one who wistfully renounces his fighting days; or as a disinterested observer. Although attempting to preserve neutrality and a peaceful life, the adventurer who witnesses injustice realizes that not fighting oppression is tantamount to accepting it. The oppressed people are unable to overcome the depredations of the villain, so they appeal to the adventurer to lead their cause. Provoked by personal or social injustice, the adventurer reacts, abandoning reluctance to spearhead a revolt, leading or joining a freedom-loving, freedom-seeking band of loyal, brave souls who help to secure their own liberty and that of society. With righteousness on their side, they commit to an ideal worth fighting and even dying for, gladly daring life and limb in the service of an admirable cause that makes such sacrifices worthwhile. Assisting the popular uprising of an exploited class, fighting for the rights of the common people, the adventurer becomes the people's benefactor by winning the battle for them, and returning to them the freedom and justice that is rightly theirs (Cohen, 58; Nerlich 1987, 113; cf. Wright, 46). While evil may be ascendant temporarily, by pursuing the conflict to its end the proper state of affairs is restored. Invariably, as *Lorna Doone* (1922) notes, "The pent-up fury of a peaceful people carries all before it."

The hero of the uprising is largely selfless in his motives, never desiring power or a kingdom that does not rightly belong to him. Enemies are punished, but the leader remains aloof from any vicious reprisals that would bring him down to the villain's level. The mob, not the hero, kills his nemesis in *Scarmouche* (1923) and *The Black*

Book / Reign of Terror. In Drums / The Drum, rather than the English resident Carruthers, it is Prince Azim who kills Azim's treacherous uncle the usurper Ghul Khan. When the political goal is fulfilled, the hero steps aside in favor of the restored civil hierarchy, asking no compensation; followers are ready to disband and leave the governing to others (Hark, 15). Only if injustice again threatens may the leader be prevailed upon to once more carry the people's banner. Leaders who flaunt their positions to create personal advantage violates the adventurer's code and become ambiguous or evil figures, as with Yasmini in The Black Watch, Dravot in The Man Who Would Be King, Ahab in Moby Dick, or the title characters in The War Lord; Anne of the Indies; Captain Kidd; and Zarak.

The hero may have a personal interest at stake, however. Revenge sometimes becomes a subsidiary motive even when politics is foremost, with the hero trying to avenge a wrong perpetrated against his or her family (Captain Kidd; Captain from Castile; The Black Shield of Falworth). The hero also may be the victim of the villain's private vendetta, opposition to oppression causing misfortune to be inflicted on family or associates, further personalizing the conflict, as in The Black Arrow / The Black Arrow Strikes (1948). Yet personal motivations must become political before victory is achieved, as when Scaramouche unites forces with representatives of the French Revolution to defeat a murderous member of the nobility. While an avenger may fail to realize the full political ramifications, in either type of story the political pattern is much the same: the status quo is unbalanced by an injustice that must be corrected. The avenger's commitment to justice and duty are equal in fervor to that of the patriotic adventurer, both bringing justice closer.

Conflicts are acted out in a number of ways, depending on the nature of the injustice and the extent of the hero's alienation from society (Cohen, 52). They range from overthrowing a military dictatorship (The Mark of Zorro) to foiling Cardinal Richelieu's plan to undermine the French monarchy (The Three Musketeers) to returning a just king, such as Richard the Lion-Hearted, to power. If those with brutal, dictatorial tendencies gain power, the adventurer rebels and undertakes subversion (The Prince Who Was a Thief). Or a ruler may learn the burdens of his subjects; The Prince and the Pauper is primarily concerned with a fictitious episode that supposedly cements young Edward VI's consciousness to that of his people, involving him with adventurer Miles Hendon. A similar pattern occurs in efforts to defeat the threat of foreign enemies; the theme of national independence resonates throughout adventure (*Quebec*; *Captain Lightfoot*; *Fire over England*). The cause may even be unrelated to the hero's homeland, instead taken up from purely altruistic reasons—as when an Englishman impersonates King Rudolf, his cousin and double, to protect Ruritania from the plotting of Black Michael (*The Prisoner of Zenda*). As the *Son of Monte Cristo* proclaims, "When justice is crushed in one land, men of other lands spring up to defend it."

Frequently, the outcome of the revolt is that a former system of acknowledged justice and legitimacy is restored, nostalgically returning fairer rulers from previous years, exemplified when King Richard resumes the throne seized by Prince John in tales of Robin Hood and *Ivanhoe*. Some event often intervenes before the revolt is carried to its logical conclusion, and the two sides are brought together peacefully with a minimum of bloodshed. For example, the return of King Richard forces Prince John to relinquish his throne without a battle, or a change occurs in the status quo as a result of the uprising, causing the removal of the villain or the modification of the political system (*The Fighting Prince of Donegal*). Justice is frequently achieved through replacing corrupt men, oppression having been the result of an abuse of power. Injustice is overcome by the death or exile of those responsible, and correction becomes a matter of ousting a flawed officeholder: Philippe takes the throne from Louis in *The Fifth Musketeer / Behind the Iron Mask*, Umbopa succeeds Twala in *King Solomon's Mines*. In such cases, the hero's instincts are closer to those of a reformer or a rebel rather than a true revolutionary. The adventurer may not examine the underlying causes that allowed adverse conditions, especially when avenging a personal wrong; neither *Captain Blood* nor *The Sea Hawk* (1940) oppose the thriving slave trade that brought about their tortuous odysseys. Occasionally, the adventurer's actions may be parochial, failing to see issues in a broader context, and not always extended to outsiders who may be equally victims of injustice; the loyalty of the tribal mountain rebel *Zarak* is limited to his followers.

On occasion a usurper or tyrant has yet to gain control, and the adventurer follows conventional patriotism by defending his government against villains undermining legitimate authority (*Drums*). Either rebellion or conquest is celebrated by adventure, so long as an oppressive regime is overwhelmed, fighting oppression whether from the political right or left. Loyalty to the crown (or the raj), even if the monarch is foolish, may be a virtue since the ruler represents national hope and stability (*The Three Musketeers; Adventures of Don Juan*). Royalty with flaws is usually preferable to a conspiratorial grab for power, such as the duplicitous Black Michael makes in *The Prisoner of Zenda*. Also, the adventurer's code—gentlemanliness and duty to homeland—demands that the musketeers protect the queen, despite her indiscretions, from Cardinal Richelieu's schemes. Such pictures portray one more way of avoiding an abuse of power, by opposing a potential usurper instead of one already in place. While the restoration of "proper" authority may seem the more conservative manifestation of adventure's political current, there are radical overtones even here. For all the apparent fealty to the reformed establishment, henceforth it will have greater need to be justified. There is an awareness of the limitations on power, which, if breeched, may provoke a revival of the rebellious spirit.

Spiking an incipient revolt becomes as worthy as initiating one when it threatens a reversion to a more barbarous state, as in the French Revolution or the bloodthirsty colonial rebellions led by religious fanatics. The theme of preventing such an outcome—fighting various forms of terrorism in or out of government—unites such disparate adventure pictures as *Omar Khayyam; Gunga Din;* and *The Black Book / Reign of Terror*. The real counterweight to the radicalism to which adventure is prone is its inherent opposition to the threat of ultimate disorder and the social disintegration that would undercut the code. The potential for anarchy, of a society unregulated by law and civilized conduct, is regarded as a menace equal to despotism (Nerlich 1987, 393; Sobchack and Sobchack, 250). Authoritarianism and the radicalism it could provoke are twin dangers, and the adventurer's need for liberty and independence is never carried to its extreme. The chaos of unchecked emotions could overthrow the code that guides the adventurer's behavior, one reason that a monarchy, even with its faults, is often supported by such adventurers as the musketeers.

When the existing regime has become corrupt and tyrannical, the entire establishment is discarded in a break with the past that removes all vestiges of tradition and foretells a more democratic, egalitarian future. Nostalgia for the hierarchies of the past is left behind; authority has grown so base that all respect for tradition is lost. In such cases the lowest, most exploited classes rise to overthrow the existing regime, forming an exclusively proletarian revolution, usually in opposition not only to the aristocracy but also to the mediating influence of the middle class, including minor nobility or ship's officers. The notion that any man may be trusted with the sweeping power of a king or a ship's captain is rejected in favor of democratic institutions. A complete change is made as feudal systems are replaced so that the future offers new hope for better lives in unmistakably sociopolitical terms. This dream, however, must usually be realized in a setting removed from outside interference, such as the remote Pacific island of Pitcairn in *Mutiny on the Bounty* or the mythicized Lombardy of *The Flame and the Arrow,* or the battle for the Magna Carta that presages the American Revolution in *Rogues of Sherwood Forest.* With a status between the government and governed, the hero becomes an intermediary who checks the excesses of authority by the willingness to lead a popular rebellion temporarily, a reminder that ultimate power resides not with the rulers but with the people. Government is dependent on a satisfied populace that has before and may again overthrow a tyrant, especially now that a precedent has been set. The new governors know they will be carefully watched by the army of former rebels entrusted with guarding a country's welfare and customs. Though disbanded, they relish the opportunity to reassemble and fight again at the first sign of injustice, as in many Robin Hood sequels and their imitations, such as *Bandit of Sherwood Forest* and *Son of Ali Baba,* respectively. Even when achieving reintegration within society, a truly rebellious life, once lived, will be impossible to forget. One-time outlaws never fully lose their aura of nonconformity, although they may become part of the establishment, as Henry Morgan and his friends discover as governors of Jamaica in *The Black Swan.* In some cases the only government a former rebel trusts is one he controls, often through high office, as in *Captain Blood* (Rosenzweig, 46).

The apparent distinction between actual revolutions and restorations of authority all but vanishes on consideration of shared incidents. The difference is founded on only one relatively minor difference, whether the oppressor already has power or only threatens to secure it. Either way, the hero is placed in the position of an outlaw, opposing a strong force attempting to gain dominion, whether the sheriff of Nottingham, the cardinal's guards, Madame Guillotine, or an Oriental tribal chieftain. The hero and his mission remain constant: ready to defend the rights of others, to oppose tyrants and oppression no matter the source, whether the hero favors or opposes the incumbent, aiding a revolt or the establishment. In any case, the hero supports the underdog, the ill-treated and the displaced, against a powerful villain, as indicated by two seemingly opposite examples.

The Flame and the Arrow (1950) typifies both the personalization and the politicization of the conflicts in adventure. The movie begins in the darkest days of the twelfth century, as the local peasants, skilled at surviving, plot their liberation amidst Romanesque ruins serving as a forest hideout. At first their hoped-for champion, the archer Dardo (Burt Lancaster), fails them, preferring to avoid social commitment—until his son is kidnapped by Ulrich (Frank Allenby), the local Hessian overlord who has taken Dardo's former wife as mistress. Dardo's progression from political alienation to commitment parallels his move from outsider to an integrated member of a new, rebel society. Private motives combine with political ones, as Dardo discovers the purpose of patriotism by realizing that his son's plight is only one manifestation of Ulrich's tyranny over every phase of the people's lives. One of the memorable strengths of the movie is the emphasis on the psychological aspect of the conflict, with the *noir* style accenting the serious, darker elements of the story. Similarly, Ulrich's attempt to remold the boy according to Hessian standards, so that he will emulate his mother as a willing collaborator, is a metaphor for Ulrich's desire to subjugate the whole of Lombardy to foreign authoritarianism. (There are certainly parallels with memories of underground movements and collaboration in Europe during World War II, but as with most adventure films, the timely, "relevant" elements remain squarely within the typical generic patterns.)

During the ensuing struggle, others come to see the justice of the people's cause. Anne (Virginia Mayo), the niece of Ulrich, is abducted for revenge but becomes romantically attached to Dardo. By contrast, a pragmatic local nobleman, Alessandro (Robert Douglas), is initially dispossessed by Ulrich, then bribed to betray the peasants who gave him refuge. Ulrich and Alessandro are both oppressors, the former a tyrant, the latter a traitor. Through the use of tricks and disguise Dardo's band eventually gains access to Ulrich's castle. After a battle dominated by acrobatics and the homespun weapons so beloved of adventurers, Dardo kills Alessandro in a sword fight and saves his son by skillfully sending an arrow through Ulrich's heart. Dardo is united with his son and Anne in a love that will trample class lines and combine all levels of Lombardy society in freedom.

Offering an ostensibly more conservative view is *The Scarlet Pimpernel* (principally the 1934, 1948, and 1982 versions, but others along with sequels and imitations). Yet the dissimilarity vanishes on a closer consideration of the ideals of adventure that provide motivation. Like Dardo, Percy Blakeney as the Pimpernel is concerned with saving the defenseless, a universal trait of the adventurer, whether a pirate like *The Buccaneer* or the empire builders in *Flame over India / Northwest Frontier*. Through daring and organization, Percy epitomizes the admirable adventure hero defeating his cruel enemies with the minimal possible violence. While the victims in *The Scarlet Pimpernel* are no longer the peasants but the aristocrats, they are saved for the same reason. Many innocents, especially women and children, are threatened by tyranny, in this case the French Revolution's reign of terror. The members of the aristocracy are presented sympathetically, not because they belong to a social elite but because they are faced with arbitrary and ruthless extermination at the guillotine. The emphasis is not on the ethics of the French Revolution but whether Percy and his friends will escape the Revolutionary agent Chauvelin. To Chauvelin, Percy is an outlaw, whose exploits have made him a rebel fighting the status quo in France. Frustrating the forces behind the guillotine with his cunning and a small band of followers, Percy must also keep his identity secret even from his aristocratic French wife, by the same foppish, supercilious act with which he disarms French suspicion. Percy is, in effect, Zorro without the mask, and the difference between Percy, Zorro, or Dardo is a matter of context, not beliefs.

The terror Percy fights is presented as an instance of oppression more bloody than any other, even more cruel than the social system the revolution overthrew. The French Revolution occupies a unique niche within the genre as the epitome of the event to be feared, a governmental change more destructive than constructive and an affront to the standards of the code. The dream of an orderly progression toward a just and democratic society is replaced by mob violence, spawning a dictatorship that violates the very rights and liberties it claims to champion. The new rulers prove even more heartless than the aristocrats of old, savagely fueling the popular desire for revenge, violating the code by trampling the tradition of chivalry that was the one redeeming virtue of the aristocrats. This glorification of revenge allows the French Revolution to be judged an affront to the code. In such other films as *Swords and the Woman* / *I Will Repay*; *A Tale of Two Cities*; *The Black Book*; and *The Purple Mask*, the French Revolution is the exception to the relatively bloodless, respectable rebellions lauded in adventure. Yet the revolution is supported by *Scaramouche* and *The Fighting Guardsman*, which depicts the king as a greedy, overweight, lecherous fool, unable to adapt to the changing times, whose "whole being is filled with the venom of despotism."

A third example from another adventure form synthesizes these tendencies. The historical incident of the mutiny on board the *Bounty* has been the subject of numerous works, including the famous trilogy by Charles Nordhoff and James Norman Hall that inspired the 1935 and 1962 screen interpretations, *Mutiny on the Bounty*; other film versions include two made in Australia, *The Mutiny on the Bounty* (1915) and *In the Wake of the Bounty* (1933), along with *The Bounty* (1984). The many tellings of the *Bounty* mutiny, and similar adventure stories indicate the resonance of its fundamental theme of revolution and renewal in a new, preordained land. The 1935 movie is one of the most archetypal, and political, adventure films, demonstrating the persistence of the overriding ideological beliefs expressed in the genre. Even the French Foreign Legion tale *Adventure in Sahara* (1938) is a desert remake of *Mutiny on the Bounty*, indicating how the same basic plot could be utilized in various adventure forms.

Mutiny on the Bounty opens with First Mate Fletcher Christian (Clark Gable) seizing men to serve on the vessel, raiding a tavern indiscriminately to impress men into the crew, even separating a newlywed couple expecting a baby. The first sight on deck is equally brutal, as Captain Bligh (Charles Laughton) orders the flogging of a sailor already dead from punishment. Combining a sea voyage, exploration, imperialism, and ultimately a revolt, the journey of the *Bounty* becomes an odyssey that takes the film's protagonists far from their usual existence, prompting them to act upon and emulate the beliefs of adventure.

At the beginning of the journey the ship is without a hero, Christian filling the vacuum as the voyage progresses. He initially obeys the captain, although not sharing Bligh's malevolent streak, and is tormented by his duty to acquiesce. Bligh has lost all grasp of hu-

The cruelty of Captain Bligh (Charles Laughton, center) extends not only to ordinary sailors but the higher ranks as well; here Fletcher Christian (Clark Gable) holds the ship's surgeon (Dudley Digges) when he dies after being forced to leave his sick bed to witness the flogging of seaman Burkitt (Donald Crisp), in *Mutiny on the Bounty* (1935).

manity, treating his men barbarically, obviating any loyalty due him. Bligh's error is not in his position as captain or in the need to impose order on the crew but rather in his unremitting refusal to respect the human dignity of the sailors. Christian is a cynical, experienced man, considerate but unquestioning of the status quo, but Bligh's excesses force him to discover the need for ideals. As months pass, the tyranny grows too extreme, and Bligh's conduct goes beyond what can be hopefully rectified by an appeal to the admiralty on the return to port.

The narrative of *Mutiny on the Bounty* seeks to unify Fletcher Christian's character and live up to his surname, by reconciling his two halves, the gentle and liberal side with the traits that tie him to the ship's hierarchy. Christian ultimately upholds the adventurer's code, to protect the weak and defenseless, realizing his duty is to the crew members who are suffering. Bligh has broken the covenant by

The adoption of new values by Christian (Clark Gable) is culminated by the visit to Tahiti, where he is torn between his love for the island and a native girl (Movita), and his duty to return to the ship and support Bligh's oppression, in *Mutiny on the Bounty* (1935).

abusing his authority, and Christian's respect for tradition is overcome by the need for radical action. There is only one alternative, a mutiny that will make the crew members permanent outlaws and sever all ties with their homeland. At sea, a small-scale allegory of revolution occurs, espousing the right of a people to free themselves from oppression, reflecting the same political view as the land-based swashbuckler or the sea-based pirate. The kingdom in the sea adventure is the ocean-going vessel on which the captain reigns; it is totalitarianism that drives his subjects to mutiny, no less than Robin Hood is forced to fight the despotism of Prince John.

At the same time, the mutiny is controlled, the sailors only turning on those who are unjust and never randomly taking reprisals. Christian persuades the crew not to kill the officers who are now overthrown, instead ordering them set adrift in a small boat with supplies. By contrast, Bligh's subsequent achievement in steering the loyal men to safety is negated by his motivation to avenge himself on the mutineers. Christian skillfully wins and maintains the loyalty of the ship's company without the recourse to punishment

Bligh used so freely, finding an ultimate equality between all shipmates. An improved life for all is founded upon the establishing of a settlement on Pitcairn's Island, and Fletcher Christian's mutineers are safely out of reach of British ships.

Unknown to the mutineers on Pitcairn's, the reaction back home is far from a condemnation of their course; Captain Bligh is discredited by his peers for his excesses of discipline. The navy is redeemed when a royal pardon is forthcoming for the loyal Roger Byam, a victim of Bligh's vindictiveness. Byam returns to service and is gladly welcomed aboard a new ship, indicating that Bligh's ruthlessness will never be repeated. The picture announces in both the foreword and conclusion that because of the mutiny, "a new understanding between officers and men has come to the fleet." The very extremity of the mutiny and its provocation is shown as bringing about change in seafaring laws. Even though mutiny is the only answer on board the isolated ship, there is hope for a reformed order, the successful rebellion partly containing yet also thoroughly justifying the actions taken.

Some might argue that through narrative and setting, adventure films render their politics irrelevant to audiences. Adventure movies may be simultaneously radical in their politics and still serve as a perfect bourgeois entertainment, satisfying and thus containing the need for rebellion in a constructive and fulfilling way. The politics of adventure occur within the narrative, with the cause usually won during the course of the film. The potential radicalism may be contained by apparently resolving the "call to arms" for the audience, making it unnecessary for spectators to carry the "message" outside of the plot. The liberation ethic of many adventure movies is thereby robbed of most of the force it might otherwise engender. Adventure helps to secure the comforting belief that there is a direction and logic of progress to history (Bloch, 143).

However, such a dismissal would be too simplistic a reading. The readiness to attack authoritarian rule may both acquire emotional power and be deprived of some of its immediacy by its placement in a historical milieu and/or distant geographical locale. The more fictionalized the setting, the greater the latitude to portray a political establishment as evil, with unjust courts and cruel and corrupt officials all justifying a revolution—actions that might not be shown or tolerated (by studios, censors, or audiences) in a less fictive genre (Davis, 27). As well, since the adventure philosophy is far from traditional liberalism and only indirectly related to the contemporary political context, adventure's radicalism could be permitted.

Adventure films reconcile the often antithetical doctrines of protecting individual rights and the obligation to a social order. The advance of freedom balances with the simultaneous need for strong leadership and patriotism in adventure's vision of history. Adventure films belong completely neither to the left or the right; they project portions of both viewpoints. Liberation and conservatism are blended, compatibly, each making the other more palatable, lending a polysemy to the politics of adventure. (Nowhere is this more apparent than in the genre's attitude toward colonialism, the subject of the next chapter.) The genre mixes adversarial elements, the narrative sometimes contradicting the tenor of its political statement. Classic Hollywood films traditionally offer mixed messages; just as women's films are often recouped at the end into traditional lifestyles by the marriage of the heroine, so adventure offers a final scene that shows justice triumphant in a new establishment. Yet in both genres, it is the scenes of revolt and independence from the status quo that are memorable, whether they portray an outlaw hero who causes a revolution or a woman who creates a life apart from men. Despite the mitigating factors, what ultimately matters in adventure pictures is the sanctioning of revolts as heroic outlaws fight oppression and bring about political change, themes not found in other genres. The balance is weighted toward the radical potential, with the genre inherently favoring fundamental alterations in the status quo and the foundations of class and moneyed, established power on which so much of society is grounded.

CHAPTER 8 Colonialism and Adventure

The mixing of seemingly incompatible liberal and conservative ideas that is typical of adventure (and of Hollywood films generally) is nowhere more apparent than in its depiction of colonialism. Empire, fortune hunter, and to a lesser extent the sea and Oriental swashbuckler types frequently use Far Eastern locales, where the presence of imperialism gives a more conservative tinge to adventure's basic theme of the struggle between insurgencies and the status quo. Yet the relationship between adventure and colonial images is a complex one, not prone to preconceptions or easy generalizations. Imperialism was widely justified or tacitly accepted in movies through the 1940s, although by the 1950s adventure films were clearly changing, climaxing in the revisionist trend of the 1970s. When seen today, many of the older, classical films display certain backward characterizations that are now universally repugnant to spectators of all races and backgrounds. However, the movies themselves also continue to appeal to audiences and are still viewed on television and videotape. Even when the context is remembered, the suspenseful images of heroes in peril retain their power to beckon film audiences (Fisher, 329). The reason is basic to the paradoxical nature of the genre. While offering many racist undercurrents in portraying Eastern characters, colonial adventure movies have long satisfied a desire for escape, becoming one of the principal avenues for presenting views (however warped) of foreign cultures and distant lands to curious and receptive audiences. Both of these currents must be recognized; the genre is on the one hand guilty of numerous demeaning stereotypes, while at the same time manifesting an enlightened eagerness to experience different life-styles.

The pernicious results of the Western movement to colonize Eastern lands are widely known and need no elaboration here. Imperialism has been an integral part of global history for centuries, and the world is still grappling with its unfortunate consequences. Rather than point out the obvious variance from historical fact of colonial adventure films, it is more productive to map the various ways in which the genre depicts the multiple forms of imperialism. The films themselves are most fully comprehended by examining how the myth of colonial settings and native peoples is constructed through narrative devices, characterizations, and conventions. Like most classical film genres, in adventure a fictional world is constructed with little relation to the actual facts of imperialism. The fascination with foreign lands has widely impacted the popular culture of all Western nations, and one of its manifestations was in the movies. Eager to entice audiences into the theater, filmmakers search for the most popular myths to dramatize, often borrowing from other popular culture certain suppositions and narrative patterns of what is distinctively "Oriental" and "other-worldly." Indeed, many empire adventures, like other forms of the genre, seldom attempt to reflect historical fact, instead serving an allegorical function in depicting the facets of political conflicts.

Not all genres utilizing colonial settings operate in the same manner as adventure, and some embody very different attitudes. Love stories emphasize the concern with miscegenation, as in *The Sheik*; *The Rains Came*; *White Cargo*; *Bhowani Junction*; *The Rains of Ranchipur*; *A Passage to India*; and *Heat and Dust*; and the 1984 television miniseries *The Far Pavilions* and *The Jewel in the Crown*. In the post–World War II era, this genre, combined with melodrama, has emerged as the favored form in which to plumb the worst aspects of colonialism, a sociologically far more revisionist view of imperial life than was ever explored through adventure. More directly political films, from *The Guns of Batasi* to *Conduct Unbecoming* to *Gandhi* to *Mister Johnson*, explore different facets of imperialism in a less generic context. By contrast, other forms display the crude, blatant racial superiority sometimes mistakenly associated with adventure. Thrillers with native characters in Europe or Europeans abroad reveal the fear of a Fu Manchu–style "yellow peril." Similarly, jungle movies, despite their generally up-to-date temporality and frequent mixture with other generic forms, account for the worst native stereotypes found in filmmaking.[1]

In adventure films, by contrast, empire is a place of opportunity, not the menace it appears to be in thrillers or melodrama. Adventure offers colonial settings primarily as a site for courageous deeds against a background often more mythic than factual in its historical details. Adventure luxuriates in appealing, romantic locales: faraway or isolated places, distant both spatially and temporally, unexplored or belonging to a time long past. The range of iconic possibilities and the genre's vast terrain, taking place in almost any corner of the globe, is one of adventure's enticements to the viewer (Bolitho, 109). As the story moves away from what is familiar to the heroes or principal audience, the genre revels in the characteristics of the country and the distinct life-style and customs of its people. Colonial adventures often incorporate documentary-style location footage, as in *Killers of Kilimanjaro; King Solomon's Mines; The Lives of a Bengal Lancer; The Naked Prey; Outpost in Morocco; Sanders of the River; Stanley and Livingstone; Trader Horn;* and *Zulu Dawn*. Curiosity becomes a prime appeal, and the genre is associated with unexpected challenges amidst exotic surroundings promising a narrative outside the ordinary world (White, 98). Regions visited in imperial narratives range from India, Africa, and Arabia to the "New World" (*Captain from Castile; Mayflower: The Pilgrims' Adventure*), the Orient (*Marco Polo; Genghis Khan; 55 Days at Peking*), the South Seas (*Drums of Tahiti*), and beyond to unsettled lands, from *Scott of the Antarctic* to the uncharted islands of Robinsonades. The very names of the lands—from Bengal to Morocco—imply the appeal of the exotic, and imperial speech is studded with phrases from the local language, whether *sahib, bwana, effendi, salaam,* or references to the will of Allah or the

The colonial setting allows adventure to emphasize the lure of the East, as in *King of the Khyber Rifles* (1954).

beard of the prophet. Adventure offers a largely positive portrayal of foreign lands and cultures; the danger becomes localized in the potential for a revolt.

Just as adventure leads to many lands, the colonial adventurer may be from a variety of nations. The colonial urge was not unique to any one country or its tradition, each country taking as much land as its explorers and the competition allowed. Many of the major powers of the time participated, including England, France, Germany, Spain, Italy, and the United States. While adventure literature, written in the particular language of each of these countries, often served as a form of propaganda for imperial aims, adventure films portray the colonial efforts of different countries almost interchangeably (Green 1990, 14–15). The way in which films could serve as propaganda for the imperial aims of any particular country was limited by their intended international audiences, which included many of the countries that were rivals for control of those same colonies. Movies were shown not only throughout Europe but also in the very countries of their setting, such as India or Asia. Only rarely did films risk becoming obvious support for the aims of a single country; the most exceptional case is the Alexander Korda cycle from England in the late 1930s (*Sanders of the River; Drums / The Drum; The Four Feathers*). More often empire adventure offers a mix of characters, such as British brothers joining the French Foreign Legion in *Beau Geste*.

Most studies of colonialism and adventure in various forms of popular culture have emerged from England, concentrating on that country's history and image, with the result that empire adventure has often been looked upon almost exclusively as a form of British propaganda.[2] However, Hollywood's interest in movies depicting empire was inspired by contemporary imperialism, together with the United States' own growing role on the world scene. The inclination for stories with British backgrounds or supporting her politics can be explained more convincingly by the fact that during the peak years of adventure filmmaking, Britain was the dominant imperial power. Further, it was important commercially that Hollywood not alienate the English market, not only because British ticket sales could provide the margin of profitability but also, on occasion, because of the connotations that a picture might have for global political considerations (*The Sea Hawk* [1940]). The reverse was also true;

because of the common language, British films were frequently imported into the United States, and the presentation in British adventure movies had to be adjusted to ensure their appeal to American audiences.

Empire adventures were produced because a formula was found that won widespread commercial success. Hollywood was far less concerned with any political purpose than with the genre's consistent success at the box office. The film community in general seems to have expended little thought on the political content of adventure, and the same may also have been true of the audience. Adventure pictures were hardly intended for or received by audiences as propaganda. There would surely have been little political point in making imperial adventure films during the actual dismemberment of empires, yet they were produced into the postwar era. With the revisionist trend after World War II, there was never any hesitation in accepting negative portrayals of British imperialism either on the part of producers or of audiences in either the United States or England, whether in Hollywood's *King of the Khyber Rifles* or Britain's *The Long Duel*.[3] India and other exotic lands of the Orient were favored as settings for empire adventures primarily because of their intrinsic appeal, with their tradition of mysterious allure for the West (Richards 1973, 3). North Africa and Arabia also became a popular setting, where France held sway, through the rugged, romantic tradition of the Foreign Legion. Audiences were concerned with the territory shown, not who administered it.

While adventure films attract audiences through the promise of a provocative and edifying (but not didactic) visit to another side of the world, in the story this experience has a similar effect on the white hero. The empire adventurer has a close relationship with his surroundings. In empire adventures, especially, the hero is often introspective, filled with self-doubts, and agonizing over his duty; frequently the adventurous life is embarked upon to obscure some shameful episode in the past or a character flaw, as in Foreign Legion films and *The Four Feathers*, respectively. Colonial adventurers desire to live in a different realm, hastening to outposts along the frontier as soon as the opportunity arises. Traditional pleasures, including family and the comforts of civilization, are willingly and even eagerly forfeited to indulge this existence.

Colonialism is part of a larger aspect of adventure: the obsession with exploration of unknown lands, penetrating jungles, encountering "savages" and overcoming such characteristics of the wilds as cannibalism and Thuggee. This is one of his paradoxes; he is drawn to the site of what he perceives as the primitivism he finds both attractive and abhorrent, instincts he must suppress in himself and those around him. The adventurer never completely loses the fear that the natives will return to the local traditions that the imperial power has attempted to overcome. The colonial challenge is regarded as not only good for the native but also a worthwhile test of western culture (Katz, 44). The colonial experience is a process of self-questioning and self-discovery from which the empire builder emerges with a new awareness, heroic in compassion and understanding (Meyers, x). The real force of nature is not any native he may encounter, but the weakness and failings the adventurer fears he will find in himself, such as cowardice or insanity in *Lord Jim* and *The Lost Patrol*, respectively. The adventurers' trek to the edge of settlements becomes a way of bringing out the best within themselves, overcoming their own weaknesses. This inner discovery is the intangible compensation for life in far-off lands; the material rewards are few if any (*Beau Geste*) (Katz, 49–50). As the adventurer dispenses his civilization and its perceived benefits wherever he goes, leading such a life becomes inherently more and more difficult as wild land diminishes. This alternation of civilization and the primitive might be labeled the Robinson Crusoe dialectic: the empire builder pursues distant, atavistic lands, transforming them into his own image, before departing to new regions to repeat the process (Noyce, 46).

Adventurers are partial to seeing and exploring the world for themselves, having the explorer's curiosity to break the ordinary conventions of day-to-day existence. There is the desire to experience life to its fullest, exchanging the predictable for the unknown, broadening horizons by traveling to remote regions (*Adventures of Marco Polo*) (Nerlich 1987, 272–73). The odyssey commences when the adventurer leaves the security of his birthplace to roam, rarely settling long in one place, so that home is simultaneously everywhere and nowhere (Burnett, xi; Zweig, 32). The hero takes the necessary risks to see the world not as a tourist but living as the natives live. Frequently this leads to defiance of traditional limitations and the willingness to incur the contempt of those less imaginative. Overseas the hero experiences the freedom to practice the adventurer's skills, defeating pirates, natives, or mutinous crews, achieving a measure of heroism. At home, however, that same enterprising spirit is frustrated or deflected, as with *The Sea Hawk* (1940) (Gove, 163).

One of the typical ways of concealing the effects of imperialism was to portray colonial lands as a haven for oppressed, exploited European refugees. As Cortés pronounces at the end of *Captain from Castile*: "Before this venture is concluded, gentlemen, we will taste the joys of victory or the miseries of defeat. Many will die in the days that lie ahead. But those who survive will one day return to their homeland, rich in wisdom and gold, exonerated by his majesty, and forever secure in the knowledge that they have participated in the opening of a new world." Adventure in the colonies, leaving home to engage in exploration or military service, or reading about those who did, are fundamental expressions of a desire for freedom. Adventure stories written in the age of European imperialism—and the subsequent films—charted a very literal path of escape. Those drawn to empire range from impoverished aristocrats to younger sons and black sheep of noble families and the middle and lower classes, who found the European milieu unsatisfying (Katz, 61). For these people, there was limited economic opportunity at home, a surplus population, and little hope for a change in fortune. Adventure served as a safety valve, permitting men, and women, to escape confining social stratification and preemptive class positioning and the resultant economic fate. By adventuring, one could leap over social and economic barriers and be judged by qualities such as valor and courage, rather than ancestors and family. Adventurers found a new, more egalitarian society (at least for whites) in dangerous lands far removed from the influence of home. Colonial service, usually in the military—whether officer or lower ranks—offered a career possibility that carried a respected position and basic income to those who lacked one or both. Adventure was not an easy escape, and only a few were sufficiently adept to meet the challenge; but that was what made it viable, and enviable, for the select few who succeeded in this escape.

The empire adventurer is often motivated as much by a desire to retreat from his own world as to conquer new ones, and the remote environment of a colonial region offers the best opportunity to realize these hopes and ambitions. The colonies become an alternative, even a refuge, offering a position of security never available in the homeland. Europeans such as *Lord Jim* may be dissatisfied with the company of their own race, leaving a violent, treacherous West to find a new life in the Orient. In *Mutiny on the Bounty* (1935), a colonial mentality underlies the vessel's original mission as well as the mutineers' flight, and the Tahitians are largely perceived through the positive effect they have on the Europeans. Faced with insurmountable injustice aboard ship, the crew is inspired by the idyll of the South Seas, so different from England. As the Spaniards of *Captain from Castile* go to Mexico and find freedom from the Inquisition, they initiate the process that will eventually bring the same tyranny to the Indians. The adventurer does not notice that his own search for liberty may very well impinge on the liberty of others, and this inherent contradiction results in the ultimate deficiency of the adventurous activity.

Imperialism is rarely an overt goal of the adventurers in films but instead practiced almost subconsciously. Rather than casting the hero as a forthright jingoist promoting expansionism, empire becomes a by-product of the adventurer's desire to live in remote lands on the edge of civilization (Rowse, 55). In *Captain from Castile*, when Pedro and Coatl meet again in Mexico, it is only the friend and former slave who can finally force upon Pedro the question of why the Spaniards are invading his country. Pedro has not rationalized this moral quandary, admitting that if their roles were reversed, he too would fight the invader, and the subject is never again mentioned in the movie. Just as the empire builder's overt goal is peacekeeping rather than conquest, and bringing the advances of the modern world, so the spectator becomes less concerned with the literal political result. The significance of imperialism and the military life are elided in the genre by presenting colonialism as less an object in itself than as a means for westerners to experience the lure of the unknown. This quality is emphasized by having the adventurer be an individualist, even in the military; he is often ready to disobey orders and never fully subordinated to any particular foreign policy.

The satisfaction of the empire builder in the colony does not derive from exercising authority within the governing hierarchy. The colonizer is presented not as an exploiter but as bringing a better life to the lands he rules. Invariably outnumbered, the empire builder tries to avoid armed confrontations, maintaining sovereignty not so much through military power as through moral force and an adept strategy. Empire builders regard themselves as protectors of the people as much as do swashbucklers, if in a more paternal fashion. In the manner of the swashbuckler, fighting oppression with a certain sense of noblesse oblige, the empire builder's concern for the land and its peoples leads him proudly to defend the natives from the ravages of dissipated rajahs, Kali-worshipping priests, or pillaging bandits. Colonialism is portrayed as offering better treatment for the poor and those of low caste; no longer do the strong rule supreme over the defenseless people. With rebellions invariably more evil than the status quo, malignant, oppressive insurgencies are depicted as once more being turned back—just as in swashbucklers such as *The Prisoner of Zenda* or *The Three Musketeers*. Even the fortune hunter, who proposes to exploit rather than govern the colony, growing rich off its spoils, usually discovers his responsibility to "the ethic of empire" (*Plymouth Adventure; The Black Rose*) (Richards 1973, 12, 15). In this way the colonial endeavor and imperial presence are justified, portrayed as a natural outgrowth of the adventurer's code, especially the interest in social justice, political fairness, and patriotism.

In adventure pictures, this is the "white man's burden": dispelling the clouds of primitivism by virtue of their occupying presence. "White" referred not only to race but to modern civilization and its moral standards (Katz, 133). The clash of cultures is acknowledged, but the genre assumes natives want the supposed benefits of imperialism, as in *The Real Glory* or *Drums*, although the spread of Western ideas is questioned in recent revisionist pictures such as *The White Dawn* and *The Royal Hunt of the Sun*. An imposed but fair outside government removes the threat of conflict by rival tribes or sects. Imperialism is portrayed as carrying Western values to an Orient that may be civilized and enchanting but plagued by a decadence that curses its people. The West brings liberty to the East, as when Bosambo learns "the secret of good government" from *Sanders of the River*, "A king should not be feared but loved by his people." Bosambo is supported by the British because he is a just ruler and accepts colonialization, whereas his rival Mofalaba seeks to oust the British in order to tyrannize the tribes (Richards and Aldgate, 18–19; Richards 1978, 128; Nerlich 1987, 209).

After the adventurer's search for liberty has led to this new land, the colony is adopted as a second or even permanent home. Many empire heroes acquire a greater attachment to the colony than to their homeland. Adventurers are reluctant to leave, preferring to die abroad rather than to face eventual retirement and a return to a land of their birth that now seems foreign. The affection between colonies, their people, and the empire builder is portrayed as vital and real; in their movie biographies, heroic role models such as Clive, Gordon, Livingstone, and Rhodes gladly sacrifice their lives and energy in their all-consuming love of their adopted country (Katz, 7; Richards 1973, 138). Such figures come to represent the land they inhabit to those at home, such as Richard Burton in *Mountains of the Moon.*

The Occidental character is pleased because colonial service provides the desired opportunity for interaction with native peoples and their cultures. Although this sentiment may sometimes be tinged with condescension, there is a willingness to learn from the unfamiliar locale, coming to understand them, as *Kim* does with the lama (Meyers, x). Transcending differences, whites often learn to see the world from the viewpoint of the natives, becoming their champion regardless of the lack of understanding displayed by other characters in the film, as in *The Long Duel* and *Out of Africa* (Noyce, 200). There is frequent intermarriage with local citizens, and interracial love receives favorable treatment, even during the 1930s and 1940s, when the subject was forbidden by the production code. Such romances may fail or end in marriage, but are never treated as miscegenation, as they would be in melodrama and other genres (cf. Richards 1973, 196–200). Examples include *Around the World in 80 Days; The Black Watch; Suez; Adventures of Marco Polo* (1938); *Captain from Castile* (Cortés and Doña Marina); *Outpost in Morocco; Ten Tall Men;* and *His Majesty O'Keefe.* Usually, the lovers are a white man and a native woman, although *King of the Khyber Rifles* is a notable exception to the norm. The private, personal nature of these romances prevents the couple from becoming a metaphor of the power relation between the races, and they are typical movie love stories rather than another method of white domination of the native. Such unions are symbolic of the social mixture that results in a more egalitarian outcome, in a manner similar to the convention of a noble wedding a commoner in the swashbuckler or pirate adventure.

Traditional practices, including Indian durbars and pigsticking, are encouraged by the Europeans (Richards 1974, 87). This attitude preserves the facade of the continuity of peaceful native life under

In *Outpost in Morocco* (1948), an Arabian princess (Marie Windsor; Maria Ouspenskaya behind) and a Legionnaire (George Raft) fall in love, although he must oppose her father's plot to end French rule.

colonialism, and whites have the opportunity to compete and prove their skill and courage in native sports. Adventurers, including those of the military, find comfort in the teaching of an alien, non-Western environment (*The Sea Hawk* [1924]; *The Black Rose*; *King of the Khyber Rifles*; *Lord Jim*; *Khartoum*; *The Long Duel*; *Shogun*). Here they have the liberty to entertain sympathies and beliefs that may not be acceptable in their homeland, as with Gordon's mystical sensibilities in *Khartoum*. The empire builder is often alienated from the Christianity he supposedly serves and becomes involved in the local religion (Katz, 87). For many imperialists, Christianity had already been replaced by a more patriotic religion, a belief in manifest destiny and the duty to enlighten distant and primitive lands (Richards 1973, 10, 12). Some of the so-called Christian saints of empire, such as Clive, Gordon, Junipero Serra, or Livingstone, were visibly nonconformist in their beliefs or approach to empire and missionary work, a fact highlighted in such media biographies as *Khartoum*; *7 Cities of Gold*; *Stanley and Livingstone*; and the tele-

Occidentals may adopt Oriental customs; an Englishman (Milton Sills) flees the injustice of his homeland
and joins the Barbary pirates, becoming a Moslem, in
The Sea Hawk (1924).

vision miniseries *The Search for the Nile.* Conversion and change
from native tradition are seldom accomplished through any effort of
Christian missionaries but by the adventurer's cunning imperial
strategies; adventure films rarely offer Christianity as a primary
historical justification for empire building. Despite the standard
negative appearance of such faiths as Kali worship, adventure overall
finds Eastern religions intriguing, only disdaining them when they
manifest a perceived primitivism. Islam, especially, may create a
conducive environment for adventurers of East and West to meet on

the common ground of chivalry and mutual respect, and only a fanatic bent on conquest is capable of destroying this unique amity among gentlemen adversaries, as in *The Wind and the Lion*, *El Cid*, or films on the Crusades (Green 1979, 291).

This aspect of adventure has a certain sympathy toward mysticism: foregrounding the idea of intuition and cryptic, unexplained subjective insight. The nineteenth-century imperial wave coincided with Darwinism and a corresponding infusion of Eastern religion influenced the West in such movements as theosophy and its descendants. Such an interchange, together with raising imperialism to a substitute dogma for Christianity itself, made possible the popularization of Eastern occultism and religion in the adventure novels of H. Rider Haggard, Rudyard Kipling, and Talbot Mundy (Brantlinger, 245–46; Richards 1973, 14–15). Mysticism even appears on the border of such largely European adventures as *The Corsican Brothers*, *Black Magic*, and *The Master of Ballantrae*, with the semisupernatural powers James Durie learned in India. Mysticism is part of the larger fascination with India and the Orient on which empire adventures rely for much of their audience appeal, as in *Kim*'s search for a holy river with his lama, and *Desert Legion* with its parallels to Shangri-La (cf. Anderson, 258). In recent decades the emphasis on this aspect of adventure has grown more pronounced as part of the willingness to depict the native sympathetically—progressing from, for instance, *Adventures of Marco Polo* (1938) to *The Black Rose* to *The Royal Hunt of the Sun* to *The Mission* (1986). Perhaps no adventure film foregrounds mysticism more than *The Man Who Would Be King*. Drawn to seek wealth in a fabled land beyond India, expatriate imperialists find that relics of their Masonic brotherhood initiate them into the fulfillment of an ancient prophecy that leads to a throne and ultimate death. Mystical motifs tend to tone down the otherwise imperialistic temperament of empire adventure; by partaking of the philosophy of conquered states, empire builders make clear that they are drawn to the Far East not only for conquest but also for a new way of living and thinking, preferable to any hitherto known.

In adventure pictures, there is no sense of "never the twain shall meet"; the attitude is quite the opposite, especially in revisionist empire films (cf. Richards 1973, 187–220). East and West have already met and intermingled through the colonial activity. Racial compatibility is indicated by the ease with which many Europeans and natives live side by side. The disgruntled few in the genre are intolerant, narrow-minded colonial officers or those natives who wish to dominate their fellow countrymen, not who simply resent the foreign presence. The heroes of colonial adventure dramas are inevitably those individuals who best understand and adapt to the land in which they live, adjusting to the unique circumstances of the culture and bringing together people of all races. This ability becomes prized, and often a newcomer must learn to love the land and its people as much as the veteran. The greatest adventure hero is one who, like Gordon or King of the Khyber Rifles, combines the best of both East and West and comes the closest to treating natives as equals. Gordon of *Khartoum* and Livingstone of *Stanley and Livingston* achieve transcendence as historical figures because of their extraordinary identification with Africa, attaining mythic status because they are portrayed as men *of* the country and its people, not *apart from* them.

Worthy opponents are respected as fellow warriors, from Sikhs to Zulus (Green 1979, 289–90; Richards 1973, 203). Surat Khan in *The Charge of the Light Brigade* (1936), otherwise villainous, honors the code by repaying the debt he owes Geoffrey Vickers and setting him free, even as the other English are massacred at Jakoti. Conflicts between natives and empire builders demonstrate the mutual esteem that may develop among them, as in *Zarak, The Bandit of Zhobe*, and the distinctly revisionist *The Long Duel* (1967) (Richards 1973, 206). *The Long Duel* contrasts the approaches of two British administrators toward a revolt in India. One officer viciously suppresses the insurrection, regardless of its cause or cost. Another, Young, tries to understand his opponent and persuade both sides to negotiate. (Young is portrayed by the eminently moderate and heroic Trevor Howard, while his British adversaries are personified by the irascible Harry Andrews.) Like T. E. Lawrence, Young admires his adopted land and is thus regarded by the English as a virtual traitor, employed only because he is the only officer who can defeat the native rebel leader Sultan (Yul Brynner). However, Young is unique among his race, and he is not able to convince the other British to share his progressive views. Similarly, Sultan feels betrayed by the excessive zeal of his own followers and has difficulty controlling the habit of his bandit allies to murder and pillage. The fighting ends in a draw, and because it is Sultan who needs a victory, the British continue to rule. Young and Sultan come to feel a comradeship greater than their rapport among others of their own race. The dying Sultan turns over care of his young son to his sympathetic adversary as a sign of his regard. Although Young is the principal hero, all sympathy, including Young's, is with Sultan and his cause, creating a truly anti-imperial empire adventure.

Despite the openness to foreign cultures, there are contradictory strains. In portraying colonialism favorably, almost unavoidable racist overtones come to the fore in the presentation of native characters. Regrettably, adventurers have more open minds toward foreign lands and culture and to the people in general rather than to the specific native individual they encounter. Colonial adventure films need to be recognized both as products of the genre as well as emanating from, and portraying, the past, with the primary years of production the 1920s through the 1950s. During these years, the Western notion of equality extended to whites but not to other races. Stereotypes were the norm in Hollywood, and adventure was typical in this regard rather than unique. As well, adventure is also a genre seldom noted for its depth of characterization of individuals of any race. Characters are usually depicted two dimensionally, at best, regardless of whether they represent the Occident or Orient.

There are other factors that diminish the openness of colonial adventure. The genre requires an intriguing atmosphere, place, and situations, yet confines them within a predictable, formalized ritual. There is little or no attempt to teach the audience about these lands or the time period through the film. In adventure, exotic locales are most often used as backgrounds to familiar stories; actual entry into foreign cultures is limited. (At the same time, it should be remembered, adventure treats nearly every European country almost interchangeably, with a resemblance in both narrative patterns and atmosphere.) The exoticism of the Orient also mixes with heroes of a reassuringly familiar nationality, concentrating on the exploits of white men. The audience perceives the story through the viewpoint of its surrogate, the Western representative of empire in the movie, even when the emphasis is on the difference in locale. While the empire builder becomes acclimatized to his surroundings, he must never lose his own sense of national identity, as when *The Man Who Would Be King* disastrously begins to believe in his own myth. The films dwell on the excesses of such native rituals as India's suttee or the murderous sect of Kali or Thuggee (Richards 1973, 211). Knowledge of the colony's culture, whether the local language, customs, or religion, may also turn into part of the imperial arsenal: the white heroes manipulate the native fear of pigskins in *The Lives of a Bengal Lancer* and *The Real Glory.* The Western characters who participate in the narrative, and spectators of these adventures, are lured to these exotic lands and their people in part became they seem less real than their concerns—especially in historical period—and can provide whites with a safe field for escape. Differentiating Oriental culture has the effect of separating it from the Occidental's homeland, allowing a feeling of distance, at times even of superiority. The concern for the natives can act to salve the adventurer's conscience, providing the assurance that his motives are primarily altruistic, not selfish or nationalistic. Indeed, natives are often situated as distressed victims whose plight requires the hero to come to the rescue, in the process proving his own worth, just as a swashbuckler comes to the aid of a woman.

As the central protagonists in colonial stories are usually Europeans or Americans, a nationality shared with the primary audience, a cultural and racial feeling of commonality is instantly created between viewer and character. This emotion contextualizes the stories, since the hero's victorious culture is portrayed as advancing, representing modernism and a more progressive, hopeful future. However, nationalistic and racial pride does not necessarily lead to outright racism. While the superior demeanor of Europeans toward natives is embarrassing today, this attitude is often undercut within the film. Overbearing heroes are forced by the events of the narrative to adopt new beliefs. Overt racism, particularly as it existed among the military, surfaces only to be exposed and rejected, as in *King of the Khyber Rifles* and *The Brigand of Kandahar.* In *Gunga Din,* the audience laughs less at the aspiring Sepoy than at the pompous white men. The stress in adventure is on the interaction with the people of the country: the empire builder knows, or discovers, that his native counterpart is hardly a child of nature or an innocent savage but a product of an ancient and complex civilization, albeit one with many different values.

The treatment of natives becomes an issue in colonial adventures where exploration is the foremost goal (*Stanley and Livingstone; The Royal Hunt of the Sun; Christopher Columbus* [1985]). Inevitably, there is a dichotomy between those who display kindness and understanding and those who rule by force instead of example. The contrast is between exploitation and forced conversion to Western,

Christian habits, as opposed to the gradual offering of such benefits as medicine and an end to slavery. While the movies make no pretence as to which approach won, there is some compensation in the valiant cinematic efforts toward fairness of such individuals as Columbus, Livingstone, and Father Serra (7 *Cities of Gold*), foreshadowing wiser, more progressive thinking. In contrast with the western genre, where half-castes of mixed native and white blood generally become depraved, in adventure films they usually fulfill the position of the white in society—or else the system is condemned, as in *The Brigand of Kandahar* (Richards 1973, 214).

There is a definite difference in the treatment of various native races in historical adventure films. Each region tends to cultivate its own mythology, with an affinity for a particular variation of the empire story, for instance, imperialism in India and Africa are quite different (Green 1979, 308). Blacks receive the most negative portrayals, probably a reflection of domestic American prejudices. Burdened by myths of the dark continent, there is little attempt to understand African culture, and whites are usually the key characters. The continent is portrayed as largely unmapped, the site of slavery and Arab exploitation. Consequently, Africa is left in a seemingly timeless state of perpetual underdevelopment, one of the few domains remaining for recent adventure, such as *Trader Horn* (1931).

Africa was the continent for safaris, journeys that are perfect metaphors of the worst aspects of the colonial endeavor. Safaris may either appear as a means of exploration or provide the structure of an entire narrative, in which case they most frequently resemble the fortune hunter type of adventure rather than empire. Whites are taken on a trip of a certain duration that will allow them to see strange lands yet remain safely insulated as Europeans and provide amazing tales to tell at home. Safaris became primarily voyages of self-discovery for the white participants, with little thought given to the accompanying blacks bearing supplies. There is frequent and brutal killing of the wildlife. Ironically, the cynical great white hunter has the fewest illusions about his own race and has given up the prospect of life in Europe for a colonial life on the frontier. The hunter essentially cleans up after the safari, whether that entails dealing with animals left half-dead because of poor shots or with the psychological problems of his fellow whites.

By comparison, Orientals and those of the Indian subcontinent are treated in a more positive manner. Usually portrayed under British colonial dominion, India offers whites the promise of privilege, fame, and wealth, yet the true heroes are not those who exploit but mature individuals who come to understand the country. Unlike perceptions of Africa, India was recognized as a developed and highly structured country, with established systems of government and religion that empire builders had to consider. The colonial challenge is to preserve the peace and maintain order, not to explore or settle, as in Africa (Green 1979, 286). The civilization of India and its aura of other-worldliness prove most comprehensible to and appreciated by the mind of the Western imperialist. The same can be said of the Arabs, especially in the Oriental swashbuckler, but in the empire adventure as well. In *King Richard and the Crusaders* (1954), Christians are depicted as a quarrelsome, factious, boorish lot, and their excessive ambition is a greater danger to the own cause than the enemy Saladin, who is a gracious and honorable leader. In this picture and the earlier *The Crusades* (1935), it is Saladin who ultimately wins the respect of all as an individual greater than Richard (Dooley, 166; Connor in Parish and Stanke, 21).

Natives are characterized in different ways; when they are principal characters they tend to be placed at two opposite poles, either as the friend or ally of the white hero, or as an adversary. A clear pattern emerges from colonial adventure; when natives occupy central roles, whether in a heroic or villainous capacity, their thinking also comes to the fore. Whether portrayed in a positive or negative light, such individuals are allowed to speak for themselves, and the more fully the role is articulated the more positive it becomes. Often, however, natives play only minor characters, shunted into simple stereotypes sublimated to underlying racist attitudes. In such cases, their motivations may be left entirely unexplained or attributed to the basic conflict of empire, as in the Arab attacks in *The Lost Patrol* and *Under Two Flags*. In a few extreme cases, such as *The Naked Prey*, natives are portrayed as unfathomable, manifesting complete difference and otherness, the fear of the East as foreign and incomprehensible.

Although frequently natives portray servants, none take on this role in adventure movies out of a feeling of inferiority, and working for a colonist does not imply self-abasement. Even devoted servants are regarded as honorable and intelligent, and although there may be some condescension, adventure films treat them with a regard equal

King Richard and the Crusaders (1954) ultimately salutes Saladin (Rex Harrison) as the wisest ruler and best fighter, rather than such Europeans as the ailing Richard (George Sanders, left) and his cousin Edith (Virginia Mayo).

to what would be shown a white in the same position. Assisting whites, natives are not slavish but remain independent, following their own beliefs. In *Flame over India / Northwest Frontier*, the pacifist train conductor assists the escaping whites and the persecuted Hindu prince as a neutral humanitarian. Native motives are usually portrayed as improving their own status by simultaneously using and being used by empire builders. Umbopa offers himself as a bearer to the fortune hunters of *King Solomon's Mines*, but only until they arrive at their destination. Here he is revealed as the rightful king; accompanying the Quartermain safari was merely a way of returning to claim his birthright.

While Gunga Din (Sam Jaffe) is initially a subordinate to such British officers as those played by Douglas Fairbanks, Jr. (left) and Victor McLaglen (right), eventually he is recognized as the hero, a better man, in *Gunga Din* (1939).

King Solomon's Mines is not alone in portraying prominent, individualized natives in positive roles; some are shown as the equals or superiors of Occidentals, as in *The Wind and the Lion* or *Shogun*. In some films, comradeship between natives and whites goes beyond respect to friendship, allying to achieve a personal goal, taking each other into their confidence. Frequently, an empire adventurer's best companion is someone of another race, a native of the area the hero has adopted (Green 1991, 97). Sergeant "Billy Fish" joins the search for wealth in *The Man Who Would Be King*, and Feversham regards Abu as his better while they collaborate against the Mahdi in *The Four Feathers* (1977). *Gunga Din* (1939), while initially seeming to prove the contrary, in fact validates this point. Because of his caste, Gunga Din (Sam Jaffe) is treated with condescension at the outset not only by the trio of sahibs (Cary Grant, Victor McLaglen, Douglas Fairbanks, Jr.), but by everyone else, native and European alike. Ultimately, however, Din proves to be the most courageous of all, sacrificing his life and earning the salute of the entire regiment as the true hero. By this action he becomes a Sepoy, his goal—not to serve the British but to rise above the level of water carrier, gaining a position and status not offered within his own society. Gunga Din takes on legendary status, and the white men acknowledge that he is indeed "a better man" than they.

The stereotype of the hero's adversary, the native villain, follows the unscrupulous pattern evident throughout the genre of presenting adventure villains as the enemies of liberty and justice. Eastern villains are established as predators, indigenous destructive forces who willingly cause civil war and are even more dangerous to their own race than the forces of occupation (Richards 1974, 88). Despite advantages of birth, wealth, and education, native villains use their leadership among their people purely to increase personal power (Richards 1973, 30, 210–11). They allow free reign to barbaric instincts by promoting infighting among the tribes as well as against the colonial power. Religious fanaticism may blind them to the inhumanity of their movement, as with the bloody uprising begun by "the chosen one," the Mahdi in *Khartoum*. (However, explaining diabolical actions in terms of spiritual fanaticism is applied equally to both Christian and native in adventure films.) Rebellions are portrayed as heralding a return to precolonial primitivism, whether slavery (*Killers of Kilimanjaro*), the bid for power of a bloodthirsty tyrant (*The Lives of a Bengal Lancer; Drums*), a tool of foreign intrigue (*The Charge of the Light Brigade* [1936]; *Rogues March*), or a combination of these (*Gunga Din*).

This mythology derives from the 1857 Sepoy Mutiny in India and the considerable amount of popular literature it spawned. Unlike the swashbuckler, empire adventures find no inherent tradition of justice and democracy among colonized people (cf. Said, 172). Europeans are shown as believing that a beneficent outside regime is preferable to the withdrawal or defeat of the colonial presence and the dire consequences it could portend. The alternative to imperialism seems unacceptable, unleashing fierce social and religious tensions, such as the Hindu-Moslem conflict in *Flame over India*. The palpable fear exists that any laxity could cause a violent overthrow, resulting in atrocities against civilians, native and foreign, as in the "Black Hole" of Calcutta or the massacre at Cawnpore, a facsimile of which appears in *The Charge of the Light Brigade* (1936). Uprisings become wrong, less for the threat they pose to Western rule than as the reversion to primitive instincts they represent.

The genre's encouragement of imperialism cloaks itself in the guise of a short-term necessity; with the native villain threatening violence and torture, the colonial regime is justified as more progressive than any visible alternative. Unlike the swashbuckler or sea adventure, opponents of colonialism do not embody a legitimate desire for independence, for their efforts would then necessarily merit favorable treatment from adventure's politics (Richards 1974, 87). The fact that alternatives to colonialism are inevitably posed in negative terms indicates there is no automatic predisposition on the part of audiences to accept the desirability of imperial policies. The effort necessary in each adventure to establish the need for a colonial presence indicates the pattern never became accepted in the way that American Indian-as-savage was traditional in the western genre. Because of adventure's affinity for outlaws and rebels, it is almost obsessed with proving that imperialism is not oppressive. Such empire adventures as *Flame over India* and *Drums* deliberately attempt to disarm critics by offering British heroes protecting defenseless children from fanatical Moslems and tyrants. Similarly, in *Stanley and Livingstone*, the doctor describes the tribal warrior tradition of a young boy as he performs a medical operation.

Because of the vague similarities of some of the themes in colonial adventure, a few critics have compared the genre to the western: both genres feature horses, guns, an advancing civilization, control of the native, and conquest of the frontier. However, empire adventures do more than transfer into another realm the western's displacement of the native by an outside force.[4] The western never made any pretension that the treatment accorded the American Indian was anything other than expedient. Adventure, on the other hand, struggles to justify imperialism as altruistic and beneficial. In the western the primary interest is in taming the wilderness, while the adventurer's chief goal is not the settlement of the land but winning over other people and their politics. Whereas the cowboy displaces and eliminates the native, the empire builder must preserve the best of the native's way of life in the colony. In adventure, wild, unsettled outposts are sought not only to serve a nation's policy of expansion but also out of a sincere (if misplaced) wish to do some good for the colony itself—an attitude far different from the typical western. Seldom is the adventurer's travel similar to the western genre's vague desire for the loneliness of far horizons; in *Scott of the Antarctic* the reasons behind the trek are more nationalistic than scientific, while for Father Serra and David Livingstone

Protecting children from death in a religious conflict becomes one of the justifications for imperialism.

they are humanitarian in 7 *Cities of Gold* and *Stanley and Livingstone*. Adventure has entirely different sets of conventions, most notably in the multiplicity of different locales, periods, types of hero, and the variety of different cultures it presents, all of which have little in common with the homogeneity of filmdom's west.

Two widely divergent versions of Talbot Mundy's literary property, *King—of the Khyber Rifles* (1917), illustrate the traits of colonial adventures and the way they have changed over time. *The Black Watch* (1929), made shortly after the coming of sound, tends to nullify the adventurous elements, and action is always minimal or small-scale. *The Black Watch* never strives for spectacle, instead emphasizing emotions and a love story, all performed with labored exaggeration. Empire adventure film was still comparatively unformulated for audiences and filmmakers, a fact reflected in the title change (although it was still titled *King of the Khyber Rifles* in England); rather than an adventure in India, the Khyber Rifles nearly vanish from the plot, turning *The Black Watch* into a saga of the famous regiment of the same name.[5] Donald King (Victor McLaglen), because of his knowledge of India, is sent on a secret mission to foil the holy war planned by Yasmini, a mysterious leader of the hillmen. Mundy's imperious and charismatic Eurasian heroine was a type of woman that Hollywood simply could not understand, and Myrna Loy's performance projects her attractiveness but not the strength of character, further hindered by her stilted dialogue; she dies recognizing King has defeated her. A contrasting Indian character assisting King is Risaldar Major Mohammed Khan (Mitchell Lewis), an amusingly hypocritical bully who becomes the hero's respected sidekick. Before he kills a man, Khan always prays, "For all the violence I have displayed toward my fellow men, Allah forgive me," yet he is also heroic and never a mere caricature.

The uncertainty over how to handle empire adventure is shown by framing the action in India with long introductory and concluding scenes set in the regimental officer's mess. This contextualizes the overseas portions, grounding the excursion into an Oriental culture by showing details of another foreign tradition, Scotland. The filmmakers perhaps believed that India was too strange to viewers to become the principal setting, using the customs of the Scottish Black Watch to mediate the difference. Nearly a third of the hour and a half picture elapses before *The Black Watch* finally shifts to India, and not until well over halfway into the film does King enter the Khyber Pass. Even then, the Oriental mood is destroyed by crosscutting to the trenches of France, paralleling the Black Watch in the front lines of France and King's service in India. The film is ultimately about cultural contrasts between characters, comradeship, brotherhood, love, and fighting, for example in the relationship between King and his friend Khan, or between King and his brother Malcolm and the others of the Black Watch.

King—of the Khyber Rifles was more often in planning than in production at the Fox studio, with a remake announced throughout the late 1930s. Finally, the 1953 version was made after three years of preparation, distinctively reflecting the new revisionism in empire adventure. This time, consonant with the steadily firming generic period, the historical background was shifted into the past, to the Sepoy Mutiny of 1857. Surprisingly, this conflict had rarely been treated in films up to that time, although typically, only a fictional episode is portrayed. There are authentic details of Indian atmosphere that convey a sense of accuracy, such as the concern with bullets, the one-eyed Sepoy Ahmed, the mullahs, and barracks life.

Nonetheless, *King of the Khyber Rifles* is not nearly as successful as later films (such as *The Man Who Would Be King*) in capturing the sense of its locale and the unique beliefs that made the plot possible.

King of the Khyber Rifles has a lone hero and is without the emphasis on the group, military camaraderie, comic relief, and male high jinks that marked many similar films. There is none of the careless, *Boy's Own* tone nor is India portrayed as a primitive, savage land needing a civilizing influence, currents too often present in *Gunga Din* and *Drums*. The most intriguing shared element between Mundy's book and the films is a character of Eurasian ancestry, although instead of the heroine, half-caste status is transferred to the hero, Captain Alan King (Tyrone Power). Yasmini is eliminated entirely, and King falls in love with a white girl, Susan (Terry Moore), the daughter of the outpost's commander, General Maitland (Michael Rennie), providing an opportunity for exploring racial attitudes in a colonial setting. Focusing on a relationship between a half-caste and a white girl was, in the early 1950s, an original cinematic theme, and *King of the Khyber Rifles* was unique for presenting it in adventure. Indeed, *Bengal Brigade / Bengal Rifles*, one of the next year's follow-ups to the box-office success of *King of the Khyber Rifles*, showed the failure of an interracial romance, although one between a white officer and a native woman.

Prejudice against King emerges because of his parentage; fellow officers refuse to be billeted in the same quarters as King, and he is conspicuously not invited to the queen's birthday ball. *King of the Khyber Rifles* explores King's personal difficulties as he tries to find his own social position, living in uneasy suspension between the world of the native and the foreign sahibs, torn between them; only the adventurous experience can resolve his status. Yet King is recognized as the role model from the outset; the stress is not simply on his courage but more on the numerous challenges he must face in daily living. A social outcast at the fort, King is most secure in the home of his adopted father, Hamid Bahra, a Moslem holy man; the picture was originally to end with King returning to Bahra before joining Susan. Bahra sadly discloses to King that his foster brother has adopted the name Kurram Khan to lead a rebellion that will make him ruler of India. King impersonates a deserter to gain access to Khan, but because of childhood friendship—and the adventurer's code—King is unable to kill him. Meanwhile, King's regiment of unruly Khyber Rifles is restless due to rumors that the cartridges for

As a fellow native, King (Tyrone Power) tries to convince his Khyber Rifles that their new weapons do not use bullets greased with pig's fat in *King of the Khyber Rifles* (1954).

their new Enfield rifles are greased with pig's fat, simultaneously offending Moslem and Hindu alike. King must regain his good name by using his unique appeal as a fellow native to lead the Khyber Rifles in an attack on Khan's encampment. At the last moment, King's men resolve not to use the rifles but offer to follow him with their knives. The surprise night attack succeeds, and as King fights with his brother, Kurram Khan is killed by another member of the Rifles, Ahmed.

The Khyber Rifles are soon back at maneuvers, observed approvingly by Maitland and Susan, and King has established not just his equality within the fort but also his eligibility to marry Susan. The British outpost offers the hero the only world where his merits can win recognition, partaking of both sides of his ancestry by following in his father's military footsteps. King's birthplace and home are India, not England, and though he may serve the British, he does so for the distinction such duty may bring through association with a respected unit like the Khyber Rifles. King is in a unique position; his half-caste status, negotiating between British and Indian with a knowledge of both, has enabled a British victory. King secures greater respect than is accorded to insecure white officers like Maitland. In *King of the Khyber Rifles*, the imperial conflict is between men who are sons of India, whether Kurram Khan and his followers or King and the Khyber Rifles. Yet *King of the Khyber Rifles* ultimately evades the central question of the desire for Indian independence through depicting Kurram Khan's leadership as far more ruthless and dictatorial than British rule. While utilizing many of the incidents and motifs of *The Lives of a Bengal Lancer; The Charge of the Light Brigade; Gunga Din;* and other such movies, *King of the Khyber Rifles* also sums them up, providing both a commentary and a decisive new turn. Whereas *The Black Watch* deemphasizes the people and culture of India by stressing the Europeanized lore of a Scottish regiment, *King of the Khyber Rifles* brings Indians to the forefront, honoring the native traditions while still treating heroes and villains according to standardized patterns. While clearly an adventure of colonial India in the classical mode, *King of the Khyber Rifles* represents a shift to social consciousness, allowing the film to be watched today more easily than many other adventures of a similar vintage. By implicitly questioning racist assumptions, some of the drawbacks of imperialism are recognized, while avoiding a more directly political flavor and remaining squarely within the format of adventure.

CHAPTER 9 **Adventure and the
American Experience**

After the definition and analysis of adventure movies in the previous chapters, one basic questions remains: Why have audiences responded to these particular myths? What purpose have they served,
especially as productions of the Hollywood studio system? A number of answers have been advanced over the years, some of them
more convincing than others. Certainly the genre's attraction is not
due to any one, simple cause but a mélange of reasons. I shall note
several of these, then introduce a new explanation that best explains
why the genre has been popular, especially for audiences in the
United States and those abroad who have absorbed American mythology.

A variety of factors account for the appeal of historical adventure
films. First, and most obviously, they are a form of escape for the
romantic, would-be hero and traveler in everyone (Tony Thomas, 4).
Adventure pictures offer relief from the mundane complexities and
confinements of contemporary life. Audiences may be comforted

vicariously by enjoying a bygone, albeit anachronistic time when men and women were gallant and charming, and the sword served to uphold justice and right (Edwin Connor in Parish and Stanke, 16). Most adventure viewers are intellectually aware that this picture of history is far from accurate. Nonetheless, simply indulging the myth may permit a few moments of emotional relaxation. Focusing even for only a moment on victory in a larger situation relieves frustrations and provides hope that the viewer, too, may overcome obstacles (Noyce, 110). In this way adventure is a unique form of diversion from the constrictions of time and the pressures of our own world to a realm that formerly existed, distinctive from the escape offered in entirely other-worldly genres, such as fantasy or science fiction, or those forms ostensibly more realistic, such as melodrama or crime. Adventure clearly also projects its audience in a specific direction toward the endorsement of certain behavioral, political, and spiritual values.

Beyond wish-fulfillment elements, other explanations have been advanced. For European audiences, adventure films have much in common with long-standing local myths and story forms. The typical settings in medieval Europe may seem to offer mythicized explanations of the development of various nationalities or portrayals of key events and personalities in the national psyche. For instance, *El Cid* could be examined as a saga of a Spanish national hero. Yet this essentially literal and local explanation is largely unconvincing, because it fails to indicate why audiences all over the world respond equally to such pictures. A picture such as *El Cid* is popular outside of Spain, just as Robin Hood tales have meaning outside England.

Similar explanations claim that adventure has been a vehicle to support the policies of other nations with whom America has had much in common. Some scholars have pointed out that the many British characters and frequent use of English history as a background in Hollywood historical adventure pictures, especially in the empire type, tend to support the policies of Great Britain and celebrate her way of life.[1] A certain amount of sentiment friendly to Britain in adventure films is to be expected, considering the closeness of heritage and her status as America's own "mother" country (cf. Rossiter, 150). In the television series *The Swamp Fox*, the antagonists of the American revolutionaries are invariably referred to by such euphemisms as redcoats or His Majesty's troops, and are never called British, even in Walt Disney's historical introductions. Yet a

British bias in adventure movies cannot be squared with America's heritage as a former colony that experienced the English yoke of colonialism and won freedom through war.

The entire notion of adventure as a familial tribute to the mother country is an unconvincing explanation for the totality of adventure, especially in Hollywood. Indeed, anglophobic sentiment was evident with a favorite target the stereotypical egotism, stuffiness, and pomposity of Britishers. This attitude is viciously mocked in the characterization of Lord Tyce and the trial before the Royal Geographical Society in *Stanley and Livingstone*, which also emphasizes Stanley's adoption of America as his homeland over his native England. As well, many movies that seem on the surface to be tributes to Britain may, on reflection, be far different. *Mutiny on the Bounty*, especially the 1935 version, projects its fundamental image of the revolt at sea and the beginning of a free life in a new land in a manner that may more accurately be read as analogous to the birth of the United States than as a careful attempt to reenact an episode in naval history. This emphasis on the struggle for human dignity against a despotic captain has a thematic resonance far beyond its direct narrative context, and the entire sea adventure emphasizes the common, democratic brotherhood of humankind.

While the British and French overseas empires have perhaps appeared most often in films, empire adventure also frequently portrays imperial ventures on the American continents and the United States' own forays abroad, forming a whole stream of films with America as the site and proponent of adventurous imperialism. Some of the empires located in the New World are Spanish and Portuguese (*Christopher Columbus*; *Captain from Castile*; *The Royal Hunt of the Sun*; *The Mission* [1986]), and also include the first British colonies (*Plymouth Adventure*; *Mayflower: The Pilgrims' Adventure*). Such motion pictures include the regions of the future United States proper (7 *Cities of Gold*). The Americas are locales for adventure during the initial period of discovery, before turning into a setting for westerns. Pirate movies set around New Orleans and the dozens of versions of the Zorro myth, and such imitations as *Mark of the Renegade*, reflect the easy transferability of adventure values to the shores of the American continent. Some films of the exploration and settling of the west in colonial times are closer to adventure than most westerns, but still belong to the latter form: *Allegheny Uprising; Drums Along the Mohawk; Fort Ti; The Howards of Virginia; Hudson's Bay; The Last of the Mohicans; Northwest Passage; Unconquered.* Otherwise, movies set in the Americas during the period of westward expansion, the late eighteenth century through the beginning of the twentieth century, plainly qualify as westerns. These include films located in Latin America, like *The Treasure of Sierra Madre,* which, although similar in fortune hunter theme to *The Man Who Would Be King,* is crucially different in setting and cultural milieu. Films of the settlement of Alaska, the Yukon, and adjoining regions, such as the Northwest action of the Mounties, most closely resemble westerns in content and iconography (*Ice Palace; Call of the Wild*). Action dramas set during the American Civil War are a separate genre, different thematically from adventure in their presentation of the grim, disillusioning side of fighting, so foreign to adventure and resembling the war picture.

The rise of the United States to preeminence as a world power coincides with the cinematic century and the dominance of Hollywood in global filmmaking. America's own imperial activity around the world is illustrated by *The Real Glory, The Sand Pebbles*, and *The Wind and the Lion.* A number of other adventures, from empire to pirate pictures, feature Americans in various locales (*Yankee Pasha; 55 Days in Peking; The White Dawn; Cook and Peary: The Race to the Pole; The Man without a Country; Santiago; Tripoli* [1950]; *Yankee Buccaneer*), especially sea stories (*Old Ironsides; John Paul Jones; Captains Courageous; Souls at Sea; The Sea Wolf; Slave Ship; Reap the Wild Wind; Two Years before the Mast; Moby Dick*). On the other hand, Hollywood filmmakers have not had to add their efforts to a centuries-old propaganda machine, while those in Britain, for instance, may have felt compelled to justify history in their portrayals of empire. America kept its empire unnamed, not acknowledging that its policies were as imperial as those of Europe, spending most of its initial colonizing effort on the move west and through the Americas via manifest destiny and the Monroe Doctrine (Green 1979, 129–30). Strong opposition to jingoism has been influential in American history since at least the middle of the nineteenth century, with the decision not to annex Cuba. Most of the United States' pre-twentieth-century imperialism was manifested in the conquest of the American west, and it is the western, rather than adventure, that has reflected most of the energy of this nation's expansionist fervor. In turn, modern American imperialism has been absorbed by such war movies as *The Green Berets* (1969) and the Rambo series. By contrast, the "message" of adventure has been that the spread overseas of American ideals and institutions and respect for individual rights are more important than territorial expansion.

The essential congruity between adventures with a European background and the American experience is revealed in such pictures as *The Real Glory* (1939) and *The Wind and the Lion*. In *The Real Glory*, the empire archetypes of the second cycle of adventure films (1934–1942) are transferred to United States imperialism, in this case in the Philippines in 1906. The story is strikingly reminiscent of the India adventure *The Lives of a Bengal Lancer* (with the same star, Gary Cooper, and director, Henry Hathaway), demonstrating the similarity in attitude toward any colonial setting, no matter the particular place nor imperial power involved. *The Real Glory* contains such typical elements as native religious fanaticism tied in with bloody tyrants abusing their own people. The defenseless are protected with altruistic motives, if patronizingly, by western occupation in the name of the white man's burden.

Yet there are also key differences. *The Real Glory* emphasizes that the Americans are preparing the Philippines for self-government, through the titles, an introductory scene, and the narrative. Indeed, this transition is the source of danger; as American forces diminish, training the Philippino army to take their place, the vicious Alipang and his Moro warriors pillage the area to make Alipang the sultan of Mindinao. Dialogue notes that the battle for the Philippines hinges on the outcome at Mysang. Alipang seeks to lure the unprepared troops of the Mysang garrison into a jungle trap by sending his men on suicidal missions to kill the officers. When that fails, he cuts off the river that provides the village's water supply, and an epidemic of cholera breaks out. Appropriately, the ultimate hero among the few whites is not one of the soldiers but the doctor, Canavan (played by the star, Gary Cooper), who helps the Philippinos overcome their fear of the Moros, saves Mysang from the cholera epidemic, and reopens the river. Like other empire heroes, Canavan best understands the Philippines and the needs of its people; he is marked for heroism from the opening when he befriends a Moro boy, Miguel. The other Americans are similarly altruistic, from the two com-

The army physician Canavan (Gary Cooper) teams up with a local boy (Benny Inocencio) to evade the Moro traps (seen here) and save Mysang in *The Real Glory* (1939).

manding officers who are killed to another who is going blind. Canavan's fellow officers are presented as equally free from imperialistic motives; one dreams of a small tropical island of his own, while the other collects and breeds orchids. Indeed, the battle is finally won by the Philippinos, with Alipang killed by their new native officer, Yabo. The garrison is firmly self-governed and secure in the final scene as the last of the Americans depart. The mission accomplished, American colonialism has been presented as both protecting the natives from local dangers and actually preparing them for rule by their own kind, not simply talking about it, as in films depicting British imperialism. Needless to say, *The Real Glory* elides the actual facts of American occupation in the Philippines and local resistance, but the attitude toward final independence in the movie is a unique variation on imperial formulas, demonstrating the interconnection between empire and an acceptance of orderly evolution toward self-rule.

In addition to such fictional American characters, Europeans and

Asians are not the only ones to occupy pivotal positions as authentic heroes for films. The two most prominent Americans to function in this way were the seventh and twenty-sixth presidents, Andrew Jackson and Theodore Roosevelt, respectively utilized in *The Buccaneer* (1958 version especially) and *The Wind and the Lion* (1975). Jackson and Roosevelt stand out for a variety of shared reasons: military and patriotic activities, "strenuous" lives, belief in expanding their nation's physical boundaries and world influence, opening the government to greater participation by ordinary people instead of just the wealthy and powerful, all combined with a sense of gentlemanliness and honor. Further, Jackson is recalled for his stand against South Carolina's move toward secession, a position not unlike the adventurer's determination to maintain central control in the empire and keep it from fragmenting, distinguishing between revolts that were justified and those that were not. In a slightly more legendary sense, the names of Jackson and Roosevelt have come to stand for the advocacy of the rights of the common man against oppressive forces—be they national banks, trusts, or Spanish colonial misgovernment.

Theodore Roosevelt's position as a predominantly pre–World War I figure makes him seem the last of the true American adventurers. During his life he led men into battle as a Rough Rider, hunted game, traveled and explored the wilds, ultimately becoming the leader of his nation, and helping to build the American empire. Yet he also turned peacemaker in the Russo-Japanese war, combining adventure with a scholarly bent as historian and writer. As president he was a profoundly moral figure, embodying chivalry and the adventurer's code and carrying them into the political arena, identifying his policies with expansionism, reform, and a virtuous, sportsmanlike spirit of good government involving fairness for all (John Fraser, 122, 123, 119).

The conflict against the Barbary Pirates has been a popular theme for adventure as the first major manifestation of American power beyond her own shores. *Old Ironsides, Tripoli*, and *Barbary Pirate* were set in the nineteenth century, while *The Wind and the Lion* was set at the outset of the twentieth century. *The Wind and the Lion* carries further the theme of true adventure as intrinsically American in nature, as opposed to the crude, selfish imperialism of European powers. Not only is there the growing overseas power of the United States as a global policeman at the beginning of the twentieth century, but parallels are drawn between the adventure spirit and American ideals. This is conveyed through weaving together portrayals of a Moroccan bandit chieftain, Rasuli (Sean Connery), and President Theodore Roosevelt (Brian Keith). Caught between them are an American mother (Candace Bergen) and her children abducted by the Arab, not simply for ransom, but to reveal how his nation has become hostage to western imperialism. Yet Rasuli fails to realize how his scheme promotes what he seeks to end, allowing a foreign invasion. The victims of Rasuli's escapade come to esteem him, since his own code, very similar to that of the adventurer, unexpectedly turns him into their protector, ultimately causing the Americans to liberate Rasuli when he is taken prisoner. The two distinct nationalities realize their common love of freedom in their separate domains, Rasuli and Roosevelt as leaders sharing the gentlemanly virtues of the swashbuckler and the warrior faults of the empire builder. Although representing the clash of elemental forces stemming from very different cultural backgrounds, Roosevelt and Rasuli are compared to reveal the adventurous spirit that lies at the heart of both men, including their vanity and belief that God favors them, with Rasuli from a more primitive but nonetheless dignified tradition. Imperialism is seen as a result of the impetus toward expansionism on the part of all nationalities, less in a deliberate planned clash than a natural outgrowth of the inclination to action and political crusades. These instincts inevitably move from the homeland to foreign shores, empire emerging as the logical next step for the adventurer after swashbuckling.

In these examples, adventure embodies a blend of liberalism and conservatism, even a tinge of radicalism, combining nationalism, imperialism, and social justice in a manner most reminiscent of early twentieth-century Progressivism. Adventure belongs to the style of politics promulgated by Theodore Roosevelt, rather than FDR, and is inextricably bound with activism and a belief in intervention abroad. This ideology was consonant with the freedom so prized by the adventurer, containing all of the inherent contradictions introduced when it is combined with imperialism—a blend found in the various adventure types. Further, Progressivism was a political view uniquely appropriate to a person of action like Roosevelt, one that the adventure genre demands. Yet there is also a more than passing resemblance between adventure's ideology and the goal of the four freedoms enunciated by Franklin Roosevelt at the start of

1941: speech and expression, to worship in one's own way, and freedom from want and freedom from fear. Adventure is not clearly connected to either end of the American political spectrum nor to any political party.

However, on a deeper and more pervasive level, beyond any particular historical moment, adventure has resonances with attitudes and history unique to the development and self-perception of the United States. The consistent concerns of the genre are found in America's own heritage and are compatible with the values inherent in the nation's history. Americans see aspects of their own past and national virtues reflected in the myths offered by adventure films, regardless of their ostensible setting. Just as the life-style presented in adventure pictures represents action as of the essence, this same restlessness is part of the American culture and spirit.[2] Adventure is central to the national consciousness through its echoes with America's historical past. Indeed, there has probably never been a nation so founded by, and built upon, the spirit of adventure, as the United States, and it has remained with the country to this day (Hawthorne, 177).

Many of the same, seemingly incompatible crosscurrents exist and thrive within both American politics and that of the adventure movie. Numerous aspects of adventure philosophy may be regarded as attempts to cope with the tensions, ambiguities, and contradictions, placed in a global context, that seem to be typically American characteristics. The adventure film's overriding political motif, the overthrow of tyranny and injustice, can be related to the American experience through the Revolution. It is above all this spirit and event that adventure indirectly celebrates and emulates, rather than the history of England or a parallel with the western genre (Richards 1973, 4; Richards, Summer 1977, 18–19; Rosenzweig, 61–65). Adventure celebrates the triumph of the political values that underlie democratic institutions. Through the vehicle of adventure movies, Americans see their own development in the portrayals of the evolution of other countries and their social systems (Durgnat in Grant, 108). This is why adventure films frequently make no pretence at enunciating political attitudes that were viable in the time of the movie's setting, such as the dissonance between beliefs and era in *The Black Knight*, set in Arthurian England. The effort is not to retain period realities but instead to underline certain democratic and egalitarian sentiments by expressing them in another time.

This grounds the genre's ideals, giving them credence and support in various eras and settings other than the American Revolution.

Adventure movies serve as a metaphor, reenacting by analogy the Revolution. Conveying a sense of freshness and change, the adventure genre dramatizes the overthrow of oppressive rule. The narrative movement is invariably toward greater freedom, with respect for human rights and equality gaining a firm footing that will eventually have its culmination in democratic forms of government. Such historical phrases as, "Give me liberty or give me death," "No taxation without representation," or "Life, Liberty, and the Pursuit of Happiness," could well serve as slogans for the genre, forming the basis for the rhetoric that expresses the politics of adventure. In colonial America, as in adventure pictures, *liberty* was a key word, defined as freedom from subjugation so far as order will permit (Rossiter, 4, 141, 10).

An analysis of the beliefs underlying the Revolution is simultaneously an overview of the specific ideology of adventure films. The conflicts in adventure pictures are revolts to reassert tradition against imposed authority, by winning back legitimate rights lost to a usurper and at the same time establishing a more democratic government with a system of justice under law. Rather than a truly proletarian uprising against the entire establishment, these revolts seek to restore liberty once enjoyed but now endangered. Similarly, George III's historical attempt to assert stronger British control over the American colonies after the laxity induced by the French and Indian Wars—in effect, usurping the accustomed autonomy—was a key factor in precipitating the Revolution.

In Hollywood adventure films, the ambivalence toward revolts, despite the acceptance of the right to overthrow a tyrannical regime, derives from the belief of Americans that their rights were virtually preordained, with the Revolution an attempt to defend rather than to establish them. As Clinton Rossiter has written in *Seedtime of the Republic*, this sentiment and historical fact underlie the American Revolution (the following citations are from this book). A large measure of liberty and prosperity was already part of the colonists' way of life, and such rights as equality before the law; opportunity and social mobility; liberty of individual conscience and the right to dissent; separation of church and state, and religious tolerance, were expected throughout the colonies (4). Even though these principles appeared radical to outsiders, domestically they seemed to preserve traditional life, conserving the form of government the colonists had known, although it was a system unlike anything Europeans would experience for decades to come (448). Consequently, the American revolutionaries were the first in modern history to defend, rather than seek liberty (440). Our revolution was an unusually reluctant, limited, measured, and successful event, struggling to defend what had already been achieved, making it a radical event occurring in a conservative framework (448).

Americans became radicals by chance rather than by choice, forced ironically into this path by their own essential conservatism and unwillingness to lose what had already been gained (347). As in adventure, there was little desire to create a truly new social system by breaking completely with all that already existed, despite its faults. Prior to the call for independence, resistance was to restore the old order, to return to the days before the usurpation of liberties (347). Beginning with protest before turning to war, as in adventure films, Americans avoided resorting to arms until allegiance to the government and their liberty became incompatible (349). The same pattern is often seen in the genre; revolts restore the old king, or the previous regime, whose justice had been overturned by a pretender.

Americans considered themselves freeborn subjects of the crown, who had the right of political self-determination (7). As in adventure, a high value was placed on patriotism and interest in military activity, and a need for governmental authority was recognized, resistance occurring only if it grew authoritarian. Government, certainly free government, was good, beneficial, and popular, the product of purposeful men acting in pursuit of universal principles (142). The Revolution was not against the idea of order per se but was intended to organize and substitute the old order to effect the safety and happiness of the people (397). Good government was a free association of free and equal citizens giving their allegiance for certain defined purposes, to protect the people and their property from danger (especially evident in colonial adventure) and to foster freedom and humankind's best instincts and proclivities in an egalitarian environment (442–44). Government was simply a means, rather than an end, to securing what was good for the people (445, 413, 414). The responsibility of government to promote the well-being (happiness, welfare, liberty, equality) of the governed is still celebrated uniquely by adventure. The concern is less with abstract politics than with practical ways toward good government, regarded primarily as a matter of selecting the proper ruler and keeping despots from acquiring power.

As in adventure, subjects who are conscious of government's origin, purpose, limits, and authority will not endure a regime that is arbitrary, corrupt, or oppressive (413). In the Revolution obedience to government was a matter of consent, not duty (407). The authority of government was granted by the people in a fashion that was always free and revocable. Tyranny immediately dissolved the compact between the people and their government, leaving its subjects free to unseat a ruler (359, 413, 364). The ultimate ruler is not the officeholder but the law itself; tyranny is not a result of government but an abuse of it (420, 413).

The adventurer's code reflects the American assumption that democratic principles are based on self-discipline and morality (55). A patriotic, moral, temperate, and courageous people deserves liberty, while corruption leads to enslavement (447). Moral standards govern private conduct, guiding and restricting behavior in such a way that a natural order evolves (368, 440–41). Humankind is endowed with certain natural rights and the political and social realms are governed by laws every bit as universal, immutable, and inescapable as nature (440–41). There is no natural right giving one person dominion over another (442). Hence government is an attempt to replicate as closely as possible the laws of nature in the political sphere; simultaneously, the transgression of that order becomes a violation not only of political order but of nature as well (369). The public good demanded the preservation of the natural rights of man as the chief end of government (142).

One result of the conservative reverence for tradition found in adventure is the limitation on the degree of revolt sanctioned in the genre, based on a fear of the potential chaos unwarranted change can bring about. The dominant American ideology, as well as that found in adventure pictures, avoids both extremes of the political spectrum. A location within the political center is desired, but it is a center that is dynamic and progressive. Its advocates are not content to stand pat so long as there are wrongs to be corrected or necessary reforms to be made. The political philosophy of the Revolution sought a balance between extremes of anarchy and autocracy, individualism and statism, liberty and order, resulting in a form of ordered liberty (402).

The respect for authority causes a reluctance to rebel, and the adventurer and American revolutionary were forced into this option when oppression becomes too severe and all other avenues to overcome it are exhausted. The American Revolution is regarded as an isolated instance, of colonies driven to rebel by an improper imposition of authority. Without an overriding discipline, the fear exists that a revolt can lead to the brutal bloodshed typified by the French Revolution, its even greater heritage of injustice causing a swing to a dangerous extreme. This eventuality the empire builder explicitly tries to prevent. The anxiety over such an event also has a derivation in the American experience. Balancing the key importance of the Revolution is the memory that the nation's other great trauma was a civil war to assert the importance of national government and to restore a union of states threatened by the secession of an aristocratic, slave-based South (Fraser, 6). In adventure, those who have the same desire as the Confederacy, without the moral provocation of the American Revolution, are condemned. America becomes uneasy regarding the revolutions of others to change conditions, especially for the first time. Resistance is a solemn duty, the last refuge of the people to protect lives, liberty, and property, and not the effort of a pretender to justify a revolt or a coup d'état, as seen in empire films (Rossiter, 445). Adventure movies do not advocate radical action without having a higher loyalty to another authority, as a swashbuckler has in restoring the rightful ruler to power. The ready endorsement of colonial authority may stem from such logic, adventure depicting primarily rebellions to secure rights of human freedom and dignity, so long as they are already implicitly won and in the position of being defended.

Adventure is not only ideologically parallel to the Revolution but it is also similar in the type and class of heroes offered. The ragtag rebellions of swashbucklers lead toward the goals of a middle-class insurrection. The adventure hero's milieu, whether aboard ship or in Sherwood Forest, is American in spirit and organization, simultaneously offering equality and a social hierarchy (Rosenzweig, 49). Although the colonies reflected a well-defined class structure, it was open-ended, more fluid than in Europe, with a New World insistence that each person should rise or fall by their own virtues and capacities (Rossiter, 86, 110, 93). Nonetheless, there is a strong tendency within the genre toward preferring patrician, rather than truly popular, leadership. The most politically influential are the best educated and locally respected, generally men whose property gave them a stake in community affairs (Rossiter, 447). Hence there is a natural propensity to look to the established aristocracy to take a guiding, wise position; notions of suffrage were an afterthought (Rossiter, 425).

There is no reason for decision makers to attain position by accident of birth, but a liberty-loving people continues to need gifted leaders. Officeholding was a privilege and a duty, not a right of the elite (Rossiter, 446, 447). The same is true in adventure, and leaders almost always concern themselves with the needs, rights, and happiness of all the people, not solely the upper class. Magistrates were regarded as servants rather than rulers of the people, to be chosen by the community and remain accountable to it. As in adventure, the colonies believed in the virtues of government while simultaneously deploring those who misuse it, finding a solution in officeholders of integrity. It is not the fact of having a strong leader that will be objected to, only an unwise imposition or abuse of authority by that individual.

Other secondary aspects of adventure are reflected in colonial America before the Revolution. Religion was personalized as a matter of individual choice, rather than institutionalized; it was acceptable within its place but potentially dangerous should it enter the secular realm (Rossiter, 38). Family structure was patriarchal, and the unmarried individual was regarded as a suspicious luxury, just as adventurers frequently end their exploits with a wedding (Rossiter, 93). Like their Revolutionary predecessors, cinematic adventurers such as *Scaramouche* often disseminate their philosophy through pamphlets and orations (Rossiter, 329–31). Although liberty must be shared equally by all, anyone can accumulate whatever property they may so long as they do not impinge on another's freedom (Rossiter, 416–17). Liberty did not guarantee economic equality or property—never part of the radicalism of adventure films—only the right to accumulate property (Rossiter, 416–17). The genre's concern with preserving property may well be a result of the importance of security in homes and the right to defend them from confiscation and occupation during the Revolution.

Despite all that adventure shares in common with the American Revolution, there are few portrayals of this conflict in the cinema, especially compared to other occurrences of similar significance, such as the French Revolution. Indeed, by contrast, there have been hundreds of pictures exploring every facet of the Civil War. Films portraying the American Revolution have been as consistently unpopular with the domestic audience as they have with the British.[3] Movies (*The Midnight Ride of Paul Revere; Scouting for Washington; The Spirit of '76; Cardigan; America* [1924]; *The Scarlet Coat; Johnny Tremain / Johnny Tremain and the Sons of Liberty; John Paul Jones; Lafayette* [1963]; *Revolution* [1985]) and television (*The Swamp Fox; The Young Rebels;* the miniseries *George Washington*) based on this conflict rarely achieve commercial or critical success. Perhaps this fact has led Hollywood to prefer turning films set in this period of American history into westerns, providing an easier generic framework by emphasizing the conflict with Indians rather than British, settlers rather than independence, such as *Drums along the Mohawk* and *Allegheny Uprising.*

Generally those productions on the Revolution with some adventurous content fall closest to the swashbuckler, dealing with the struggle for liberty and independence. Hovering over these films is the almost saintly memory of George Washington, whose absence in adventure films is notable yet whose ideals and model of leadership are constantly imitated. The creators of *John Paul Jones,* one of the rare adventure movies in which Washington is featured, felt so constrained by his presence that they awkwardly kept his back to the camera throughout a long dialogue scene with Jones. Yet Washington's example is constantly invoked in the selfless, reluctant hero who saves the people's rights. Often adventure heroes resemble not the historical individuals on whom they are ostensibly patterned, but the legendary virtues of George Washington as founder of our country. Cinematic adventurers never strive for power of their own, always gladly making way for the restoration of civil authorities, constantly emulating the legendary example of George Washington and the Continental Army. Other Revolutionary leaders are also invoked; *The Black Book / Reign of Terror* introduces the side of justice by identifying it with the Marquis de Lafayette, indicating the French Revolution has exiled him, thereby highlighting the excesses of France by comparison with our own revolution.

The adventure movie may be said to be a metaphorical manifestation of ideas and myths in American history because there is an immediacy and sanctity about these events themselves, especially the Revolution, that renders them difficult to adapt directly for the cinema. The motivations for the American Revolution may have been too complex, its incidents too sacred, to be condensed for the cinema. The American Revolution, as opposed to, for instance, the more geographically removed French Revolution, is better known to American audiences, assured of at least a measure of instant historical recognition of where fact and fiction separate. Above all, American audiences may be uncomfortable with depictions of the degree of radicalism of which they were once capable. Movies about this event would also require the implicit admission that the United States was once a colony, subject to an overseas power, an admission made doubly difficult because of the imperialism since engaged in by America in her own right. Simultaneously honoring the founding fathers and yet practicing the very policies they fought against would be a hypocrisy difficult to admit.

The Revolution is also the one historical conflict in which Americans still have a nationalistic, emotional stake, that differs completely from audiences in England. A cinematic representation of the American Revolution inevitably divides audiences, placing the United States and France against the United Kingdom and Germany, if the role of Hessian mercenaries in the Revolution is included. By contrast, more fictional narratives, or the use of a more remote time, whose nationalistic implications are less relevant, allow all audiences to participate equally in applauding a hero of any background against his enemy. Similarly, American audiences need not worry about the use of European settings and the lack of authenticity and accuracy involved, since there is no compelling reason to know about them. The Revolution brings impressions that are just the reverse and may easily resemble school textbook lessons.

Perhaps for parallel reasons, pictures about the English Revolution have also never been especially popular. While America celebrates George Washington, Oliver Cromwell elicits a more ambiguous response, his revolution leading to a dictatorship and ultimately a restoration. The few adventure films to portray the conflict usually do so from a royalist perspective (*The Exile* [1947]; *Moonraker* [1958]; *The Crimson Blade / The Scarlet Blade; The Return of the Musketeers*). Indeed, the difficulty for American audiences to celebrate royalists is understandable. England and the United States have drawn sharply different lessons from their respective revolutions, making each difficult for the other to cheer.

The implicit comparison between the swashbuckler and the American Revolution has become so commonplace that an unpretentious Robin Hood sequel, *Rogues of Sherwood Forest* (1950),

Robin (John Derek, center), his band, and the nobles pledge with the Archbishop (Donald Randolph) to fight for their basic rights in *Rogues of Sherwood Forest* (1950).

could easily tell the entire story almost unconsciously. *Rogues of Sherwood Forest* begins by noting: "The Bill of Rights and the Liberty and Justice we enjoy today stem from the Magna Carta, the great charter that the oppressed people of England forced from their tyrannical King John. In the year 1215, King John was secretly planning to crush all who stood in the way of his ruthless ambition." This is, of course, the very same King John, younger brother of Richard the Lion-Hearted, who has been mythologized as the ultimate usurper in countless versions of the Robin Hood saga. *Rogues of Sherwood Forest* crystallizes the comparison between adventure and the American Revolution by casting John (George Macready) as the George III figure. The comparison is reinforced as John hires a mercenary army, in this case Flemish, to enforce his power. John plans to pay their leader by marrying him to Robin's true love, Marianne (Diana Lynn). Now that tyranny threatens again, the Merrie Men reunite under the archetypal revolutionary leader, in this case Robin's son and namesake (John Derek).

As part of his plan to rule the kingdom single-handedly, John plans

After King John (George Macready, left) signs the Magna Carta, observed by the Archbishop (Donald Randolph, center), Robin (John Derek, right) is united with Marianne (Diana Lynn), as the conclusion merges the political, heroic, and romantic elements in *Rogues of Sherwood Forest* (1950).

to eliminate the nobles, the intermediaries between the king and his mercenaries and the people they rule. John arranges their massacre, planning to blame Robin, but one of the barons accidentally survives to tell the true story. The remaining nobles meet with Robin and the archbishop, uniting to resist John's tyranny. They draw up a compact that will guarantee their security, rights, and property, and plan to force John to sign. They spontaneously articulate the rights they need: "Every man shall be held innocent until proven guilty"; "no imprisonment for debt"; "every man shall have the right to dispose of his own property by will"; "women must not be forced into marriage without their consent." "Aye, all of those things and more," replies the archbishop to this litany of basic adventure—and American revolutionary—values, and he is asked to put it into writing. The nobles promise that John shall sign such a document, and they come to represent the individual colonies, realizing that the king must be prevented from moving against them singly; in Benjamin Franklin's analogy, they must all hang together or assuredly they will hang separately. In order to gain time to raise an army, Robin's banditry must divert John's forces.

Ultimately, with Robin's rescue of Marianne, John's mercenaries abandon him on the field of battle, and his military surrender follows a bloodless confrontation. Nonetheless, John tries to reassert his authority, offering pardons while perusing the Magna Carta. However, the united forces of church, nobility, and people, represented by Robin, tell him they seek no pardon, only an answer to their demands. John asserts, "Demands? No man, no power on earth, may make demands upon me. I rule by divine right." However, the archbishop replies, "The church denies your claim. You rule by the consent of your subjects." Without any other recourse, John is compelled to admit defeat and sign the Magna Carta. John may only continue to wear the crown by sealing the covenant, and the camera moves into an extreme close-up of the process, emphasizing that it is a document on paper, a virtual declaration of independence. The archbishop requires the king to "swear by your sword that you will abide by this charter, this Magna Carta you have just sealed." (Such references are not unusual; Jean Lafitte in *The Buccaneer* (1958) is outspoken in his admiration for the Declaration of Independence, and *The Fighting Guardsman* tries to abduct the French king to force him to recall the parliament and make a constitution for all.) As cheers arise and bells ring, Robin kisses Marianne, unifying the political and personal nature of the change in power. *Rogues of Sherwood Forest* tells of the revolution, from the need for liberty, to fighting mercenaries, finally acknowledging their freedom, making it perhaps the most comprehensive yet analogous movie reenactment of the Revolution. *Rogues of Sherwood Forest* is even more important in that it is so typical of the conventions of adventure and hardly exceptional or unusual, to such a degree that it has remained almost entirely overlooked to date.

Earlier in this book I resisted the temptation to attempt a broad narrative formula that would apply to all adventure films, preferring to note the diversity of types along with the thematic treatment that unified them. At this point, however, it is appropriate to indicate that there is a basic pattern or formula that may be applied to all adventure films, from an existing document. This document has been read, revered, and considered by schoolchildren and adults alike for generations, especially in the United States but also around the world, making a cinematic manifestation almost inevitable. Not only may the spirit of the American Revolution be said to underlie adventure movies, their formula is crystallized by, and indeed seems to have been taken directly from, the Declaration of Independence. The second paragraph, after the famous enumeration of self evident rights, reads as follows.

> To secure these rights, governments are instituted among men, deriving their just powers from the consent of the governed. That, whenever any form of Government becomes destructive of these ends, it is the Right of the People to alter or abolish it, and to institute new Government, laying its foundation on such Principles, and organizing its Powers in such form, as to them shall seem most likely to effect their Safety and Happiness. Prudence, indeed, will dictate that Governments long established should not be changed for light and transient causes; and, accordingly, all experience hath shewn, that mankind are more disposed to suffer, while evils are sufferable, than to right themselves by abolishing the forms to which they are accustomed. But, when a long train of abuses and usurpations, pursuing invariably the same Object, evinces a design to reduce them under absolute Despotism, it is their right, it is their duty, to throw off such Government, and to provide new Guards for their future Security.

Adventure perfectly reflects both this patience not to sanction subversion of regimes that are not fully justified along with the determination to overthrow those governments or governors that have been judged oppressive. Further on, the Declaration notes that "a prince whose character is thus marked by every act which may define a tyrant is unfit to be the ruler of a free people." All of these characteristics define, in a broad sense, not only the spirit but the conventions of adventure films, whether a swashbuckler or a pirate, a captain leading his crew, an empire builder saving his people from the threat of oppression, or a Monte Cristo–style fortune hunter seeking vengeance. No better summing up of adventure films can be offered than the Declaration of Independence itself.

Perhaps it is only through such indirect, mythicized, and metaphoric, less immediate, and personal means as the adventure movie that American filmgoers can fully grasp the ideals and also the ambiguities underlying the nation's birth. As well, adventure films may have offered a way for audiences worldwide to experience the hopes and aspirations of the Revolution and the American dream of democracy and equality in a dramatized, action-filled generic form, iconographically approximating the Revolutionary period and its sabres and muskets. Many of these non-American audiences find similar comfort in these same ideals. Hence, it is perhaps not surprising that the revival of adventure during the fourth cycle of the 1970s peaked at the time of the celebration of the American Bicentennial, especially of the Declaration of Independence. While some of these correlations are inherently speculative, it is indisputable that the adventure genre is based on many of the same concepts as promulgated in the American Revolution. In this way the genre of historical adventure pictures plays a significant role in American culture, both in understanding ourselves and in helping others to grasp the American vision.

CONCLUSION

In attempting to map the parameters of adventure films for the first time, my goal has been to lay a foundation for future studies by examining the totality of the genre. One result has been to preclude commentary on the larger issues of genre study and some of the less basic methodologies. Nonetheless, there are a number of other directions that offer potentially promising results. The influence of literature on Hollywood filmmaking needs to be enlarged to consider not only the direct source of adaptations but also the similarities between Hollywood formulas and popular literature, especially the pulps. Similarly, studies of the relationship between films and history must be expanded beyond dwelling on specific cinematic interpretations of various eras to construct broader ways of interpreting how myth and legend are transmuted into popular culture. Another possible line of inquiry would take an anthropological and behavioral perspective that could include the themes of isolation, survival, Darwinism, and initiation, found in films from *The Lost Patrol* to *Zulu*; *The Sands of the Kalahari*; and *Lord of the Flies*. Further probing of the issues of characterization would include the manner in which race and gender roles are constructed and how adventure relies upon bipolarities and ideas of otherness that both invoke and violate stereotypes. For instance, although natives and women may appear as imperiled objects for the hero's rescue, either may also be brave protagonists. A more ideological reading could be made of the genre's political strains, and doubtless more will be heard from various types of Marxist and sociological readings, whose depth I have only had the opportunity to suggest. Work remains to be done on the types of non-Hollywood adventure films indigenous to Europe and elsewhere.

To begin the discussion, this book has defined the genre largely by content; adventure movies manifest themselves in five distinct forms, the swashbuckler, pirate, sea, empire, and fortune hunter adventures. They are differentiated by narrative formulas, varied geographical locales and, to a lesser degree, the types of character and their motivations. What unites adventure is less the precise narrative conventions than the treatment of history, characters, conduct, and the attitudes toward issues of government and politics. By adopting a generic perspective, it has been possible to trace these themes through the various types of adventure narratives.

Among the key motifs are adventure's use of a distinct period of history, from the Middle Ages until the outbreak of World War I. The genre is both subsequent to the time of belief in the gods and magic, and ends when technological and industrial warfare introduced a new level of violence. Adventure belongs to the years of faith in the human endeavor, taking an optimistic worldview. Morality is drawn in sharp relief, arranging characters around the polarity of hero and villain. Heroes often thrive as leaders of small groups, although these associations do not constrain their individualism. A woman is typically an object, the hero's consort, although increasingly independent female heroes have emerged.

The several strands that combine to create the dominant thematic content of adventure films and the manner in which it portrays history and characters can best be termed its philosophy. Adventure propounds a code of conduct, an almost secular religion emphasizing gentlemanliness and patriotism to a chosen cause. The code prompts adventurers to undertake a search for liberty, often involving them in subversion of an oppressive political system. Unlike much of the genre's literary precursors, adventure films center around a political dialectic, most frequently presented as oppression, rebellion, and the establishment of a just government. Yet while revolutionary movements are often valorized, many adventurers are also imperialists, who justify exploration and colonialism in the belief that they spread the benefits of their civilization to supposedly unenlightened lands.

Only in the historical adventure genre does Hollywood combine all these themes. Adventure's concern with a period backdrop for depicting revolts against an unjust status quo, and the creation of a new society with rights for all, must be placed within the American context from which Hollywood product largely emerged. Adventure pictures have addressed nationalism and freedom from both radical and conservative perspectives, managing to unite these seemingly antithetical tendencies in a narrative that creates ideological unity. The genre may be regarded as an unconscious attempt to cope with the tensions of American political thought, especially by creating a metaphor for the one great event of our national consciousness that has never found a secure home on the screen: the American Revolution. Through this realization a new understanding of adventure movies is possible, one that explains the apparent contradictions within the genre.

APPENDIX

Chronological List of Adventure Films by Type

This list of movies, serials, and television series and mini-series in the genre by type is compiled through the author's screenings and, for those pictures not seen, information from sources in the bibliography. Alternate titles for British or television release are indicated.

THE SWASHBUCKLER ADVENTURE

Year	Title	Distributor or Producer
1906	*Dick Turpin's Last Ride to York*	
1906	*Dick Turpin's Ride to York*	Hepworth
1908	*The King's Messenger*	Biograph
1908	*The Standard Bearer*	Unique
1908	*Swash-buckler*	Selig
1908	*When Knights Were Bold*	Biograph
1909	*Gambling With Death*	Vitagraph
1909	*Richelieu or the Cardinal's Conspiracy*	Biograph
1909	*Robin Hood and his Merry Men*	Clarendon
1909	*1776, or the Hessian Renegades*	Biograph
1909	*A True Patriot*	Lubin
1909	*The Two Sons*	Imp
1909	*When the Flag Falls*	Lubin
1910	*The Call to Arms*	Biograph
1910	*The Duke's Plan*	Biograph
1910	*Nursing a Viper*	Biograph
1910	*The Oath and the Man*	Biograph

1911	*Ivanhoe*	J.S. Blackton
1911	*The Prince and the Pauper*	Vitagraph
1911	*Richelieu*	Pathé
1911	*The Three Musketeers*	Edison
1912	*The Flag of Freedom*	Kalem
1912	*The Midnight Ride of Paul Revere*	Kalem
1912	*Robin Hood*	Eclair-Universal
1912	*Shamus O'Brien*	Imp
1912	*When Kings Were the Law*	Biograph
1913	*In the Days of Robin Hood*	Kineto
1913	*Ivanhoe*	Imp
1913	*The Prisoner of Zenda*	Famous Players
1913	*Rebecca the Jewess / Ivanhoe*	Zenith
1913	*Robin Hood*	Thanhouser
1913	*Robin Hood—Outlawed*	British & Colonial Kinematograph
1914	*Cardinal Richelieu's Ward*	Thanhouser
1914	*Francis Marion—the Swamp Fox*	Kalem
1914	*Kidnapped*	
1914	*The Reign of Terror*	Eclectic
1914	*Richelieu*	Universal
1914	*Rogues of Paris*	Solax-Eclair
1914	*The Spy*	Universal
1914	*The Three Musketeers*	Aquila
1914	*The Three Musketeers*	Film Attractions
1914	*Washington at Valley Forge*	Universal
1914	*William Tell*	Greene
1915	*Brigadier Gerard*	Barker
1915	*The Prisoner of Zenda*	Jury
1915	*The Prince and the Pauper*	Famous Players
1915	*Rupert of Hentzau*	Cromelin/London/Jury
1916	*Beau Brocade*	Lucoque
1916	*Beverly of Graustark*	Biograph
1916	*D'Artagnan / The Three Musketeers*	Triangle
1916	*The Heart of a Hero*	World
1916	*Rupert of Hentzau*	Universal
1917	*Barnaby Lee*	Edison
1917	*Kidnapped*	Edison
1917	*The Midnight Ride of Paul Revere*	Edison
1917	*Scouting for Washington*	Edison
1919	*The Scarlet Pimpernel / The Elusive Pimpernel*	Stoll
1920	*An Adventuress*	Republic
1920	*If I Were King*	Fox
1920	*The Mark of Zorro*	United Artists
1921	*The Black Tulip*	Rollandia
1921	*Bluff*	Hardy

1921	*The Tavern Knight*	Steiner
1921	*The Three Musketeers*	United Artists
1922	*Captain Fly-by-Night*	FBO
1922	*Cardigan*	American
1922	*Dick Turpin's Ride to York*	Stoll
1922	*Fortune's Fool*	Wallace Heaton
1922	*Lorna Doone*	Ince
1922	*The Prisoner of Zenda*	Metro
1922	*Rob Roy*	Gaumont
1922	*Robin Hood*	United Artists
1922	*The Three Must-Get-Theres*	United Artists
1923	*The Fighting Blade*	First National
1923	*The Prince and the Pauper*	
1923	*Richard the Lion-hearted*	APD
1923	*Rupert of Hentzau*	Metro
1923	*Swords and the Woman / I Will Repay*	Ideal
1923	*Under the Red Robe*	Cosmopolitan
1924	*Claude Duval*	Gaumont
1924	*Robin Hood's Men*	Regent
1925	*Dick Turpin*	Fox
1925	*Don Q Son of Zorro*	United Artists
1925	*The Eagle*	United Artists
1926	*Bardelys the Magnificent*	Metro-Goldwyn-Mayer
1926	*Don Juan*	Warner Bros.
1927	*The Beloved Rogue*	United Artists
1927	*The Fighting Eagle / Brigadier Gerard*	Pathé
1927	*The King's Highway*	Stoll
1927	*The Magic Flame*	United Artists
1928	*The Man in the Iron Mask*	British Filmcraft
1928	*The Scarlet Daredevil / The Triumph of the Scarlet Pimpernel*	British & Dominion
1929	*The Iron Mask*	United Artists
1930	*The Vagabond King*	Paramount
1931	*The Lash / Adios*	First National
1933	*Dick Turpin*	Gaumont
1934	*The Affairs of Cellini*	United Artists
1934	*The California Trail*	Columbia
1934	*The Scarlet Pimpernel*	United Artists-Korda
1935	*The Bold Caballero / The Bold Cavalier*	Republic
1935	*Lorna Doone*	Associated Talking Pictures
1935	*The Three Musketeers*	RKO
1937	*The Californian*	20th Century-Fox
1937	*Dr. Syn*	Gaumont
1937	*Fire Over England*	United Artists-Korda
1937	*The Prince and the Pauper*	Warner Bros.

1937	*The Prisoner of Zenda*	United Artists-Selznick
1937	*Under the Red Robe*	20th Century-Fox
1938	*The Adventures of Robin Hood*	Warner Bros.
1938	*The Face Behind the Mask / The Masked Prisoner*	Metro-Goldwyn-Mayer
1938	*If I Were King*	Paramount
1938	*Kidnapped*	20th Century-Fox
1938	*The Return of the Scarlet Pimpernel*	United Artists-Korda
1938	*Sharpshooters*	20th Century-Fox
1939	*The Three Musketeers / The Singing Musketeer*	20th Century-Fox
1940	*Aloma of the South Seas*	Paramount
1940	*The Mark of Zorro*	20th Century-Fox
1940	*Son of Monte Cristo*	United Artists-Small
1944	*Gypsy Wildcat*	Universal
1945	*The Fighting Guardsman*	Columbia
1946	*Bandit of Sherwood Forest / The Son of Robin Hood*	Columbia
1946	*Don Ricardo Returns*	Producers Releasing Corp.
1946	*Son of the Guardsman / Outlaws of Sherwood Forest* (serial)	Columbia
1946	*The Wife of Monte Cristo*	Pathé
1947	*Bonnie Prince Charlie*	United Artists-Korda
1947	*Captain Boycott*	Universal
1947	*The Exile*	Universal
1947	*The Pirates of Monterey*	Universal
1947	*Slave Girl*	Universal
1948	*Adventures of Casanova*	Eagle-Lion
1948	*Adventures of Don Juan*	Warner Bros.
1948	*The Black Arrow / The Black Arrow Strikes*	Columbia
1948	*The Elusive Pimpernel / The Fighting Pimpernel*	United Artists-Korda
1948	*The Gallant Blade*	Columbia
1948	*Kidnapped*	Monogram
1948	*The Prince of Thieves*	Columbia
1948	*Sword of the Avenger*	United Artists
1948	*The Three Musketeers*	Metro-Goldwyn-Mayer
1949	*The Adventures of Sir Galahad* (serial)	Columbia
1949	*The Black Book / Reign of Terror*	Eagle Lion
1949	*The Gay Swordsman*	International
1949	*The Pirates of Capri / The Masked Pirate / Captain Sirocco*	Film Classics
1949	*The Secret of St. Ives*	Columbia
1950	*The Flame and the Arrow*	Warner Bros.

1950	Rogues of Sherwood Forest	Columbia
1950	Shadow of the Eagle	British Lion
1951	The Highwayman	Allied Artists
1951	The Lady and the Bandit / Dick Turpin's Ride	Columbia
1951	Lorna Doone	Columbia
1951	Mark of the Renegade	Universal
1951	Mask of the Avenger	Columbia
1951	Quebec	Paramount
1951	Robin Hood and the Golden Arrow	Roach
1951	The Sword of Monte Cristo	20th Century-Fox
1952	At Sword's Point / Sons of the Musketeers	RKO
1952	The Brigand	Columbia
1952	Ivanhoe	Metro-Goldwyn-Mayer
1952	The Lady in the Iron Mask	20th Century-Fox
1952	Prince of Pirates	Columbia
1952	The Prisoner of Zenda	Metro-Goldwyn-Mayer
1952	The Story of Robin Hood / The Story of Robin Hood and His Merrie Men	Buena Vista
1952	The Sword of D'Artagnan	Roach
1952	Sword of Venus / Island of Monte Cristo	RKO
1952	The Tales of Robin Hood	Roach
1953	The Bandits of Corsica / The Return of the Corsican Brothers	United Artists-Small
1953	Blades of the Musketeers	Roach
1953	Captain Scarlett	United Artists
1953	Knights of the Round Table	Metro-Goldwyn-Mayer
1953	The Master of Ballantrae	Warner Bros.
1953	Sea Devils	RKO
1954	The Black Knight	Columbia
1954	The Black Shield of Falworth	Universal
1954	Casanova's Big Night	Paramount
1954	Crossed Swords	United Artists
1954	The Iron Glove	Columbia
1954	Men of Sherwood Forest	Hammer
1954	Prince Valiant	20th Century-Fox
1954	Rob Roy—the Highland Rogue	Buena Vista
1954	The Saracen Blade	Columbia
1954	Star of India	United Artists
1955	The Adventures of Gil Blas	
1955	Captain Lightfoot	Universal
1955	The King's Thief	Metro-Goldwyn-Mayer
1955	Kiss of Fire	Universal
1955	Moonfleet	Metro-Goldwyn-Mayer

1955	*The Purple Mask*	Universal
1955	*Quentin Durward / The Adventures of Quentin Durward*	Metro-Goldwyn-Mayer
1955	*The Scarlet Coat*	Metro-Goldwyn-Mayer
1955	*The Three Musketeers* (series)	ABC
1955	*The Warriors / The Dark Avenger*	Allied Artists
1955–8	*The Adventures of Robin Hood / Adventures in Sherwood Forest* (series)	CBS
1956	*The Court Jester*	Paramount
1956	*The Son of El Cid*	
1956–7	*The Adventures of Sir Lancelot* (series)	NBC
1957	*The Gay Cavalier* (series)	Associated Rediffusion
1957	*Johnny Tremain / Johnny Tremain and the Sons of Liberty*	Buena Vista
1957	*The Pride and the Passion*	United Artists
1957	*The Sword of Freedom* (series)	Official Films
1957	*The Women of Pitcairn Island*	20th Century-Fox
1957–9	*Zorro* (series)	Disney
1958	*The Adventures of William Tell* (series)	NTA
1958	*The Curse of Zorro*	Buena Vista
1958	*Dangerous Exile*	Rank
1958	*The Iron Mask* (series)	
1958	*Ivanhoe* (series)	Associated Rediffusion
1958	*Moonraker*	Associated British
1958	*The Scarlet Pimpernel* (series)	Towers of London
1959	*The Son of Robin Hood*	20th Century-Fox
1959–60	*The Swamp Fox* (mini-series)	Disney
1960	*Adventures of Mandrin / Captain Adventure*	
1960	*The Hellfire Club*	Regal
1960	*Kidnapped*	Buena Vista
1960	*The Scarlet Pimpernel* (mini-series)	CBS
1960	*The Sign of Zorro*	Buena Vista
1960	*The Son of D'Artagnan*	
1960	*Sword of Granada*	Manson
1960	*The White Warrior*	Warner Bros.
1960	*Zorro the Avenger*	Buena Vista
1961	*El Cid*	Allied Artists
1961	*The Pirate of the Black Hawk*	Film Group
1961	*Sword of Sherwood Forest*	Columbia
1961	*The Treasure of Monte Cristo / The Secret of Monte Cristo*	Regal
1961	*Zorro*	
1962	*Duel at the Rio Grande*	Regal
1962	*Hero's Island*	United Artists

1962	*The Huns*	Producers International
1962	*The Prince and the Pauper*	Buena Vista
1962	*Prisoner of the Iron Mask*	American International
1962	*The Secret Mark of D'Artagnan*	Columbia
1962	*Seventh Sword*	New Realm
1962	*The Shadow of Zorro*	Compton Cameo
1962	*Taras Bulba*	United Artists
1963	*The Crimson Blade / The Scarlet Blade*	Hammer
1963	*Lafayette*	Maco
1963	*Richard the Lionheart* (series)	Associated Rediffusion
1963	*The Scarecrow of Romney Marsh* (US mini-series) / *Dr. Syn Alias the Scarecrow* (UK feature)	Disney
1963	*Siege of the Saxons*	Columbia
1963	*Son of the Red Corsair*	Medallion
1963	*Sword of Lancelot / Lancelot and Guinevere*	Universal
1964	*Behind the Mask of Zorro*	
1964	*The Hundred Horsemen*	Domiziana International/ Cinemat.-Procusa-International Germania
1964	*The Sword of El Cid*	Producers Releasing/ Eldorado
1964	*The Three Swords of Zorro / Swordsmen Three*	Hispamer
1965	*The Legend of Young Dick Turpin*	Buena Vista
1965	*The Revenge of Ivanhoe*	Tevere Films
1965	*Sword Without a Country*	Silvio Scarpellini
1965	*The War Lord*	Universal
1966	*The Fighting Prince of Donegal*	Buena Vista
1967	*A Challenge for Robin Hood*	Hammer
1967	*The Lion of St. Mark*	Liber
1969	*A Walk With Love and Death*	20th Century-Fox
1970	*Start the Revolution Without Me*	Warner Bros.
1970–1	*The Young Rebels* (series)	ABC
1971	*Kidnapped*	American International
1971	*The Adventures of Gerard*	United Artists
1972	*Ivanhoe* (mini-series)	Ogilvy & Mather
1972	*The Last Valley*	Cinerama
1972–3	*Arthur of the Britains* (mini-series)	ITC
1973	*King Arthur—the Young Warlord*	Heritage
1973	*The Fortunes of Sir Nigel* (series)	20th Century-Fox
1973	*Wolfshead—the Legend of Robin Hood*	Hammer
1974	*Lancelot du Lac / Lancelot of the Lake*	Mara Films-Laser

1974	The Mark of Zorro	20th Century-Fox
1974	The Three Musketeers—the Queen's Diamonds	20th Century-Fox
1975	Robin Hood Junior	Almi
1975	The Four Musketeers—Milady's Revenge	20th Century-Fox
1975	Zorro	Allied Artists
1976	Robin and Marian	Warner Bros.
1977	New Adventures of Robin Hood (series)	Trident
1977	The Man in the Iron Mask	ITC
1978	Crossed Swords / The Prince and the Pauper	Warner Bros.
1978	The Duellists	Paramount
1979	Kidnapped / The Adventures of David Balfour	TV West
1979	The Fifth Musketeer / Behind the Iron Mask	Columbia
1979–82	Dick Turpin (series)	ITC
1981	The Talisman (mini-series)	BBC
1981	Zorro—the Gay Blade	20th Century-Fox
1982	Ivanhoe	CBS
1982	The Scarlet Pimpernel	CBS
1983	The Adventures of Young Robin Hood	Filmworld TV
1984	The Black Arrow	Buena Vista
1984	The Master of Ballantrae	CBS
1984	The Zany Adventures of Robin Hood	CBS
1985	Revolution	Warner Bros.
1986	Crossbow—the Adventures of William Tell	RAI
1989	The Lady and the Highwayman	CBS
1989	The Return of the Musketeers	Universal
1989	Zorro—the Legend Begins (pilot feature)	New World
1990–	Zorro / The New Zorro (series)	New World
1991	Robin Hood	Fox
1991	Robin Hood—Prince of Thieves	Warner Bros.
1992	Covington Cross (series)	ABC

The Oriental Swashbuckler

1942	Arabian Nights	Universal
1943	Ali Baba and the Forty Thieves	Universal
1944	The Desert Hawk (serial)	Columbia
1945	Sudan	Universal
1950	Bagdad	Universal
1950	The Desert Hawk	Universal
1951	Flame of Araby	Universal

1951	*The Golden Horde*	Universal
1951	*The Prince Who Was a Thief*	Universal
1952	*Son of Ali Baba*	Universal
1952	*Thief of Damascus*	Columbia
1953	*Prisoners of the Casbah*	Columbia
1953	*The Veils of Bagdad*	Universal
1954	*The Adventures of Hajji Baba*	20th Century-Fox
1954	*Princess of the Nile*	20th Century-Fox
1955	*Son of Sinbad / Nights in a Harem*	RKO
1957	*Omar Khayyam*	Paramount
1964	*Sword of Ali Baba*	Universal

THE PIRATE ADVENTURE

1912	*The Pirate's Daughter*	Selig
1912	*Treasure Island*	Edison
1916	*Daphne and the Pirate*	Triangle
1916	*To Have and to Hold*	Paramount
1917	*The Slave Market*	Paramount
1918	*Peg of the Pirates*	Fox
1918	*The Sea Panther*	Triangle
1918	*Such a Little Pirate*	Paramount
1918	*Treasure Island*	Fox
1920	*Dead Men Tell No Tales*	Vitagraph
1920	*Miss Nobody*	National Federated
1920	*Treasure Island*	Paramount
1921	*Wet Gold*	Goldwyn
1922	*Captain Kidd* (serial)	Star Serial Corp.
1924	*Captain Blood*	Vitagraph
1924	*The Sea Hawk*	First National
1926	*The Black Pirate*	United Artists
1926	*The Eagle of the Sea*	Paramount
1927	*The Road to Romance*	Metro-Goldwyn-Mayer
1928	*Blockade*	FBO
1929	*The Delightful Rogue*	RKO
1929	*Pirates of Panama* (serial)	Universal
1934	*Pirate Treasure* (serial)	Universal
1934	*Treasure Island*	Metro-Goldwyn-Mayer
1935	*Captain Blood*	Warner Bros.
1935	*China Seas*	Metro-Goldwyn-Mayer
1938	*The Buccaneer*	Paramount
1939	*Jamaica Inn*	Paramount
1942	*The Black Swan*	20th Century-Fox
1944	*Frenchman's Creek*	Paramount
1944	*The Princess and the Pirate*	Paramount
1945	*Captain Kidd*	United Artists
1945	*The Spanish Main*	RKO

1947	*The Sea Hound* (serial)	Columbia
1948	*The Wreck of the Hesperus*	Columbia
1949	*The Mutineers / Pirate Ship*	Columbia
1950	*Buccaneer's Girl*	Universal
1950	*The Fortunes of Captain Blood*	Columbia
1950	*The Last of the Buccaneers*	Columbia
1950	*Pirates of the High Seas* (serial)	Columbia
1950	*Treasure Island*	Buena Vista
1951	*Anne of the Indies*	20th Century-Fox
1951	*Double Crossbones*	Universal
1951	*The Crimson Pirate*	Warner Bros.
1952	*Against All Flags*	Universal
1952	*Blackbeard the Pirate*	RKO
1952	*Captain Pirate / Captain Blood— Fugitive / Captain Blood Returns*	Columbia
1952	*Caribbean / Caribbean Gold*	Paramount
1952	*The Golden Hawk*	Columbia
1952	*Hurricane Smith*	Paramount
1952	*Yankee Buccaneer*	Universal
1953	*The Great Adventures of Captain Kidd* (serial)	Columbia
1953	*Raiders of the Seven Seas*	United Artists
1953	*Sangaree*	Paramount
1954	*Captain Kidd and the Slave Girl*	United Artists-Small
1954	*Long John Silver / Long John Silver's Return to Treasure Island*	New Trends Associates
1955	*The Black Pirates*	Lippert
1955	*Moonfleet*	Metro-Goldwyn-Mayer
1955	*The Pirates of Tripoli*	Columbia
1956	*Adventures of Long John Silver / Return to Treasure Island* (series)	ABC
1956–7	*The Buccaneers* (series)	CBS
1958	*The Buccaneer*	Paramount
1960	*Fury at Smuggler's Bay*	Hammer
1960	*Morgan the Pirate*	Metro-Goldwyn-Mayer
1960	*Queen of the Pirates*	Columbia
1961	*Guns of the Black Witch*	American International
1961	*Pirate and the Slave Girl*	Crest
1961	*The Pirates of Tortuga*	20th Century-Fox
1961	*Sandokan the Great / Pirates of the Seven Seas*	Empire
1962	*Night Creatures / Captain Clegg*	Hammer
1962	*Pirate Warrior / Black Pirate / Rage of the Buccaneers*	Colorama
1962	*The Pirates of Blood River*	Hammer
1962	*Son of Captain Blood*	Paramount
1963	*The Devil-Ship Pirates*	Hammer

1964	Cold Steel for Tortuga / Adventure for Tortuga	Empire
1964	Tiger of the Seven Seas	Embassy
1965	A High Wind in Jamaica	20th Century-Fox
1967	The King's Pirate	Universal
1967	The Sea Pirate	Paramount
1971	The Light at the Edge of the World	National General
1972	Treasure Island	National General
1976	Swashbuckler / The Scarlet Buccaneer	Universal
1983	Nate and Hayes / Savage Islands	Paramount
1983	Yellowbeard	Orion
1985	Jamaica Inn	CBS
1986	John Silver's Return to Treasure Island (mini-series)	ITC
1986	Pirates	Cannon
1990	Treasure Island	TNT
1991	Shipwrecked	Buena Vista

The Viking Pirate

1928	The Viking	Metro-Goldwyn-Mayer
1958	The Vikings	United Artists
1959	Tales of the Vikings (series)	Bryna/United Artists
1962	Erik the Conqueror / Fury of the Vikings	American International
1962	The Last of the Vikings	Medallion
1964	King of the Vikings	American International
1964	The Long Ships	Columbia
1965	Vengeance of the Vikings	Nike Cinematografica-Asfilms
1966	Hagbard and Signe / Knives of the Avenger	World Entertainment
1967	The Red Mantle	Steve Prentoulis
1978	The Norseman	American International

THE SEA ADVENTURE

1913	The Sea Wolf	Bosworth
1915	The Mutiny on the Bounty	Crick and Jones
1917	The Sea Master	Mutual
1920	The Mutiny of the Elsinore	Metro
1920	The Sea Wolf	Paramount
1922	Down to the Sea in Ships	W.W. Hodkinson
1923	All the Brothers Were Valiant	Metro
1925	The Sea Wolf	PDC
1926	Old Ironsides	Paramount
1926	The Sea Beast	Warner Bros.
1930	Moby Dick	Warner Bros.

1930	*The Sea Wolf*	Fox
1932	*Tiger Shark*	Warner Bros.
1933	*In the Wake of the Bounty*	Expeditionary
1934	*Midshipman Easy*	Associated British
1935	*Eight Bells*	Columbia
1935	*Mutiny Ahead*	Majestic
1935	*Mutiny on the Bounty*	Metro-Goldwyn-Mayer
1936	*Drake the Pirate / Drake of England*	United Artists
1936	*I Conquer the Sea*	Academy/Halperin
1936	*Dangerous Waters*	Universal
1937	*Captains Courageous*	Metro-Goldwyn-Mayer
1937	*Mutiny on the Elsinore*	Associated British
1939	*Rulers of the Sea*	Paramount
1940	*Little Old New York*	20th Century-Fox
1940	*Captain Caution*	United Artists
1940	*The Sea Hawk*	Warner Bros.
1941	*Mutiny in the Arctic*	Universal
1941	*The Sea Wolf*	Warner Bros.
1942	*The Adventures of Martin Eden*	Columbia
1942	*Reap the Wild Wind*	Paramount
1943	*The Ghost Ship*	RKO
1946	*Two Years Before the Mast*	Paramount
1949	*Captain China*	Paramount
1949	*Down to the Sea in Ships*	20th Century-Fox
1950	*Barricade*	Warner Bros.
1950	*Tyrant of the Sea*	Columbia
1951	*Captain Horatio Hornblower*	Warner Bros.
1952	*Mutiny*	United Artists
1952	*The World in His Arms*	Universal
1953	*All the Brothers Were Valiant*	Metro-Goldwyn-Mayer
1953	*Botany Bay*	Paramount
1956	*Moby Dick*	Warner Bros.
1958	*Wolf Larsen*	Allied Artists
1959	*John Paul Jones*	Warner Bros.
1961	*Ferry to Hong Kong*	20th Century-Fox
1962	*Billy Budd*	Allied Artists
1962	*Damn the Defiant! / H.M.S. Defiant*	Columbia
1962	*Seven Seas to Calais*	Metro-Goldwyn-Mayer
1962	*Sir Francis Drake* (series)	NBC
1963	*Mutiny on the Bounty*	Metro-Goldwyn-Mayer
1977	*Captains Courageous*	Norman Rosemont
1984	*The Bounty*	Orion
1985	*Drake's Voyage*	BBC
1993	*The Sea Wolf*	TNT

THE EMPIRE ADVENTURE

1898	*Tearing Down the Spanish Flag*	Vitagraph
1906	*How a British Bulldog Saved the Union Jack*	Walturdaw
1908	*Michael Strogoff*	Essanay
1910	*The Dawn of Freedom*	Selig
1910	*The Highlander's Defiance*	Selig
1910	*Michael Strogoff*	Edison
1910	*The Sepoy's Wife*	Vitagraph
1912	*The Charge of the Light Brigade*	Edison
1912	*The Coming of Columbus*	Selig
1912	*The Fall of Montezuma*	Essanay
1912	*For Valour*	Edison
1912	*The Relief of Lucknow*	Edison
1912	*The Revenge of the Fakir*	Eclair
1912	*Richard the Lionhearted*	Cines
1912	*Under Two Flags*	Gem
1912	*Under Two Flags*	Thanhouser
1913	*Robinson Crusoe*	Bison
1914	*The Boer War*	General
1914	*Michael Strogoff*	Famous Players
1914	*Soldiers of Fortune*	All Star Feature
1915	*The Four Feathers*	Metro
1915	*Mutiny in the Jungle*	Selig
1915	*Under Two Flags*	Biograph
1916	*A Message to Garcia*	Edison
1916	*Robinson Crusoe*	Warner Bros.
1916	*Under Two Flags*	Fox
1917	*Robinson Crusoe*	Universal
1919	*Soldiers of Fortune*	Realart
1919	*The Man Who Turned White*	Hampton
1921	*The Four Feathers*	Stoll
1922	*The Adventures of Robinson Crusoe (serial)*	Universal
1922	*Under Two Flags*	Universal
1922	*With Stanley in Africa (serial)*	Universal
1923	*Columbus*	Yale
1923	*A Man's Man*	FBO
1923	*Masters of Men*	Vitagraph
1924	*Love and Glory*	Universal
1924	*Richard the Lionhearted*	First National
1924	*Robinson Crusoe*	Universal
1924	*South of the Equator*	Bud Bartley
1924	*The Song of Love*	First National
1924	*The White Panther*	Goldstone

1926	Across the Pacific	Warner Bros.
1926	Beau Geste	Paramount
1926	Michael Strogoff	Universal
1926	The Silent Lover	First National
1927	Robinson Crusoe	Epic
1928	Beau Sabreur	Paramount
1928	The Cossacks	Metro-Goldwyn-Mayer
1928	Foreign Devils	Metro-Goldwyn-Mayer
1928	The Foreign Legion	Universal
1928	White Shadows Over the South Seas	Metro-Goldwyn-Mayer
1929	The Black Watch / King of the Khyber Rifles	Fox
1929	The Four Feathers	Paramount
1930	Renegades	Fox
1930	The Legionnaire	Fox
1930	Women Everywhere	Fox
1931	Beau Ideal	RKO
1933	Laughing at Life	Mascot
1933	The Rebel	Universal
1934	The Lost Patrol	RKO
1935	Clive of India	Fox
1935	The Crusades	Paramount
1935	The Lives of a Bengal Lancer	Paramount
1935	Sanders of the River	United Artists-Korda
1936	The Charge of the Light Brigade	Warner Bros.
1936	A Message to Garcia	20th Century-Fox
1936	Rhodes of Africa / Rhodes	Gaumont British
1936	Robinson Crusoe	Guaranteed
1936	Under Two Flags	20th Century-Fox
1937	I Cover the War	Universal
1937	Legion of Missing Men	Monogram
1937	Outlaws of the Orient	Columbia
1937	The Soldier and the Lady / Michael Strogoff / The Bandit and the Lady / Adventures of Michael Strogoff	RKO
1937	Trouble in Morocco	Columbia
1937	We're in the Legion Now / Rest Cure	Grand National
1938	Adventure in Sahara	Columbia
1938	Adventures of Marco Polo	United Artists-Goldwyn
1938	Drums / The Drum	United Artists-Korda
1938	Old Bones of the River	Gainsborough
1938	Storm Over Bengal	Republic
1938	Suez	20th Century-Fox
1939	Beau Geste	Paramount
1939	Chasing Danger	20th Century-Fox

1939	*The Four Feathers*	United Artists-Korda
1939	*Gunga Din*	RKO
1939	*The Real Glory*	United Artists-Goldwyn
1939	*The Rebel Son*	United Artists
1939	*Stanley and Livingstone*	20th Century-Fox
1940	*Swiss Family Robinson*	RKO
1941	*Jungle Man*	Producers Releasing Corp.
1943	*Adventure in Iraq*	Warner Bros.
1947	*Tangier*	Universal
1948	*Captain From Castile*	20th Century-Fox
1948	*Outpost in Morocco*	United Artists-Moroccan
1948	*Scott of the Antarctic*	Ealing
1949	*Christopher Columbus*	Rank
1949	*Song of India*	Columbia
1950	*Barbary Pirate*	Columbia
1950	*Kim*	Metro-Goldwyn-Mayer
1950	*Tripoli*	Paramount
1951	*Soldiers Three*	Metro-Goldwyn-Mayer
1951	*Ten Tall Men*	Columbia
1952	*Drums of Tahiti*	Columbia
1952	*Bwana Devil*	United Artists
1952	*Plymouth Adventure*	Metro-Goldwyn-Mayer
1952	*Rogues' March*	Metro-Goldwyn-Mayer
1953	*Desert Legion*	Universal
1953	*Flame of Calcutta*	Columbia
1953	*Fort Algiers*	United Artists
1953	*Men Against the Sun*	Monarch-Kenya
1953	*Royal African Rifles / Storm Over Africa*	Allied Artists
1954	*The Adventures of Robinson Crusoe*	United Artists
1954	*Bengal Brigade / Bengal Rifles*	Universal
1954	*Charge of the Lancers*	Columbia
1954	*Khyber Patrol*	United Artists
1954	*King Richard and the Crusaders*	Warner Bros.
1954	*King of the Khyber Rifles*	20th Century-Fox
1954	*Yankee Pasha*	Universal
1955	*The Scarlet Spear*	United Artists
1955	*7 Cities of Gold*	20th Century-Fox
1955	*Storm Over the Nile*	United Artists-Korda
1955	*Untamed*	20th Century-Fox
1955–7	*Captain Gallant of the French Foreign Legion* (series)	NBC
1956	*The Conqueror*	RKO

1956	*Pacific Destiny*	British Lion
1956–7	*Tales of the 77th Bengal Lancers* (series)	NBC
1957	*The Mighty Crusaders*	Grand National
1957	*Naked Earth*	20th Century-Fox
1957	*Zarak*	Columbia
1958	*The Bandit of Zhobe*	Columbia
1958	*Desert Hell*	20th Century-Fox
1958	*Legion of the Doomed*	Allied Artists
1959	*Goliath and the Barbarians*	Standard-American International
1959	*Killers of Kilimanjaro*	Columbia
1959	*The Cossacks*	Universal
1960	*Flame Over India / Northwest Frontier*	Rank
1960	*Michael Strogoff / Revolt of the Tartars / Secret Mission to Siberia*	Continental
1960	*The Mongols*	Colorama
1960	*The Savage Innocents*	Paramount
1960	*The Stranglers of Bombay*	Hammer
1960	*Swiss Family Robinson*	Buena Vista
1961	*The Savage Hordes*	Eagle
1961	*Sword of the Conqueror*	United Artists
1962	*Marco Polo*	American International
1962	*The Sword of Islam*	
1962	*The Tartars*	Metro-Goldwyn-Mayer
1963	*Cavalry Command*	Parade
1963	*Drums of Africa*	Metro-Goldwyn-Mayer
1963	*55 Days in Peking*	Allied Artists
1963	*Kali-Yug—Goddess of Vengeance*	British Lion
1963	*Temple of the White Elephant*	Compton Cameo
1964	*East of Sudan*	Columbia
1964	*Robinson Crusoe* (mini-series)	
1964	*The Triumph of Michael Strogoff*	Films Modernes
1964	*Zulu*	Embassy
1965	*Adventure of the Bengal Lancers*	Eagle
1965	*The Brigand of Kandahar*	Columbia
1965	*Genghis Khan*	Columbia
1965	*The Sand Pebbles*	20th Century-Fox
1966	*Beau Geste*	Universal
1966	*Khartoum*	United Artists
1966	*Marco the Magnificent*	Metro-Goldwyn-Mayer
1966	*The Naked Prey*	Paramount
1967	*The Long Duel*	Rank
1968	*The Charge of the Light Brigade*	United Artists
1968	*Fury of the Khybers / Slaughter on the Khyber Pass*	Duca International/ P.C./Hispamer

1969	*Alfred the Great*	Metro-Goldwyn-Mayer
1969	*Fight for Rome / Battle for Rome / The Last Roman*	Constantin Films
1969	*The Royal Hunt of the Sun*	National General
1969	*Strange Holiday*	Mende-Brown
1969	*The Young Rebel / Cervantes*	American International
1970	*Burn!*	United Artists
1971	*The Red Tent*	Paramount
1973	*The Search for the Nile* (mini-series)	BBC
1973	*Trader Horn*	Metro-Goldwyn-Mayer
1974	*The White Dawn*	Paramount
1975	*Man Friday*	ITC
1975	*Swiss Family Robinson* (pilot feature)	ABC
1975	*Swiss Family Robinson* (series)	ABC
1975	*The Wind and the Lion*	Metro-Goldwyn-Mayer
1977	*The Four Feathers*	Norman Rosemont
1977	*March of Die*	Columbia
1979	*Mayflower—the Pilgrims' Adventure*	CBS
1979	*Zulu Dawn*	Warner Bros.
1980	*Shogun* (mini-series and feature condensation)	ABC
1982	*Marco Polo* (mini-series)	RAI
1983	*Cook and Peary—the Race to the Pole*	CBS
1984	*Kim*	CBS
1985	*Christopher Columbus* (mini-series)	CBS
1985	*The Last Place on Earth* (mini-series)	BBC
1985	*Out of Africa*	Universal
1986	*The Mission*	Warner Bros.
1987	*Walker*	Universal
1988	*Crusoe*	Island
1988	*The Deceivers*	Warner Bros.
1989	*Captain Cook* (mini-series)	TNT
1990	*Mountains of the Moon*	Tri-Star
1992	*Christopher Columbus—the Discovery*	Warner Bros.
1992	*1492—Conquest of Paradise*	Paramount

THE FORTUNE HUNTER ADVENTURE

1898	*The Corsican Brothers*	G.A. Smith
1902	*The Corsican Brothers*	
1908	*The Corsican Brothers*	Cameraphone-Film
1909	*The Count of Monte Cristo*	Selig
1910	*The Count of Monte Cristo*	Challenge
1911	*A Tale of Two Cities*	Vitagraph
1911	*The Count of Monte Cristo*	Powers
1912	*The Corsican Brothers*	Edison

1913	*Monte Cristo / The Count of Monte Cristo*	Famous Players
1915	*The Corsican Brothers*	Universal
1917	*Soldiers of Chance*	Vitagraph
1917	*A Tale of Two Cities*	Fox
1919	*A Man of Honor*	Yorke
1919	*Miss Adventure*	Fox
1919	*The Corsican Brothers*	Mutual-Universal
1922	*Monte Cristo*	Fox
1923	*Around the World in 18 Days* (serial)	Universal
1923	*Scaramouche*	Metro
1925	*The Man Without a Country / As No Man Has Loved*	Fox
1926	*Danger Quest*	Bayart
1926	*The Only Way*	United Artists
1930	*The Sea God*	Paramount
1931	*Trader Horn*	Metro-Goldwyn-Mayer
1934	*The Count of Monte Cristo*	United Artists-Small
1935	*A Tale of Two Cities*	Metro-Goldwyn-Mayer
1936	*Anthony Adverse*	Warner Bros.
1936	*Lloyd's of London*	20th Century-Fox
1937	*Ebb Tide*	Paramount
1937	*Elephant Boy*	United Artists-Korda
1937	*King Solomon's Mines*	Gaumont British
1937	*Slave Ship*	20th Century-Fox
1937	*Souls at Sea*	20th Century-Fox
1939	*Mutiny on the Blackhawk*	Universal
1940	*Safari*	Paramount
1940	*Typhoon*	Paramount
1941	*The Corsican Brothers / Vendetta*	United Artists-Small
1942	*Son of Fury*	20th Century-Fox
1943	*Isle of Forgotten Sins*	Producers Releasing Corp.
1944	*Nabonga / The Jungle Woman*	Producers Releasing Corp.
1946	*The Return of Monte Cristo / Monte Cristo's Revenge*	Columbia
1947	*Adventure Island*	Paramount
1947	*Queen of the Amazons*	Screen Guild
1947	*The Swordsman*	Columbia
1948	*Man-Eater of Kumaon*	Universal
1948	*Wake of the Red Witch*	Republic
1949	*Black Magic*	United Artists
1949	*Prince of Foxes*	20th Century-Fox
1949	*The Fighting O'Flynn*	Universal
1950	*King Solomon's Mines*	Metro-Goldwyn-Mayer
1950	*The Black Rose*	20th Century-Fox

1952	*Scaramouche*	Metro-Goldwyn-Mayer
1952	*The African Queen*	United Artists
1953	*Fair Wind to Java*	Republic
1953	*His Majesty O'Keefe*	Warner Bros.
1953	*Treasure of the Golden Condor*	20th Century-Fox
1953	*Tropic Zone*	Paramount
1953	*White Witch Doctor*	20th Century-Fox
1954	*Green Fire*	Metro-Goldwyn-Mayer
1954	*Jivaro / Lost Treasure of the Amazon*	Paramount
1954	*Tanganyika*	Universal
1955	*The Count of Monte Cristo* (series)	Roach
1956	*Around the World in 80 Days*	United Artists-Todd
1956	*Santiago*	Warner Bros.
1957	*Hell Ship Mutiny*	Republic
1958	*A Tale of Two Cities*	Rank
1959	*Watusi*	Metro-Goldwyn-Mayer
1960	*The Corsican Brothers*	Flora Film-Variety/ Mediteranee
1961	*Swordsman of Siena*	Metro-Goldwyn-Mayer
1962	*Samar*	Warner Bros.
1962	*The Story of the Count of Monte Cristo / The Count of Monte Cristo / The Story of Monte Cristo*	Warner Bros.
1963	*Rampage*	Warner Bros.
1964	*Adventures of Scaramouche*	Embassy
1964	*Cartouche / Swords of Blood*	Embassy
1965	*Lord Jim*	Columbia
1967	*Legend of the Lost*	United Artists
1969	*The Southern Star*	Columbia
1973	*Call It Courage*	Buena Vista
1973	*The Man Without a Country*	ABC
1975	*Royal Flash*	20th Century-Fox
1975	*The Count of Monte Cristo*	ITC
1976	*The Man Who Would Be King*	Allied Artists
1981	*A Tale of Two Cities*	CBS
1983	*High Road to China*	Warner Bros.
1985	*The Corsican Brothers*	CBS
1987	*Casanova*	ABC
1989	*Around the World in 80 Days* (mini-series)	Harmony Gold
1989	*A Tale of Two Cities* (mini-series)	PBS
1992	*Indiana Jones and the Curse of the Jackal*	ABC

NOTES

CHAPTER 2: Five Forms of Adventure

1. A similar breakdown is used for serials by Cline. My divisions indicate films that share much in common but have seldom been previously related to one another, a more useful typology than most of the traditional methods. For instance, Jeffrey Richards's work usually divides the genre along such lines as the temporal period of the plot, the nationality of the characters, or the source of the narrative, whether literature or legend. Green has developed a contrasting methodology for his broad definition of adventure literature in *Seven Types of Adventure Tale,* but it has no relation to film.

2. Jones, 43. Some commentators have used this convention to justify a shallow approach to the swashbuckler, concentrating on the sword play and minimizing other elements: "The films themselves are essentially forms without any serious pretentions," asserts Jones, 42 (cf. Gow 1972; Sobchack and Sobchack, 252). Jones has gone so far as to claim content is subsidiary. Even Richards 1977 dwells on the mechanics of sword fights in his analyses of individual films. However, the swashbuckler is not a style of filmmaking but a distinct narrative form of the historical adventure genre.

3. For comparison, see the comments on the western genre's revenge hero in Wright, 59–68, 155–62.

CHAPTER 3: The Evolution of the Adventure Genre

1. Many ideas in this summation of romanticism are adapted from Kenneth Allott, *Jules Verne* (London: Crescent, 1940), 244–58.

2. "No. 1 Pulp," *Time* 26 (October 21, 1935): 40. See also "*Adventure* Is 25 Years Old," *Publishers Weekly* 128 (November 2, 1935): 1667; "Adven-

ture: Dean of the Pulps Celebrates Its Silver Jubilee," *Newsweek* 6 (October 26, 1935): 23.

3. Arthur Sullivant Hoffman, "The Camp-Fire," *Adventure* 94 (November 1935): 164.

4. *The Lion's Skin* (Boston: Houghton Mifflin, 1926), x; cf. *The Historical Nights' Entertainment* (Boston: Houghton Mifflin, 1924), v.

5. Green 1984, 163. The change can be seen in critical evaluations of Talbot Mundy. Until 1919 all his work won esteem, while afterward his adventure was dismissed and only his novels of the ancient world and his philosophical fantasies received praise. For a detailed analysis of the impact this had on Mundy, see Taves, "Philosophy Into Popular Fiction."

6. All box-office figures in this chapter are from Paul Michael, ed., *The American Movies Reference Book—The Sound Era* (Englewood Cliffs, N.J.: Prentice-Hall, 1969), 617–20. Admittedly, determining the profitability of a movie was a highly problematic factor during the era of the studio system. For instance *Gunga Din*, while a box-office champion, showed poor returns in 1939 in relation to its high cost, yet in later releases became a reliable money-maker. Box-office success as a measure of generic popularity is also distorted by the impact of stars.

CHAPTER 4: The Era of Adventure

1. One of historical fiction's ingrained constraints is that it must conform not so much to facts as to the audiences's often mistaken preconceptions of a certain era or individual, derived from works of history, novels, or even previous movies. When ideas of certain situations, individuals, or motivations exist in the popular imagination by tradition, no matter how inaccurately, it will be difficult to overturn them, a factor that is inevitably considered in making a picture seeking box-office support (Sheppard, 229–31). It is on the basis of "common knowledge" that accuracy is judged, and the story must seem to have at least an element of expected truth about it, no matter how far that truth may stray from the historical facts (cf. Sheppard, 142).

CHAPTER 5: Characters and Their Traits

1. V. F. Perkins in Cameron, 123; Nottridge, 9; a similar dichotomy is pointed out by Thomas Sobchack in Gehring, 14.

2. Mundy, "Argonotes: *When Trails Were New,*" *Argosy All-Story* (October 27, 1928):861.

CHAPTER 6: The Code of Adventure

1. The tradition of matching individual will against adversity has been the subject of such books as Victor Hugo's *The Toilers of the Sea*, Sir Arthur

Conan Doyle's *The Tragedy of the Korosko / A Desert Drama*, Talbot Mundy's *The Hundred Days*, Jules Verne's *Michael Strogoff*, Charles Nordoff and James Norman Hall's *Men against the Sea* (the second part of the "Bounty" trilogy), and the whole genre of Robinsonades.

2. "The Camp-Fire," *Adventure*, December 10, 1921, 174. This quote first appeared in the May 3, 1921, issue and was reprinted on countless occasions in *Adventure* over the near quarter century.

3. Talbot Mundy, "In Winter Quarters," *Adventure* 4 (September 1912):6–7.

CHAPTER 7: The Politics of Adventure

1. See Nerlich, *Ideology of Adventure*, 61, 214 n. 7, 219 n. 3. I do not use politics to imply the inherently bourgeois ideological nature of cinema as formulated in post–May 1968 critical discourse, nor to indicate that films in the genre represent an oppositional style to classical filmmaking. Instead, politics is simply invoked as a broad term to cover the adventurer's disposition toward government and authority.

CHAPTER 8: Colonialism and Adventure

1. Although this point is not made in Richards's study of films about the British empire, *Visions of Yesterday*, his variety of examples validates my assertion. However, Richards's general term, *cinema of empire*, is an appropriate one, especially for adventure movies of this type, so it will be retained here.

2. This argument can be found in nearly all of Richards's work, especially "Korda's Empire," " 'Patriotism with Profit,' " and is the weakness of the British viewpoint found throughout *Visions of Yesterday* (i.e., 3–4).

3. Richards maintains that "in films the empire is unchanged and unchanging . . . it will always be 1890," a statement at odds with the predominant trend since World War II (1974, 81, 88).

4. Cf. Fraser, 28; Jeffrey Richards in MacKenzie 1986, 158. Richards's main reason for supporting the comparison seems to be a few remakes of adventure pictures as westerns, such as *The Lost Patrol* into *Bad Lands* (1939) and *Gunga Din* into *Sergeants Three*, and Gary Cooper's frequent appearance in both genres (1973, 4).

5. Today the Black Watch is best known for its work as ambassadors of goodwill, performing bagpipe music and routines for audiences in the United Kingdom and abroad. A more detailed discussion of the making of these films, along with all other movies derived from Mundy novels, will appear in the author's forthcoming book on Talbot Mundy. I am grateful to

William K. Everson for lending me his print of *The Black Watch*, which allowed detailed analysis of this film.

CHAPTER 9: Adventure and the American Experience

1. Richards 1974, 79–81. Elsewhere Richards equivocated (Richards 1973, 4).

2. Harold J. Laski in Robin M. Williams, Jr., *American Society: A Sociological Interpretation*, 2d ed. (New York: Alfred A. Knopf, 1960), 421; Noyce, 94.

3. Tony Thomas, *Cads and Cavaliers* (New York: A.S. Barnes, 197), 195; cf. Jowett, 804; Fraser, 171, 179.

BIBLIOGRAPHY

Adcock, St. John. *The Glory That Was Grub Street: Impressions of Contemporary Authors.* London: Sampson Low, Marston, [n.d.].

Altman, Rick. "A Semantic/Syntactic Approach to Film Genre." *Cinema Journal* 23 (Spring 1984):6–18.

Altman, Rick, ed. *Genre: The Musical.* Boston: Routledge and Kegan Paul, 1981.

Anderson, J. R. L. *The Ulysses Factor: The Exploring Instinct in Man.* New York: Harcourt Brace Jovanovich, 1970.

Andrew, Dudley. *Concepts in Film Theory.* New York: Oxford University Press, 1984.

Armes, Roy. *A Critical History of the British Cinema.* New York: Oxford University Press, 1978.

Barthes, Roland. "Historical Discourse." In *Introduction to Structuralism,* edited by Michael Lane, pp. 145–55. New York: Basic Books, 1970.

Basinger, Jeannine. *The World War II Combat Film: Anatomy of a Genre.* New York: Columbia University Press, 1986.

Baxter, John. "Books." *Film* (British Federation of Film Societies) no. 10, series 2 (January 1974):11.

Behr, Edward. "God Save the Colonial Way." *Newsweek* 105 (February 25, 1985):69.

Belton, John. "Book Review: *Swordsmen of the Screen." Filmmaker's Monthly* 11 (October 1978):49.

Bender, Bert. *Sea-brothers.* Philadelphia: University of Pennsylvania Press, 1987.

Beuselink, James. "*Adventures of Don Juan." Classic Images,* No. 127 (January 1986):13–14.

Blackburn, William, ed. "Special Section: Adventure." *Children's Literature Association Quarterly* 8 (Fall 1983):7–34.

Bloch, Ernest. *A Philosophy of the Future.* Translated by John Cumming. New York: Herder and Herder, 1970.

Bolitho, William. *Twelve against the Gods: The Story of Adventure.* New York: Readers Club, 1941.

Brantlinger, Patrick. "Imperial Gothic: Atavism and the Occult in the British Adventure Novel, 1880–1914." *English Literature in Transition* 28 (1985):243–52.

Brombert, Victor, ed. *The Hero in Literature.* New York: Fawcett, 1969.

Buck, Frank, with Ferrin Fraser. *All In a Lifetime.* New York: Robert M. McBride, 1941.

Buhler, Wolf-Eckart. "Der Piratefilm." *Filmkritik* 17 (October 1973), [special issue].

Burnett, Whit, ed. *The Spirit of Adventure.* New York: Henry Holt, 1955. pp. ix–xiv.

Cagin, Seth, and Philip Dray. *Hollywood Films of the 70s.* New York: Harper and Row, 1984.

Callenbach, Ernest. "Comparative Anatomy of Folk-Myth Films: *Robin Hood* and *Antonio das Mortes.*" *Film Quarterly* 23 (Winter 1969–1970):42–47.

Campbell, Joseph. *The Hero with a Thousand Faces.* Princeton: Bollingen, 1949.

Cameron, Ian. *Adventure in the Movies.* New York: Crescent Books, 1978.

Carlyle, Thomas. *On Heroes, Hero-worship and the Heroic in History.* New York: AMS Press, 1969.

Cassiday, Bruce. "Write Me an Adventure Novel." *The Writer* 82 (March 1969):11–14.

Cawelti, John G. *Adventure, Mystery and Romance.* Chicago: University of Chicago Press, 1976.

Cline, William C. *In the Nick of Time: Motion Picture Sound Serials.* Jefferson, N.C.: McFarland, 1984.

Cohen, Mayda Lynn. "An Examination of the Second Cycle of the Swashbuckler Genre." Master's thesis, University of Southern California, 1977.

Comolli, Jean-Louis. "Historical Fiction—A Body Too Much." Translated by Ben Brewster. *Screen* 19 (Summer 1978):41–53.

Connor, Edward. "The Genealogy of Zorro." *Films in Review* 8 (August–September 1957):330–33, 343.

Cripps, Thomas. *Slow Fade to Black.* New York: Oxford University Press, 1977.

Darrach, Brad. "Rapier Envy, Anyone?" *Time,* August 9, 1976, pp. 70–72.

Davis, John. "*Captain Blood.*" *The Velvet Light Trap,* No. 1 (June 1971):26–32.

Dooley, Roger. *From Scarface to Scarlett.* New York: Harcourt Brace Jovanovich, 1979.

Doyle, Sir Arthur Conan. *The Tragedy of the Korosko.* In *The Original Illustrated Arthur Conan Doyle,* compiled by Frank Oppel, pp. 381–460. Secaucus, N.J.: Castle, 1980.

Dumas, Alexandre. *The Three Musketeers.* 2 vols. Illustrated by F.C. Tilney. Philadelphia: John C. Winston [n.d.].

Dumont, Herve. "Les 3 Mousquetaires à l'écran." *Travelling revue du cinema* 41 (February–March 1974):18–50.

Durand, Jacques. "La Chevalerie à l'écran." *L'AvantScene / Cinématheque,* No. 221 (February 1, 1979):29–40.

Durgnat, Raymond. *A Mirror for England.* London: Faber and Faber, 1970.

Elley, Derek. *The Epic Film: Myth and History.* London: Routledge and Kegan Paul, 1984.

Everson, William K. *The Bad Guys: A Pictorial History of the Movie Villain.* New York: Citadel, 1964.

Eyles, Allen. "The State of the Legion." *Focus on Film,* No. 28 (October 1977):5–8.

Farson, Negley. "In Search of Adventure." In *Traveller's Quest,* edited by M. A. Michael, pp. 177–205. London: William Hodge, 1950.

Fiedel, Robert. "Recordings." *Take One* 5 (August 1976):25.

_____. "Buckle and Swash cont." *Take One* 5 (October 1976):36.

Fisher, Margery. *The Bright Face of Danger.* Boston: The Horn Book, 1986.

Fraser, George MacDonald. *The Hollywood History of the World.* New York: William Morrow, 1988.

Fraser, John. *America and the Patterns of Chivalry.* Cambridge: Cambridge University Press, 1982.

Fritze, Christoph, Georg Seesslen, and Claudius Weill. *DerAbenteurer: Geschicte und Mythologie des Abenteuer.* Reinbek bei Hamburg: Rowohlt Taschenbuch Verlag GmbH, 1983.

Frye, Northrop. *Anatomy of Criticism: Four Essays.* Princeton: Princeton University Press, 1957.

Fuller, Stanley. "Melville on the Screen." *Films in Review* 19 (June–July 1968):358–63.

Furstenau, Theo. "The Nature of Historical Films." Translated by Ann Keep. *Cultures* 2 (1974):27–41.

Gehring, Wes, ed. *A Handbook to Hollywood Film Genres.* New York: Greenwood, 1988.

Goff, Ivan. Interview on his adventure films. Malibu, California, September 9, 1987.

Gordon, Gordon. "The Lure of the Adventure Novel." *The Writer* 97 (March 1984):7–9, 47.

Gove, Philip Babcock. *The Imaginary Voyage in Prose Fiction.* New York: Columbia University Press, 1941.

Gow, Gordon. "Swashbucklers." *Films and Filming* 11 (January 1972):34–41.

_____. "The Sabatini Springboard." *Films and Filming* 23 (May 1977):10–16.

Grant, Barry Keith, ed. *Film Genre Reader*. Austin: University of Texas Press, 1986.

_____. *Film Genre: Theory and Criticism*. Metuchen, N.J.: Scarecrow, 1977.

Green, Martin. *Dreams of Adventure, Deeds of Empire*. London: Routledge and Kegan Paul, 1979.

_____. *The Great American Adventure*. Boston: Beacon Press, 1984.

_____. *The Robinson Crusoe Story*. University Park, Penn.: Pennsylvania State University Press, 1990.

_____. *Seven Types of Adventure Tale*. University Park, Penn.: Pennsylvania State University Press, 1991.

_____. "Adventurers Stake Their Claim." In *Decolonizing Tradition*, edited by Karen R. Lawrence, pp. 70–87. Urbana: University of Illinois Press, 1992.

Haggard, H. Rider. "About Fiction." *Contemporary Review* (London) 51 (February 1887):172–80.

Hanson, Earl, ed. *Highroad to Adventure*. New York: Robert McBride, 1947.

Hark, Ina Rae. "The Visual Politics of *The Adventures of Robin Hood*." *Journal of Popular Film* 5 (1976):3–17.

Hawthorne, Hildegarde. "The Spirit of Adventure." In *Modern Essays and Stories*, edited by Frederick Houck Law, pp. 176–83. New York: Century, 1922.

Hengen, Nona. "The Perception of Danger in Action Illustrations." *AV Communication Review* 18 (Fall 1970):250–67.

Henty, G. A. *In Times of Peril: A Tale of India*. New York: A.L. Burt, [n.d.].

Herman, Gerald. "For God and Country: *Khartoum* (1966) as History and an 'Object Lesson' for Global Policemen." *Film and History* 9 (February 1979):1–15.

Higham, Charles, and Joel Greenberg. *Hollywood in the Forties*. New York: A.S. Barnes, 1968.

Highet, Gilbert. *Explorations*. New York: Oxford University Press, 1971.

Hirsch, Foster. *The Hollywood Epic*. New York: A.S. Barnes, 1978.

Hough, Lynn Harold. "Adventure and Experience." *The Christian Century* 44 (January 6, 1927):9–10.

Howe, Susanne. *Novels of Empire*. New York: Cambridge University Press, 1949.

Hudgins, Morgan, writer, and Ray Freiman, producer. *Mutiny on the Bounty*. (production book) New York: Random House, 1962.

Huttenback, Robert A. "G. A. Henty and the Vision of Empire." *Encounters* 35 (July 1970):46–53.

"The Impossible." *The New Statesman* 19 (May 6, 1922):118–19.

Jones, Roy. "Swashbuckling Adventure Films." *Filmmaking* 9 (February 1972):42–44.

Jowett, Garth. "The Concept of History in American Produced Films: An Analysis of the Films Made in the Period 1950–1961." *Journal of Popular Culture* 3 (Spring 1970):798–813.

Kaminsky, Stuart M. *American Film Genres.* New York: Dell, 1974.

Katz, Wendy R. *Rider Haggard and the Fiction of Empire.* Cambridge: Cambridge University Press, 1987.

Kiely, Robert. *Robert Louis Stevenson and the Fiction of Adventure.* Cambridge: Harvard University Press, 1964.

King, Henry. Interview on his adventure films. North Hollywood, California, July 28, 1981.

Lahue, Kalton C. *Continued Next Week: A History of the Moving Picture Serial.* Norman: University of Oklahoma Press, 1964.

Lamb, Harold, et al. *El Cid.* [production book] Allied Artists Pictures and Samuel Bronston Productions, 1961.

Landers, Mary Anne. "Who Says Chivalry Is Dead? The Middle Ages Are Alive . . . On Video." *Classic Images,* No. 150 (December 1987):C23–C27.

Langman, Larry, and David Ebner. *Encyclopedia of American War Films.* Jefferson, N.C.: Garland, 1990.

Lascelles, Mary. *The Story-teller Retrieves the Past.* Oxford: Clarendon Press, 1980.

Lawrence, T. E. *Seven Pillars of Wisdom.* New York: Penguin, 1962.

Lill, James. "The Language of Adventure." *Georgia Review* 32 (Winter 1969):844–56.

Lindsay, Philip. *A Mirror for Ruffians.* London: Lindsay Drummond, 1939.

McConnell, Frank. *Storytelling and Mythmaking: Images from Film and Literature.* New York: Oxford University Press, 1979.

MacKenzie, John, ed. *Imperialism and Popular Culture.* Dover, N.H.: Manchester University Press, 1986.

_____. *Imperialism and Propaganda.* Dover, N.H.: Manchester University Press, 1984.

Mace, William H. *A Primary History: Stories of Heroism.* Chicago: Rand McNally, 1900.

Manzoni, Alessandro. *On the Historical Novel.* Translated, with an introduction, by Sandra Bermann. Lincoln: University of Nebraska Press, 1984.

Marlowe, John. *Mission to Khartoum: The Apotheosis of General Gordon.* London: Victor Gollancz, 1969.

Matthews, Brander. *The Historical Novel and Other Essays.* New York: Charles Scribner's Sons, 1901.

Meyers, Jeffrey. *Fiction and the Colonial Experience.* Totowa, N.J.: Rowman and Littlefield, 1973.

Milne, Gordon. *Ports of Call: A Study of the American Nautical Novel.* New York: University Press of America, 1986.

Moth. "Slump in Adventure." *The Spectator* 150 (April 14, 1933):531–32.

Mundy, Talbot. "A Land Where Romance Reigns." *Brentano's Book Chat* 1 (June 1921):36–37. Reprinted as "India: Paradise of the Imaginative Story-Teller," *New York Tribune*, August 21, 1921.

———. "The Things Men Fear." *Liberty* 2 (February 10, 1934):30–31.

———. *Romances of India: King—of the Khyber Rifles, Guns of the Gods, Told in the East.* New York: A.L. Burt, 1936.

———. *The Valiant View.* London: Hutchinson, 1939.

———. *I Say Sunrise.* Philadelphia: Milton F. Wells, 1949.

Neale, Stephen. *Genre.* London: British Film Institute, 1980.

Nerlich, Michael. "On the Unknown History of our Modernity." CHS Occasional Papers. Minneapolis: Center for Humanistic Studies, University of Minnesota Press, No. 3 (1986).

———. *The Ideology of Adventure: Studies in Modern Consciousness, 1100–1750.* Translated by Ruth Crowley. Minneapolis, Minn.: University of Minnesota Press, 1987.

Nesterby, James R. *Black Images in American Films, 1896–1954.* Washington, D.C.: University Press of America, 1982.

Newcomb, Horace. *TV: The Most Popular Art.* New York: Vintage, 1974.

Nordhoff, Charles, and James Norman Hall. *Men Against the Sea.* Boston: Little, Brown, 1935.

———. *Mutiny on the Bounty.* Boston: Little, Brown, 1935.

Nottridge, Rhoda. *Adventure Films.* New York: Crestwood House, 1992.

Noyce, Wilfrid. *The Springs of Adventure.* Cleveland: World, 1958.

Parish, James Robert, and Don E. Stanke. *The Swashbucklers.* New Rochelle, N.Y.: Arlington House, 1976.

Person, Ethel S. "The Passionate Quest." *The Atlantic Monthly* 261 (March 1988):71–76.

Pickard, Roy. *A Companion to the Movies.* London: Lutterworth, 1972.

Pickering, Sam. "Stevenson's 'Elementary Novel of Adventure.'" *Research Studies* 49 (June 1981):99–106.

Propp, Vladimir. *Morphology of the Folktale.* Austin: University of Texas Press, 1968.

Rahill, Frank. *The World of Melodrama.* University Park, Penn.: Pennsylvania State University Press, 1967.

Rainer, Peter. "The Epic, an Endangered Species." *Los Angeles Times Calendar*, March 11, 1990, pp. 30–31.

Richards, Jeffrey. "Discovery: *The Four Feathers.*" *Focus on Film*, No. 6 (Spring 1971):52–54.

_____. *Visions of Yesterday.* London: Routledge and Kegan Paul, 1973.

_____. "Imperial Images: The British Empire and Monarchy on Film." *Cultures* 2 (1974):79–114.

_____. "The Swashbuckling Revival." *Focus on Film*, No. 27 (Summer 1977):7–29.

_____. *Swordsmen of the Screen.* London: Routledge and Kegan Paul, 1977.

_____. "Korda's Empire: Politics and Film in *Sanders of the River, The Drum* and *The Four Feathers.*" *Australian Journal of Screen Theory* 5 and 6 (1978):122–37.

_____. "'Patriotism with Profit': British Imperial Cinema of the 1930s." In *British Cinema History*, edited by James Curran and Vincent Porter, pp. 245–56, 363–64. Totowa, N.J.: Barnes and Noble, 1983.

Richards, Jeffrey, and Anthony Aldgate. *Best of British.* Oxford: Basil Blackwell, 1983.

Roddick, Nick. *A New Deal in Entertainment: Warner Bros. in the 1930s.* London: British Film Institute, 1983.

Roosevelt, Theodore. *The Rough Riders.* New York: Charles Scribner's Sons, 1925.

Rosenzweig, Sidney. *"Casablanca" and Other Major Films of Michael Curtiz.* Ann Arbor, Mich.: UMI Research Press, 1982.

Rossiter, Clinton. *Seedtime of the Republic.* New York: Harcourt, Brace, 1953.

Rowse, A. L. *The English Spirit.* New York: Macmillan, 1945.

Rubenstein, Lenny. "Book Briefs: *Swordsmen of the Screen.*" *Cineaste* 11 (1981):47.

Sabatini, Rafael. *Bardelys the Magnificent.* Photoplay Edition. New York: Grosset and Dunlap, 1905.

_____. *Scaramouche.* Photoplay Edition. New York: Grosset and Dunlap, 1921.

_____. *Captain Blood.* Photoplay Edition. New York: Grosset and Dunlap, 1922.

_____. *Captain Blood Returns.* Boston: Houghton Mifflin, 1931.

_____. *The Black Swan.* Boston: Houghton Mifflin, 1933.

_____. "Historical Fiction." In *What Is a Book?* edited by Dale Warren, p. 23–39. Boston: Houghton Mifflin, 1935.

_____. *The Fortunes of Captain Blood.* Boston: Houghton Mifflin, 1936.

_____. *The Sea-Hawk.* Photoplay Edition. New York: Grosset and Dunlap, n.d.

Said, Edward W. *Orientalism.* New York: Pantheon, 1978.

Sandison, Alan. *The Wheel of Empire.* New York: St. Martin's, 1967.

Schatz, Thomas. *Hollywood Genres: Formulas, Filmmaking, and the Studio System.* New York: Random House, 1981.

Schlesinger, Arthur. "Foreword." In *American History / American Film*, by

John E. O'Connor and Martin A. Jackson. New York: Frederick Ungar, 1979.

Schlobin, Roger C., ed. *The Aesthetics of Fantasy Literature and Art*. Notre Dame, Ind.: University of Notre Dame Press, 1982.

Sennett, Ted. *Warner Bros. Presents*. New York: Arlington House, 1970.

Shanks, Edward. "Sir Rider Haggard and the Novel of Adventure." *London Mercury* 11 (November 1924):72–79.

Shaw, Harry E. *The Forms of Historical Fiction: Sir Walter Scott and His Successors*. Ithaca, N.Y.: Cornell University Press, 1983.

Sheppard, Alfred Tresidder. *The Art and Practice of Historical Fiction*. London: Humphrey Toulmin, 1930.

Simmel, Georg. "The Adventure." Translated by David Kettler. In *Essays on Sociology, Philosophy and Aesthetics*, edited by Kurt H. Wolff, pp. 243–58. New York: Harper and Row, 1965.

Slotkin, Richard. "The Continuity of Forms: Myth and Genre in Warner Brothers' *The Charge of the Light Brigade*." *Representations*, No. 29 (Winter 1990):1–23.

Sobchack, Thomas, and Vivian C. Sobchack. *An Introduction to Film*. 2d ed. Boston: Little, Brown, 1987.

Sobchack, Vivian. " 'Surge and Splendor': A Phenomenology of the Hollywood Historical Epic." *Representations*, No. 29 (Winter 1990):24–49.

Spears, Jack. "The American Revolution in Films." *Films in Review* 28 (January 1977):1–22.

Stedman, Raymond William. *The Serials: Suspense and Drama by Installment*. 2d ed. Norman: University of Oklahoma Press, 1977.

Street, Douglas. *Children's Novels and the Movies*. New York: Frederick Ungar, 1983.

Tangye, Nigel. "Introduction." In *British Adventure*, edited by W. J. Turner, pp. 5–9. London: Collins, 1947.

Taves, Brian. "Philosophy Into Popular Fiction: Talbot Mundy and the Theosophical Society." *Southern California Quarterly* (Summer 1985):153–86.

————, ed. *The Jules Verne Encyclopedia*. Metuchen, N.J.: Scarecrow Press, 1993.

Thomas, Lowell, ed. *Great True Adventures*. New York: Hawthorne, 1955, pp. xi–xii.

Thomas, Tony. *The Great Adventure Films*. Secaucus, N.J.: Citadel Press, 1976.

Todorov, Tzvetan. *The Fantastic: A Structural Approach to a Literary Genre*. Translated by Richard Howard. Ithaca, N.Y.: Cornell University Press, 1975.

Tudor, Andrew. "Genre and Critical Methodology." *Movies and Methods*, edited by Bill Nichols, pp. 118–26. Berkeley: University of California Press, 1976.

Verne, Jules. *Michael Strogoff: The Courier of the Czar.* Translated by W. H. G. Kingston. New York: Charles Scribner's Sons, 1906.

———. "The Mutineers of the Bounty." In *The Begum's Fortune.* Translated by W. H. G. Kingston. Philadelphia: J.B. Lippincott, n.d. [1879].

———. *Around the World in Eighty Days.* Charles Scribner's Sons, 1905.

Voorhees, Richard J. "The Return of Sabatini." *South Atlantic Quarterly* 78 (Spring 1979):195–204.

Ward, Hayden. "The 'Pleasure of Your Heart': *Treasure Island* and the Appeal of Boys' Adventure Fiction." *Studies in the Novel* 6 (1978):304–17.

Ward, L. E. "Romancing the Public." *Classic Images,* No. 112 (October 1984):26.

———. "On an Island with You." *Classic Images,* No. 153 (March 1988):C7–9.

Welsh, Alexander. *The Hero of the Waverly Novels.* New York: Atheneum, 1968.

White, Trentwell Mason. *How to Write for a Living.* 2d ed. Boston: The Writer, 1947.

Wilkinson, Clennell. *The English Adventurers.* Freeport, New York: Books for Libraries Press, 1931.

Williams, Orlo. " 'The Three Musketeers': A Defence of the Novel of Action," *Cornhill Magazine* 63 (November 1927):610–22.

Wollen, Peter. "Cinema's Conquistadors." *Sight and Sound* 2 (November 1992):21–23.

Wood, Michael. *America in the Movies.* New York: Basic Books, 1975.

Wright, Will. *Sixguns and Society: A Structural Study of the Western.* Berkeley: University of California Press, 1975.

Y.Y. "The Bright Eyes of Danger," *The New Statesman and Nation* 4 (new series) (November 19, 1932):621–22.

———. "The Quest," *The New Statesman and Nation* 5 (new series) (April 8, 1933):441–42.

Yenne, Bill. *The Legend of Zorro.* New York: Mallard Press, 1991.

Zimmerman, Patricia R. "Our Trip to Africa: Home Movies as the Eyes of the Empire." *Afterimage* 17 (March 1990):4–7.

Zweig, Paul. *The Adventurer.* Princeton: Princeton University Press, 1974.

INDEX